D0086829

EXILED WATERS

EXILED WATERS

MOBY-DICK
and the Crisis of Allegory

BAINARD COWAN

LOUISIANA STATE UNIVERSITY PRESS

BATON ROUGE AND LONDON

Copyright © 1982
by Louisiana State University Press
All rights reserved
Manufactured in the United States of America

Designer: Albert Crochet
Typeface: VIP Goudy Oldstyle
Typesetter: G & S Typesetters, Inc.
Printer and binder: Thomson-Shore, Inc.

LIBRARY OF CONGRESS CATALOGING IN PUBLICATION DATA

Cowan, Bainard.
  Exiled waters.

  Bibliography: p.
  Includes index.
    1. Melville, Herman, 1819–1891.   Moby Dick.
  2. Melville, Herman, 1819–1891—Allegory and
  symbolism.   I. Title.
  PS2384.M62C68   813'.3   81-19354
  ISBN 0-8071-1002-7   AACR2

To
Ouita Pate Shillingburg
1891–1976
and
Lucy Ouita Cowan
1976–1977

venne una donna, e disse: "I' son Lucia:
lasciatemi pigliar costui che dorme;
sì l'agevolerò per la sua via."

Longa tibi exsilia et vastum maris aequor arandum,
et terram Hesperiam venies, ubi Lydius arva
inter opima virum leni fluit agmine Thybris
                    —*Aeneid* II, 780–82

In those for ever exiled waters, I had lost the
miserable warping memories of traditions and of
towns.
                    —*Moby-Dick*, Chapter 42

CONTENTS

ACKNOWLEDGMENTS

MY PURSUIT of this subject could not have been sustained without multiple forms of help from many quarters. Thanks are due first of all to the Office of Advanced Studies and Research at Louisiana State University, which sponsored my project with a summer research grant in 1977; to the English Department, for funding the preparation of the manuscript; and to the College of Arts and Sciences for underwriting my attendance at the 1979 English Institute session on allegory. Three members of the Louisiana State University Press deserve special thanks: Marie Blanchard, Martha Hall and, most especially, Beverly Jarrett, for her encouragement and special attention to this entire project. Edgar A. Dryden and Gary Lee Stonum read the manuscript and provided helpful comments. The idea for this book was begun under the tutelage of Charles Feidelson, Jr., and John Freccero; and Lowry Nelson, Jr., diligently read and commented on the manuscript. Cleanth Brooks and Geoffrey Hartman have provided their splendid example and encouragement all along. Gale Carrithers became a vital sponsor at a crucial stage; and my friends in the English, foreign languages, and philosophy departments at LSU listened to me interminably and made many helpful suggestions.

There are finally some debts that go far beyond my ability to respond to them here with any reasonable indication of their depth. Louise Cowan could long ago have published a major reading of *Moby-Dick* but left that and several other projects undone to devote her time to creating a literature curriculum aimed at a critical understanding of the whole of literature, and to guiding a generation of students through those channels. I have always received her special care and instruction, and her colloquy with me over the years has not only illuminated a score of works but has kept me believing in the academic life. Her attention to my argument and language has been unflagging. Both she and Donald Cowan have constantly provided material and moral support, goads, commentary, and, when it was needed, an ideal seclusion for shaping the book.

Finally, Christine, my wife, has devoted as much attention to this book in its various stages—as typist, critic, editor, colloquist—as to all our children (whose loving patience bears mention, too). Her help, advice, and love have been my first and last resort.

EXILED WATERS

INTRODUCTION

THE PROBLEM of reading *Moby-Dick* never goes away, no matter how many times critics cast off in hopes of definitively bagging it. From the late 1940s until the beginning of the sixties, Melville criticism lived through a kind of golden age, the best work bringing to light the intricate structuring and overall artistic purpose of Melville's masterpiece (*e.g.*, Walter Bezanson's "*Moby-Dick*: Work of Art," 1953), its synthesis of worlds of practical and recondite learning (*e.g.*, Howard Vincent's *The Trying-Out of "Moby-Dick*," 1949), its Shakespearean and biblical language and character portrayal (*e.g.*, Charles Olson's *Call Me Ishmael*, 1947). Those discoveries came from close scanning of the work itself and were relatively independent of any preexisting critical theory, though the best interpretive ventures into the work went far beyond D. H. Lawrence's vague vision of Western apocalypse to stress the strong critiques of politics, religious attitudes, and the Western psyche that the work implies (*e.g.*, Harry Slochower's "*Moby-Dick* and the Myth of Democratic Expectancy," 1950; Henry A. Murray's "In Nomine Diaboli," 1951; James Baird's *Ishmael*, 1956).

In the last two decades those mines of significant material have virtually quit yielding new ore, and the fortunate combination of scholarship and criticism has resolved itself into the familiar two camps, wherein scholars argue about the text and the sequence of its composition in the author's life while critics bring more or less autonomous critical philosophies to bear on the meaning of the work. Perhaps inevitable in the sixties was the tendency to go be-

3

yond the levels of critique and myth previously discovered to proclaim that Melville's writing constitutes a radical critique of reality itself. Among others, Paul Brodtkorb's *Ishmael's White World* (1965), John Seelye's *Melville: The Ironic Diagram* (1970), and Warwick Wadlington's "Ishmael's Godly Gamesomeness" (1972) have drawn their readings from a view that the chief achievement of *Moby-Dick* is the creation of a consciousness in Ishmael that can withstand all buffets, transcend the strictures of any fixed system of thought, and emerge a victorious model of the competent personality in a universe devoid of all ultimate reality.

A peculiar brand of phenomenology has reigned in this pursuit. Husserl, the founder of modern phenomenological method, bracketed the question of existence, not out of a nihilistic skepticism but out of a recognition that making a defense of reality the starting point of philosophy returns one again to the very Cartesian impasse one has wanted to bridge. The American literary version of phenomenology, by contrast, links a skepticism about reality with an existentialism of anxiety that is never argued but only assumed: reading the "Whiteness of the Whale" chapter as Ishmael's final underlying conviction, they conclude that all notions of knowledge, participation in reality, or indeed survival are hopelessly deluded. Derived from a French critique of idealism, this perennially fashionable negativity has ignored the refutation of Sartre performed by structuralism, which showed his existential demands to be naïvely or perversely ignorant of the cultural predetermination of experience.

Still more recent studies of Melville have implicitly retreated from this radical stance, concentrating on single aspects of Melville's thought and writing and showing him and his fiction to be very much involved in a criticism of his time, its social temperament, and its spiritual sense (*e.g.*, T. Walter Herbert, *"Moby-Dick" and Calvinism*, 1977; Rowland Sherrill, *The Prophetic Melville*, 1979; Carolyn Karcher, *Shadow over the Promised Land*, 1980). These explorations return Melville's voice to the historical world, but they cannot avoid muting it in the process so that it comments on only one aspect of that world. While Melville's powerful social and cultural implications are thus narrowed down to historians' interests, the language of general literary criticism, which might once again

4

return his work to prominence in determining the situation of literature in our time, has come under the influence of an attractive but dimly understood French terminology and focus. American "poststructuralism" (the label, it has been pointed out, exists only in America) lacks both the long-standing intellectual tradition of skepticism and the developed sense of structure in literary and social theory which the French critics have and which provides the solid ground against which their anti-structural insights push off. That complex awareness of "undecidable," "unreadable," existence-nonexistence of structures which a Barthes or a Derrida (despite their differences) seeks to induce in the minds of French readers may tend to be viewed by American eyes, with favor or opprobrium, as a simple nihilism.

As it narrows down progressively to a duet of the "I" and the void, American criticism has had to ignore increasingly the vast network of texts and structures that interlock to form the heart of *Moby-Dick*. The novel's wealth of literary, historical, and mythological material is in fact part of its essence, turning its readers into poor devils of sub-subs all in their efforts to grasp the work. The experience of *Moby-Dick* is an experience of a text in its textuality, as a weaving of the many discourses of its past into its complex unity in the present.

The dimension of past and present has also been the victim of critical inattention. In other precincts of critical thought, the category of history has undergone a serious reconsideration. For decades a term designating sheer opposition to intrinsic analysis of literary texts, history has recently come to be seen, through various terms such as *trace* and *effective-history* and through the shift of perspective implicit in the term *discourse*, as inextricably involved in the shaping of the literary work. No longer is the historical dimension of the text viewed only at the comparatively crude level of milieu; it is now recognized as entering into the determination of generic form, the linguistic structure and figural relationships, and the overall sense of lived time and space. It is now possible—though few enough critics have taken this step—to move into realms of cultural criticism without deserting the close view of the literary text which the New Criticism initiated and which semiotic criti-

5

cism has sharpened, and without losing sight of the difference of the literary work from life, the sense of form which makes literary analysis possible.

It is for this reason that the name of Walter Benjamin appears so frequently on the pages to follow. Though he may seem an alien intruder at this gam of American ships, he is arguably the exemplary critic in merging the study of cultural history with the discussion of genre, aesthetic intention, and figurative language. The fact that he died some forty years ago only increases the exemplary nature of his writing. The relations between temporality and the relatively timeless realm of art lie at the foundations of most of the major terms in his writings. Notable for our purposes is that the terms *allegory* and *symbol* do not for him express the temporal and the timeless respectively, but that, after his demolition of the Romantic symbol in *Ursprung des deutschen Trauerspiels* (1928), allegory comes to stand for the complex relation between those two dimensions of existence.

It is essentially for this reason that I see the term *allegory* as applicable to *Moby-Dick*: not as a word designating a set of literary conventions, nor as an honorific title meaning that the work is profound, but as a mode of discourse employed in past Western literate societies to come to terms with a crisis in the imagining of the relation between the timely and the timeless. *Moby-Dick* both expresses and examines this crisis as it has emerged in our time, and it holds out the possibility of at least a limited recovery—or a first discovery—of a vital tradition, a cultural habitus both unconstraining and civil, a place for memory to come to the fore and interact with imagination. The distance gained from land on the "exiled waters" of his voyage allows Ishmael to reenvision the Western past and the natural present, freed from their enforced New England interpretation, as an allegory. And at the ever-present second level of the narrative, Ishmael the writer is already portraying this transformation of himself as an allegory of allegory.

These assertions open up a number of questions, and I hope I will be forgiven for not stopping to pursue them here, since they are the questions to which I continually return in the chapters that follow. What I hope will do for the time being is an indication of the path my inquiry is to take: to begin with, the two matrices out of which my reading of *Moby-Dick* arises. The first is the relatively more permanent category of genre. Although allegory arises, as I see it, in response to specific historical conditions, these conditions can occur in a variety of ways, and hence the structure of allegory bears certain important characteristics more or less constantly over its two-thousand-year history. Beginning with Benjamin's re-formulation of allegory as especially suited to express the historical experience of loss and decay, then, in the first chapter I work toward a theory of allegory as a cultural activity that arises at moments of crisis in the history of a literate people, when a text central to a people's identity can neither command belief any longer nor be entirely abandoned.

The second matrix is the general problematic of signification in Melville's own time. Chapter II is devoted, then, to a rather broad sketch of the form this textual crisis takes in Melville's century, when the discontinuous nature of signification begins to be realized more fully than before and corresponds to a growing recognition of more specific discontinuities in social and cultural practice. I go on to give an indication of the forms that the response to this awareness takes in some of the major writers in the nineteenth century.

The final five chapters proceed from a single premise, that *Moby-Dick* presents the central drama of exile—from being, from tradition, and from community—that shaped the nature of allegory in the Romantic epoch. Together the chapters subdivide the narrative into five sections, in each of which the mode of allegory uncovered takes on a different character. Each one, in turn, is constituted by a transforming event in Ishmael's path and by the change occurring in his understanding of, and personal relation to, the historical and communal aspects of human experience.

Finally, a credo which I do not explicitly argue in these chapters, but which all my readings of individual passages go in hope of proving, is that Ishmael's character and understanding progressively deepen, both in the process of the voyage and in the process of writing the book. Ishmael's understanding is cumulative and, like the imagination in allegory, endows all events with meaning by recalling them as part of lived history. Hence, "The Whiteness of the

Whale," for instance, in addition to its profound ambivalence, does not lose its overtone of naïveté, because it is the product of Ishmael's still relatively unversed imagination during the early part of the voyage. The deaths of whales and men which he is to witness, like so many passion plays, leave him far from a vision of "dumb blankness"—they leave no space in his memory that is not written on.

I

~~~

TEXT AND BODY:
THE CULTURAL ORIGIN
OF ALLEGORY

MOBY-DICK gives testimony to three epochal revelations in Melville's century: in the sperm whale, the discovery of nature as an inexhaustible text for contemplation; in Ahab, the downfall, however magnificent, of the masters at the helm of a machinelike civilization; and in Ishmael, the recovery of tradition as the truth of the outcast, along with the restoration of community as the brotherhood of isolatoes. Though none of these positions would meet unanimous agreement from the world's "deep readers" of Melville, at least the first two would elicit general assent, as would the recognition that Ahab's role is subordinate to Ishmael's and that Ahab's interpretation of the white whale as evil is in error. It is the third testimony that may be the most arguable—Ishmael's recovery of tradition and community—though I see it as inextricably linked to the other two; and thus this book on the allegory of *Moby-Dick* is, to begin with, about Ishmael's sense of tradition.

Even to speak of tradition in the same sentence with the unconventional Ishmael—or the unorthodox Melville—requires a radical redefinition. The perspective of the German essayist Walter Benjamin provides possibly the best available vantage point from which to approach such a definition of tradition. Throughout his writings Benjamin was concerned with "reclaiming" and "appropriating" the past in ways antithetical to historicism. For him tradition is not to be equated with history; in fact, a "fundamental aporia" exists between them, an opposition which compels him to view tradition "as the discontinuum of the past in contrast to history as the continuum of events"; to consider "the history of the oppressed as a discontinuum": and finally to assert that the "task of history is to claim the tradition of the oppressed."[1] The sense and extent of Marxism in Benjamin's thought is problematic, perhaps insolubly so, but at least one can say that his intent would exclude a doctrinaire program for action or interpretation. The experience of the "oppressed" that he has in mind is not so much the economic exploitation of workers as the dispersion and persecution of the Jews; their circumstances, however, are advanced less as a special claim than as a model of the human predicament in general. The paradigm which they provide indicates that neither truth nor community can be securely passed on to the next generation as a legacy, as "the continuity and renewal of the truths of the fathers by the sons."[2] What can be passed on, unfortunately, are the quite tangible keys to institutional power: thus, in a radical sense, "the continuum of history is that of the oppressor."[3] The truth and the notion of community, by contrast, must be rediscovered and recreated by each individual. Though these two precious entities become lost in the onslaught of history, they leave behind traces and fragments of their existence—testimonies—that can be found only in history. Against the grain of apparent continuous progression, then, the task of the historian, essentially an isolato (a sub-sub-librarian, as Melville portrays him), is to go to history "motivated by the urge to re-collect the broken past, to remember the dismembered."[4]

This last idea—to remember (and re-member) the dismembered —has always been the defining concern of allegory. It is preeminently the purpose of Melville in his great whaling novel. But preliminary to such a consideration of *Moby-Dick* it seems necessary to

1. Walter Benjamin, notes to "Über den Begriff der Geschichte," *Gesammelte Schriften*, ed. Rolf Tiedemann and Hermann Schweppenhäuser (4 vols.; Frankfurt/Main, 1972–77), I, 1236.
2. Anson Rabinbach, "Critique and Commentary/Alchemy and Chemistry: Some Remarks on Walter Benjamin and This Issue," *New German Critique*, No. 17 (Spring, 1979), 9.
3. Benjamin, notes to "Über den Begriff der Geschichte," 1236.
4. Irving Wohlfarth, "On the Messianic Structure of Walter Benjamin's Last Reflections," *Glyph*, III (1978), 154. See Walter Benjamin, "Theses on the Philosophy of History," *Illuminations*, trans. Harry Zohn (New York, 1968), 257–68.

reexamine the allegorical tradition in the light of its cultural context. This attempt will require some penetration of the aura of otherworldly unconcern surrounding allegory and a clarification of its vital function in reanimating the despised and rejected past.

Allegory has arisen at moments in history when a people has found itself in a crisis of identity, its members seeing themselves as inheritors of a past tradition of such authority that the tradition is identified with their very name as a people, yet on the other hand finding much of that tradition morally or factually unacceptable. Allegory thus arises out of the dawning of what Hans-Georg Gadamer calls the "hermeneutic consciousness"; at such a time, he writes, tradition "must have become questionable in order for an explicit consciousness of the hermeneutic task of appropriating tradition to have been formed."[5] A culture that has reached the point of recognizing its necessary discontinuity with received tradition is also confronted with the problem of its own identity. However, this "hermeneutic consciousness" may not necessarily produce allegory. Protestantism gains its identity by turning away from the body of Catholic theology and exegesis and proposing a return to the Bible to find its real meaning. The Bible, it was assumed (though mistakenly, as the Enlightenment would soon show), would offer a haven of unproblematic reading. But it is when a text has become problematic that allegory is born. Werner Jaeger asserts that allegory "has always been at that moment of intellectual development when the literal meaning of the sacred books has become questionable but when the giving up of those forms was out of the question, because that would have been a kind of suicide." These forms were retained because of "a sociological necessity having something to do with the fact that the continuity of life depends on form."[6]

The culture that resorts to allegory thus finds itself called in two opposing directions, by an allegiance to its history and by an allegiance to truth. The allegorical interpreter feels this conflict as a

5. Hans-Georg Gadamer, *Truth and Method*, trans. Garrett Barden and John Cumming (New York, 1976), xxi.

6. Werner Jaeger, *Early Christianity and Greek Paideia* (Cambridge, Mass., 1961), 127–28. Cf. Joseph A. Mazzeo, *Varieties of Interpretation* (Notre Dame, Ind., 1978), 52–56, on seeking a reading that is *theoprepes* (befitting a god).

conflict of readings, for the philological-rhetorical method of reading stresses the specific historicity of language whereas the philosophical method stresses its alignment to truth.[7]

Paul de Man's studies of rhetoric identify allegory as the locus of the "unreadability" of a text, the place where the impossibility of reading it asserts itself.[8] In a similar sense on a cultural scale, the crisis of allegory arises when an authoritative text becomes unreadable to a whole reading community. If a text simply loses its authority and is no longer believed, as for instance Greek mythological poetry was diminished by the early Christians, it does not exert this generative power of unreadability; instead, it may simply be glossed as lies and falsehood. Allegory, in contrast, cannot dismiss the text. The allegorist stands at the cutting-edge between two imperatives, on a thin line that marks the convergence of two disciplines just as it demarcates the separation of two historical epochs. His cultural situation is structurally similar to the linguistic "double-bind" of the schizophrenic, who, in Gregory Bateson's analysis, is caught in a persistent familial situation that places two equal and opposing demands on him. Eventually the double-bind causes the meanings of all statements to be undeterminable.[9] But whereas the schizophrenic often evades his double-bind by creating verbal fantasies, the persistent impulse of allegory is to evade cultural psychosis by creating a "higher" sense in which the original text can be taken—that is, a sense clearly not inherent in the signifying system of the text itself.

At the heart of allegorical interpretation is an impulse that is both liberalizing and conservative, preserving the old text while extending its meaning beyond the old bounds. It asserts a continuity in order to mask the obvious fact of a dangerous discontinuity between past and present. Heraclitus (or Pseudo-Heraclitus—not the great Presocratic), the chief Stoic allegorizer of Homer, proceeds

7. Cf. Mazzeo, *Varieties of Interpretation*, 53. On the opposition of sophists and logicians in Greek education, see Henri-Irénée Marrou, *A History of Education in Antiquity*, trans. George Lamb (2 vols.; New York, 1956), Vol. I, Chs. 6–7.

8. Paul de Man, *Allegories of Reading: Figural Language in Rousseau, Nietzsche, Rilke, and Proust* (New Haven, 1979), 205, 209.

9. Gregory Bateson *et al.*, "Toward a Theory of Schizophrenia," *Behavioral Science*, I, 4 (1956), 251–64.

from the premise that Homer, "to whom we entrust the education of our children from their earliest years," was either the most impious of all men or must be understood allegorically. Since the alternative is too frightening, Plato must be wrong and Homer must be reinterpreted.[10] Even this pragmatic conservatism, however, is based on a clear faith, if also pragmatic, in the trustworthiness of Homer.

For allegory to make its appearance, a society cannot seek to safeguard an older text merely out of empty piety, nor out of the urge toward "continuity of life," nor even out of the desire to preserve its identity. That text must still be felt to have something yet unheeded to say, to be "the cipher of a saving truth."[11] It must possess an excess of significance which one's own time needs and by which, it is hoped, one's own time can be redeemed. Usually that excess stems from the intuitive compactness of the system of thought out of which the text arose, one free from the comparative rationalism of the later age which receives it and tries to elucidate it. The notion of divine inspiration was useful in this way, not only to the Jews but to the Greeks as well. Dio Chrysostom justifies the continued reading of Homer despite moralists' objections: "To the poets sometimes, I mean the very ancient poets, there came a brief utterance from the Muses, a kind of inspiration of the divine nature and truth, like a flash of light from an unseen fire."[12]

This faith in inspiration is immeasurably strengthened when Hellenistic allegorizing turns to the Jewish scriptures. Philo's voluminous commentary on the Septuagint proceeds from the premise with which he advises his readers: "Do not let any subtle point escape your notice, for you will not find a single pointless expression."[13] If scripture is divinely inspired, he argues, then it must not be found to contradict itself or to lie at any point. Hence it cannot mean some things literally, as when it is written that Cain took a

10. Jaeger, *Early Christianity*, 127.

11. Mazzeo, *Varieties of Interpretation*, 57, referring to what the "desacralizing" character of modern textual interpretation does *not* see in the text.

12. Dio Chrysostom, *36th Discourse*, quoted in Edwin Hatch, *The Influence of Greek Ideas on Christianity* (1888; rpt., New York, 1957), 51.

13. Philo Judaeus, *Legum Allegoriae*, in F. H. Colson and G. H. Whitaker (trans.), *Philo*, Loeb Classical Library (10 vols.; New York, then Cambridge, Mass., 1929–62), I, 398–401 (III. 147). This edition is hereinafter cited as "Loeb."

wife (because no woman besides Eve had yet been created). Since this assertion cannot contradict scriptural fact, it must be read figuratively. Hence Philo sees Cain as the vain and uninstructible man who has "wedded his own opinion."[14] Furthermore, Philo insists, the allegorical reading of the passage cannot be merely an arbitrary escape; the passage must have been *meant* as an allegory originally. Factual self-contradiction then becomes a signal imbedded in the text that a philosophical truth is being portrayed. Thus the text subject to allegoresis has actually already begun allegorizing itself, and it provides "the clues for the use of this method." In Eden, for instance, "there are trees in no way resembling those with which we are familiar, but trees of life, of Immortality, of Knowledge, of Apprehension, of Understanding, of the conception of good and evil." They cannot therefore be "growths of earthly soil, but must be those of the reasonable soul."[15]

Philo is moved by his argument to assert the continuity of intention between the literal and allegorical meanings. Modern scholars speak of his "two-level view" of scripture, a layered structure of which he gives ample evidence in his methodological asides: "the hidden truth which can be traced under the surface meaning of the words"; "when we interpret words by the meanings that lie beneath the surface, all that is mythical is removed out of our way, and the real sense becomes as clear as daylight."[16] The process of uncovering the deeper meaning of the text is a kind of inspiration or illumination, always depicted as a gradual and gentle progression: an opening up, a pressing on, an anointing, an allowing light to shine. "Press on to allegorical interpretations," he counsels his readers, for "the letter is to the oracles but as shadow to the substance." God is enjoined to "be our prompter and preside over our steps and never

14. Ronald Williamson, *Philo and the Epistle to the Hebrews*, Arbeiten zur Literatur und Geschichte des hellenistischen Judentums (Leiden, 1970), IV, 526. See also Samuel Sandmel, *Philo of Alexandria: An Introduction* (New York, 1979), 18: "A chief purpose of allegorical interpretation is to enable one to continue to bind himself to a textual passage that is both sacred and troubling."

15. Philo Judaeus, *De Plantatione*, in Loeb edition, III, 230–31 (§36). Cf. Williamson, *Philo and Hebrews*, 522–23.

16. Philo Judaeus, *De Confusione Linguarum*, in Loeb edition, IV, 86–87 (§143); *De Agricultura*, Loeb, III, 108–203. On the "two-level view" see Sidney G. Sowers, *The Hermeneutics of Philo and Hebrews* (Richmond, Va., 1965), 28–34.

tire of anointing our eyes, until conducting us to the hidden light of hallowed words." [17]

Philo's affirmation of continuity takes place in an epoch attempting to continue or extend an old tradition rather than to begin a new movement. With a fundamentally "conservative" approach, this view structures allegory as a progression or an evolution, a continuous journey, rather than as the sharp turn that occurs in St. Paul. Here such symbols as the veil, the inner temple, the pilgrimage or voyage, and rites of initiation mark the stages of enlightenment in the allegorical process. These images abound in works not only of Philo's century but also of the next two, even in profane settings such as *The Golden Ass*. Only when the older tradition is perceived as having exhausted its plenitude (the continuous progression ended) does the vision of layers to be mined for new meaning cease to have any compelling force.

Philo's terms *shadow* and *substance* suggest a familiarity with Plato's allegory of the cave, but Philo ignores the drama implicit in these metaphors. He misses the complex structure of allegory contained in Plato's image and opts instead for a simpler, straightforward progression. Plato's account depicts a dramatic turning away from the cave and toward the light, rejecting an old way of life for a new one oriented to the truth. Thus the Platonic progress of the soul calls for a radical turn *away* from an old tradition in order to begin anew. The very absoluteness of this decision, however, makes him reject allegoresis entirely. Just as the freed prisoner turns away from the darkness of the cave, Socrates turns away from Homeric poetry in turning to his vision of the ideal state: "Hera's bindings by her son, and Hephaestus' being cast out when he was about to help out his mother who was being beaten by his father, and all the battles of the gods Homer made, must not be accepted in the city, whether they are made with a hidden sense or without a hidden sense." [18] It is this drastic turn or departure that marks later allegory, opening the possibility for a thoroughgoing reinterpretation of real-

---

17. Philo Judaeus, *De Confusione Linguarum*, IV, 114–15; *De Somniis*, in Loeb edition, V, 382–85 (I. 164). On "light" in Philo see Erwin R. Goodenough, *By Light, Light: The Mystic Gospel of Hellenistic Judaism* (New Haven, 1935).

18. Plato, *The Republic*, trans. Allan Bloom (New York, 1968), 56 (II. 378d).

ity. The turn is a physical image of the disjunction of signification inherent in the use of "a style speaking something and meaning other than what it says" (Heraclitus' definition of *allegoria*).[19] In this movement of will the assertions of continuity with the original text finally reveal themselves for what they are: attempts to conceal the impossibility of reconciling tradition with reality.

Plato's universe, moreover, advanced the ontological framework for a radically disjunctive allegory. The allegory of the cave testifies to an earthly world of privation and distance from being. The ascent up the mountain from the cave implies that true being can at least be approached; however, the *Phaedrus* portrays the realm of true being as existing beyond the heavens, inaccessibly far from the grasp of mortal man. Similarly, the republic—the image of the community to which Plato turns when he rejects received tradition —he admits to be something that might exist only in heaven and in discourse.[20]

These insights were lost on the neoplatonists. In the context of Christianity, however, they were taken over and transformed. No longer merely an endeavor inspired by idealism, full of risk, and rewarded by a solitary felicity, the Platonic turn became a discovery of new life for an existing people and an existing text. For Christianity the other meaning of the scriptures is neither an extension of the original literal meaning nor an embedded, hidden meaning already there and awaiting illumination. The radically new character of allegorical meaning in early Christian interpretation is explainable only by the close connection of this new meaning to Christ's death and resurrection. An event that is both the central event in history and a gratuitous gift of God, in no way necessitated by the past, changes the significance of the past, marking a clean break while at the same time reordering the past in retrospect so that it leads up to and anticipates the break.

No one was more conscious of these paradoxes than St. Paul, who practiced the art of reinterpretation on numerous scriptural passages of both large and small import. Beneath the intentions of

---

19. Heraclitus, *Quaestiones Homericae*, 5, quoted in Sowers, *Hermeneutics of Philo and Hebrews*, 11.

20. Plato, *The Republic*, trans. Allan Bloom, 274 (IX. 592a-b).

the inspired authors Paul detects a hidden intentionality pointing toward the redemption of the people. When he cites the Mosaic injunction, "Thou shalt not muzzle the mouth of the ox that treadeth out the corn," he responds, "Doth God take care for oxen? . . . For our sakes, no doubt, this is written: that he that ploweth should plow in hope; and he that thresheth in hope should be partaker of his hope."[21] This spiritual interpretation of a particularly unspiritual verse emphasizes the openness—toward a "higher" meaning and toward an eschatological future—inherent in even the most specific and proscriptive of passages. As he writes in Romans: "For whatsoever things were written aforetime were written for our learning, that we through patience and comfort of the scriptures might have hope" (Rom. 15:4).

The radical openness to the future that constitutes hope is precisely what Paul sees to be lacking in the narrow and legalized interpretation of the Old Testament. A solely literal reading of scripture, by its refusal to adapt received forms to their unexpected configuration in actual occurrence, prevents signification from becoming a living act. A legalistic reading excludes hope altogether and can only conclude in the logical *reductio* of legalism, the death sentence. This is the essence of Paul's treatment of the law in Romans and Galatians. "Therefore by the deeds of the law there shall no flesh be justified in his sight"; "And the commandment, which was ordained to life, I found to be unto death" (Rom. 3:20; 7:10); "For as many as are of the works of the law are under the curse: for it is written, cursed is every one that continueth not in all things which are written in the book of the law to do them" (Gal. 3:10). Only if scripture is written "in the hearts" of believers—understood interpretively—can it be freed from its petrifying spell of condemnation.

The metaphor of writing on the heart combines the faculties of intellect and will in a single image that implies an indelible change in the inmost being of the person. Paul receives the images of writing on the heart and of replacing stone with flesh from the era of the prophets, who take the voice of God in condemning the complacent uncharitableness of the people. Jeremiah proclaims, "After

21. I Cor. 9:9–10. Quotations from the Bible are from the King James version, the version which Melville read and marked.

17

those days, saith the Lord, I will put my law in their inward parts, and write it in their hearts; and will be their God, and they shall be my people" (Jer. 31:33). And Ezekiel: "And I will give them one heart, and I will put a new spirit within you; and I will take the stony heart out of their flesh, and will give them an heart of flesh" (Ezk. 11:19).

Paul adds to this opposition of images an opposition of letter and spirit which makes explicit the necessity of an allegorical reading of scripture: "But he is a Jew, which is one inwardly; and circumcision is that of the heart, in the spirit and not in the letter" (Rom. 2:29); "we should serve in newness of spirit, and not in the oldness of the letter" (Rom. 7:6). In II Corinthians this opposition is most strongly expressed: as "ministers of the new testament," those who trust in Christ are ministers "not of the letter, but of the spirit: for the letter killeth, but the spirit giveth life" (II Cor. 3:6). The killing power of the letter is associated with the stone tablets of the Mosaic law and the severity of its penalty, "the ministration of death, written and engraven in stones" (II Cor. 3:7).

In a further association, the veil that covered Moses' glowing face when he returned to the people from Sinai becomes the emblem of a blindness equivalent to the hardening of the hearts of the people:[22]

> Seeing then that we have such hope, we use great plainness of speech: And not as Moses, which put a vail over his face, that the children of Israel could not stedfastly look to the end of that which is abolished: But their minds were blinded: for until this day remaineth the same vail untaken away in the reading of the old testament; which vail is done away in Christ. But even unto this day, when Moses is read, the vail is upon their heart. Nevertheless when it shall turn to the Lord, the vail shall be taken away. (II Cor. 3:12–16)

The act of reading is the central metaphor in this chain of associations. Paul presents Christianity as a drama of cultural crisis in which an entire people failed to respond adequately to the task of reading in the spiritual sense. The Hellenistic imagery of veil, light,

22. See John Freccero, "Medusa: The Letter and the Spirit," in Dante della Terza (ed.), *Yearbook of Italian Studies: 1972* (Florence, 1974), 1–6.

and blindness reinforces the emphasis on allegorical reading. It is the turn to Christ, however, rather than any intrinsic enlightenment, that will remove the veil. The older imagery is appropriated to play its part in a historical drama of conversion. Paul's thorough sense of history is brought out in his amplifying the image of Moses' shining face as "the end of that which is abolished" (*eis to telos tou katargoumenou*—literally, "to the end of what was fading")—that is, the reign of the Law.

Paul's figures suggest the revolutionary cultural implication of allegorical reading: to begin to read an authoritative text in a new way is to begin a new historical epoch, discontinuous with the old. The letters to the Corinthians focus on this because the divisiveness and moral backsliding among the Christians at Corinth caused Paul to consider the nature of a Christian community. In the first letter he develops the analogy to the body: "For as the body is one, and hath many members, and all the members of that one body, being many are one body: so also is Christ" (I Cor. 12:12). In II Corinthians he uses the letter itself as a metaphor, saying that he needs no letter of introduction to them because "Ye are our epistle written in our hearts, known and read of all men: Forasmuch as ye are manifestly declared to be the epistle of Christ ministered by us, written not with ink, but with the Spirit of the living God; not in tables of stone, but in fleshy tables of the heart" (II Cor. 3:2–3). This association of body and text is new and henceforth fundamental for allegory. It states a concern for the identity of a people in metaphors which assert their unity. Furthermore, by the image of writing on (or in) the body the turn away from the old, petrifying tradition becomes a reappropriation of it, bringing it fully into the present and into new life.

Finally, the image of the body is significant for its incompleteness. Unlike the inscribed text, the body represents something unfinished: "whilst we are at home in the body, we are absent from the Lord" (II Cor. 5:6); the body is "our earthly house of this tabernacle," and "we that are in this tabernacle do groan, being burdened," whereas in heaven "we have a building of God, an house not made with hands, eternal in the heavens" (II Cor. 5:1, 4). The body is the realm of process. To transfer writing onto it is to replace the finished inscription of the stone tablets with a project wherein the truth of the allegory will have to be worked out in living.

The new sense of allegory developed in Christianity, in short, is one of turning away from a petrified text to embrace a body and to reinscribe the text on the body. The body to be embraced is preeminently Christ: the veil will be taken away from the children of Israel when they "shall turn to the Lord." Elsewhere in the New Testament Christ is depicted as one who not merely lifts but tears the veil of the text. In the crucifixion narrative this image combines with others suggesting a breaking out of imprisonment: "And, behold, the veil of the temple was rent in twain from the top to the bottom; and the earth did quake, and the rocks rent; and the graves were opened; and many bodies of the saints which slept arose, and came out of the graves after his resurrection, and went into the holy city, and appeared unto many" (Matt. 27:51–53). The temple and the city, signifying the two dimensions of cultural life, are both disrupted. In the letter to the Hebrews, Christ becomes the torn veil itself, as he forges a path for the people "to enter into the holiest by the blood of Jesus, By a new and living way, which he hath consecrated for us, through the veil, that is to say, his flesh" (Heb. 10:19–20). Christ is "the mediator of the new testament" (Heb. 9:15).

These patterns become fully incorporated into the Christian poetic imagination in *The Divine Comedy*. Dante's journey through the realms of the afterlife is structured as a series of thresholds he must cross. Although the pilgrimage in its overall shape is a progress of the soul, in structure it is a series of discontinuous regions, at the meeting-points of which Dante several times finds himself challenged and barred from entry. It is at these moments that the discontinuity of his experience presents itself most fully: time seems to dilate as he retreats within himself in fear from the challenge. The threat of fear, which seems able to defeat him by itself, makes the passage of these thresholds an allegory of the act of interpretation. In it Dante is forced to revise or reenvision himself and his weakness regarding the threat in the light of the theology of salvation. This is not to suggest that Dante's progress in the poem is only a matter of his refining an already resident interpretive power. In the

Inferno especially, his passage is most often a result of a mere act of giving himself over to Virgil's wisdom, even to his actual physical presence, as guide. The turn not to the mind but to the body of Virgil for shelter, especially emphatic since Virgil's poetry is the greatest of all influences on Dante's mind, restates Paul's insistence that an act of will, rather than any intellectual manipulation, constitutes the leap out of a literal into a spiritual sense. The volitional, imaged in both Paul and Dante as the physical, constitutes the chief disjunction in reading the allegory of Christianity.

The first passageway in which the act of reading plays an explicit role is the entrance to hell. The final words of the inscription over the archway, "All hope abandon, ye who enter here," strike fear in Dante's heart.[23] He expresses his consternation to Virgil: "Master, these words import / Hard meaning." The word *hard—duro—*associated with meaning (*senso*) amplifies the combination of letters and stone in the inscribed archway. Since the inscription is the final testimony of the severity of God's law, the Pauline association of letter and stone with the law comes into play in this passage. Dante remains a literal reader, applying the message to himself and thus spreading a veil of fear over his will. Virgil replies to Dante "as one prepared" and demonstrates the radical rereading required for a journey through hell: "Here thou must all distrust behind thee leave; / Here be vile fear extinguished." The words of his admonishment follow almost literally the last line of the inscription, but reverse their meaning, directing Dante to abandon not "hope" (*speranza*) but its opposites, "distrust" (*sospetto*) and "vile fear" (*viltà*).

The episode at the entrance to the City of Dis, the fullest the-

23. Henry Francis Cary (trans.), *The Vision: or, Hell, Purgatory, and Paradise of Dante Alighieri* (New York, 1845). Quotations are from the text identical to the edition owned and marked by Melville. See Merton M. Sealts, Jr., *Melville's Reading: A Check-List of Books Owned and Borrowed* (Madison, Wis., 1966), 55, Item 174; J. Chesley Mathews, "Melville's Reading of Dante," *Furman Studies*, n.s., VI (1958), 1–8. The explicit role given to Cary's Dante in *Pierre* (1852), Melville's next novel after *Moby-Dick*, attests clearly to Melville's attentive reading of the *Inferno*; for evidence that he also read the *Purgatorio* and *Paradiso* with care, see Howard Schless, "*Moby-Dick* and Dante: A Critique and Time Scheme," *Bulletin of the New York Public Library*, LXV (May, 1961), 304n, and Merrell R. Davis, *Melville's "Mardi": A Chartless Voyage* (New Haven, 1952), 85, 86n, 150n.

Quotations of *The Divine Comedy* in Italian are from the edition of Charles S. Singleton (6 vols.; Princeton, 1970–75).

matic treatment of the crossing of allegory in the entire poem, expands like a commentary on this first threshold scene of reading.
Dante and Virgil are forbidden entry into nether hell by the Furies,
who threaten to reveal Medusa and turn the travelers to stone. Virgil counsels Dante:

> "Turn thyself round, and keep
> Thy countenance hid; for if the Gorgon dire
> Be shown, and thou shouldst view it, thy return
> Upwards would be for ever lost." This said,
> Himself, my gentle master, turn'd me round;
> Nor trusted he my hands, but with his own
> He also hid me. Ye of intellect
> Sound and entire, mark well the lore conceal'd
> Under close texture of the mystic strain.   (*Inf.* IX, 55–63)

Henry Francis Cary's translation improvises at an important point:
the last line is *sotto 'l velame de li versi strani*, "under the veil of the
strange verses." John Freccero, detecting the hidden presence of II
Corinthians in the episode, has shown that the passage is a comment on the nature of Christian allegory.[24] The Medusa, who if unveiled would petrify the wayfarers, is in direct contrast with Moses,
whose remaining veiled signifies the hardened minds of the children of Israel. The turn to Virgil parallels the turn to Christ which
the Jews are exhorted to make. The exhortation to read what is
"conceal'd" reproduces Paul's concern with reading spiritually. Finally, the address to the reader brings to the fore the presentation of
this scene as an allegory of allegorical reading, Dante's closed physical eyes—closed to literal representation—exactly corresponding
to the reader's open intellectual eye ("mark well," *mirate*, literally
"look at"), to signify the choice of spirit over letter.

The disjunction in Dante the poet's turn away from his fictional
scene to address the reader makes evident an underlying disjunction
in the entire poem: between Dante pilgrim and Dante poet. The
distance between the two views, unknowing and knowing, makes
allegory a perpetual possibility in the structure of the poem; for an
event that has a simple meaning—or obscurity—to the earlier

---

24. Freccero, "Medusa," 1–18.

Dante has acquired a deeper sense to the later one. The difference is also temporal and, although it is only in a single life, it thus implies the temporal movement in the salvation of the human race. Dante's own allegorical reading of his poem, in the letter to Can Grande, links the progress of the soul and the deliverance of the Jews and of mankind as parallel levels of a single action. The pilgrim's rescue and the fulfillment of his understanding have no guarantee in advance but, once they are accomplished, take on retrospectively a continuity with the pattern of sacred history.

One further pattern reenacted in the Medusa episode is the entry of the mediator-figure to rend the veil and open the passageway to a new, saving truth. Virgil can save Dante from petrification, but to cross the threshold into Dis they both must wait for the descent of an angel to open the gate. In first mentioning this necessity to Dante, Virgil recalls the descent of Christ into hell to liberate the souls waiting for deliverance. Implicit in the legend of the harrowing of hell is an act of violence, staunchly resisted but carried through:

> This their insolence, not new,
> Erewhile at gate less secret they display'd,
> Which still is without bolt; upon its arch
> Thou saw'st the deadly scroll.   (*Inf.* VIII, 124–27)

The descending angel is similarly referred to as "one whose strong might can open us this land." The resistance of the devils, however, is so strong that Virgil says to Dante, "We may not enter without rage" (*Inf.* IX, 33). The angel's belated entry is awesome:

> Loud-crashing, terrible, a sound that made
> Either shore tremble.
>
> . . .
>
> Ah me! how full
> Of noble anger seem'd he. To the gate
> He came, and with his wand touch'd it, whereat
> Open without impediment it flew.   (*Inf.* IX, 65–66, 88–90)

The inexplicability of this event—the angel says not a word to the travelers, "but wore / The semblance of a man by other care / Beset, and keenly prest"—combines with its violence to present a model of allegorical interpretation quite different from Philo's serene illumination. The entry into a deeper understanding is accomplished only by the will of God, for unknowable reasons, in an action clearly not deserved by the petitioner. The truth can be reached only by passing through the perilous arch of the literal, the petrified text of the Law; in that text, however, an opening must be forced. It must be read against the grain, even, if necessary, in exactly the opposite sense from its assumed meaning. Recently Giuseppe Mazzotta, finding the drama of interpretation enacted in several episodes of Dante's poem, has concluded that "the process of interpretation by which the past is handed over seems to imply that violence is the genuine and fruitful mode of preserving the past and that revision is inevitably an act of betrayal, a metaphor of appropriation." In the *Commedia*, he argues, "the act of reading emerges as the fundamental metaphor upon which Dante's view of history depends." As Francesca's book-induced adultery demonstrates, "to take the metaphors of the text literally . . . is to die. At the same time, reading is also the experience by which the reader resists the seductive authority of the text by doing violence to and interpreting the letter." [25]

The peculiar logic of allegory from the beginning of Christianity onward is: violate to preserve. For Dante, who appropriates Paul and the author of Hebrews in their insistence on hope and openness to the future, their use of threshold and veil imagery, and their concern with letter and spirit, the process of interpretation is not a serene or scholarly *Aus-legung*, a careful laying-out of the text. It is instead a perilous and powerful event. It does violence to the physical surface of things by interpenetrating them with spirit. It does violence to the uniform fictional time of lived experience, superimposing upon it further dimensions of author's and reader's time. Finally, it does violence to the supposed integrity of the self and the self-constituting power of the intellect, because the intellect under its own power cannot force open the doors of passage. A mediator—Christ, the Holy Spirit, or some special emissary—must intervene, carrying the key that is actually a wand to strike, like Moses,

25. Giuseppe Mazzotta, *Dante, Poet of the Desert: History and Allegory in the "Divine Comedy"* (Princeton, 1979), 190–91.

24

the unyielding rock of the letter and transform it into the fluidity of significance.

The image of the community is not readily evident in the allegory of the *Inferno*. In the midst of this great anti-community Dante's embrace of Virgil must stand for the desertion of self and trust in another which are essential to community. Several times Dante must physically clasp Virgil in order to cross a threshold: in facing Medusa, in riding on Geryon's back down into Malebolge, in escaping the devils at the ruined bridge, in passing into lowest hell in the palm of Antaeus' hand, and finally and most graphically, in leaving hell itself by crawling down Satan's body.

In purgatory, however, the achievement of community becomes no longer a desperate solution but a problem on a larger scale. The souls crossing the water and singing "In exitu Israel de Aegypto" indicate that the true community, which has existed in history only as an image, is achieved as a reality in the afterlife. In political life on earth, however, it remains something distant. The simple model of unified believers projected by St. Paul in Corinthians cannot operate for Italy. Dante is thoroughly of the Western cast of mind on the separation of church and state: in purgatory Marco Lombardo sees the two in a tour-de-force image as "two suns, whose several beams / Cast light on either way, the world's and God's" (*Purg.* XVI, 107–108). These two thus form two separate communities of earthly allegiance. One may allegorically represent the other; indeed, the only possible relation between the two on earth is an allegorical one, for Dante follows St. Augustine in seeing the earth as a "little threshing-floor" which will separate the City of God from the City of Man only at the end of time.

Whether his hope was for the political community to be an image of the City of God or for an earthly polity that simply did not actively prevent the virtual community of the City of God from functioning, Dante saw unmistakably that the two embodiments of community to which he had devoted his life and his passion—Florence and the Church—were in states of crisis. His exile from Florence naturally magnified the elements of sacred history he could see reenacted in his own political life. But Dante saw clearly that Flor-

ence was in an irreversible state of faction; in his once open and
hospitable city reigned a political viciousness that was the direct
cause of his exile, and he could return only if the viciousness were
somehow to disappear. This chance seemed so remote that he does
not mention it until the late canto of the *Paradiso* in which he is
examined on hope. Canto XXV begins:

> If e'er the sacred poem, that hath made
> Both heaven and earth copartners in its toil,
>   . . . be destined to prevail
> Over the cruelty, which bars me forth
> Of the fair sheep-fold, where, a sleeping lamb,
> The wolves set on and fain had worried me;
> With other voice, and fleece of other grain,
> I shall forthwith return; and, standing up
> At my baptismal font, shall claim the wreath
> Due to the poet's temples.   (*Par.* XXV, 1–9)

Clearly the prospect of the political situation righting itself, tied
as it was to the pope's interests, was out of the question. Dante's
only hope—and the unconditional theological quality of that hope
is the focus of this canto—was that his poem itself might work a
magical transformation on his sentencers. He depicts a transformation also in himself, but one already accomplished: from lamb to
mature poet. If he is to return it will be on his own terms, and he
imagines himself in a triumphant entry into the city, returning to
the place of his spiritual origin to reclaim it to his present life.
These transformations are absolute, and the "other voice" (*altra
voce*) Dante attributes to himself is virtually a literal translation of
allegoria, sometimes termed in Latin *alieniloquium* or "other-speech."
When the genuine perspective of allegory enters, the fulfillment of
sacred historical models in secular experience becomes an ambiguous and uncertain promise, not to be brought about by gradual im-
provement of conditions already known but only by a sudden transfiguration into the unexpected.[26]

At times such a unification is anticipated in the *Commedia* by

26. See Walter Benjamin, *The Origin of German Tragic Drama*, trans. John Osborne
(London, 1977), 233–35, on the "miracle" in baroque allegory.

Dante's allusions to the model of the Roman Empire under Julius Caesar. Dante's treatise *De Monarchia* is based on a hope of a united Italy according to the plan of the empire. In the *Commedia*, however, the allusions to Caesar reveal the structure of this desire for political unity as allegorical—referring to a past entity which through legend has become a model of totality. The achievement of that model in concrete time is left to the domain of pure hope.

Sometimes, in addition, that model is inserted into the text in such a way that it invokes its religious counterpart, that other community to which Dante belonged, and the one that in the poem takes precedence. This happens in Canto IX of *Purgatorio*, at the entrance to purgatory—a scene that may serve as the résumé of the structural features of Christian allegory, for it is one of the most momentous threshold-crossings in Dante's journey, parallel to his entrance into the City of Dis in *Inferno* IX. The descending angel is here, but the angel has become an institution—he regulates the entry into purgatory, trying the gate with a key of gold and a key of silver, allegorical devices probably representing the Church's power to remit sin and the actual penitence of the individual. This is clearly an allegorical moment: Dante has just dreamed of being lifted up into the Empyrean by an eagle; at the same time he is actually carried to the level before the gates by St. Lucy, who descends from heaven as another mediator figure to transport him across a boundary. The dream at the threshold provides a text which the rest of the action in the canto explicates.[27] The steps leading to the gate are of three colors, emblems of theological dogma. Here, as in St. Paul, the crucial act is a form of writing on the body. As a signal of the difference between infernal and purgatorial allegory, however, the images of text and body are not opposed but united: the angel traces seven *P*s on Dante's brow (for *peccata*, sin), marks that are to be effaced only as he performs his penance on each level. As Dante is instructed to enter through the gate he is reminded by the angel, "he forth again departs who looks behind." A threat of petrification remains in this allusion to Christ's warning about the sec-

27. On the pattern of threshold dream and explication, see Edwin Honig, *Dark Conceit: The Making of Allegory* (Evanston, Ill., 1959), 71–78.

ond coming: "he that is in the field, let him likewise not return
back. Remember Lot's wife" (Lk. 17:31–32).

Caesar's moment comes next, in a curious detail. As the gate is
opened to let Dante in, the metal pivots sound against the hinges so
loudly that "harsh was the grating; nor so surlily/ Roar'd the Tarpeian, when by force bereft / Of good Metellus, thenceforth from
his loss / To leanness doom'd" (*Purg.* IX, 135–38). Dante always
refers to Julius Caesar's accession to power and his uniting of Italy as
if they were part of salvation history. In *Purgatorio* XVIII an instance from one of Caesar's victories is cited side by side with an
instance from the life of the Virgin Mary as examples against sloth.
Here, as in that later citation, the reference is to an event depicted
in Lucan's *Pharsalia*, the epic of the struggle between Caesar and
Pompey: "When Metellus had been led away, forthwith the temple
was flung open. Then did the Tarpeian Rock re-echo, and with a
loud peal bear witness to the opening of the door" (*Pharsalia*, III,
153–68). The Roman Treasury was being kept in the Temple of
Saturn on the Tarpeian Rock in Rome and the tribune Metellus ap-
pointed to keep it safe; Caesar's "liberation" of it was the unofficial
sign of his triumph in Rome. His forcible entry makes him a type of
Christ the mediator, descending into hell and opening the treasury
of the afterlife, countermanding the guardian figure sworn to protect it from spoliation. With this act a community is brought home
to itself; so, the analogy suggests, Dante has reentered his true
homeland like an exiled Caesar returned. But this obscure, hidden
reference to a political community redeemed to itself is invoked, it
seems, only to indicate the remoteness of the possibility of its happening as an earthly political event in Dante's lifetime. And the
final detail in the canto describes the uncertain, "indistinct" status
of the community in the view of allegory:

> Attentively I turn'd,
> Listening the thunder that first issued forth;
> And "We praise thee, O God," methought I heard,
> In accents blended with sweet melody.
> The strains came o'er mine ear, e'en as the sound
> Of choral voices, that in solemn chant

With organ mingle, and, now high and clear
Come swelling, now float indistinct away.   (*Purg.* IX, 139–45)

What this brief survey has attempted to show is a dynamic moment in the origin of allegory. This moment is a peripeteia, a turning away and then back upon itself that is the essence of figural language.[28] This structure underlies allegorical interpretation, or allegoresis: it is the origin of the "other meanings" given to a text. Even if the interpreter wants to assert that the meaning is inherent in the text and continuous with the movement of its intention, it is the break of that movement, caused when it brushes against an opposing text, that engenders the allegorical meaning.

Similar structures reveal themselves in fictional allegories. A frequent motif is the moment in which the protagonist must choose between two alternatives, often two paths. This threshold moment, presenting a radical divergence in the line of action, resembles in its outlines the discontinuous moment of allegorical interpretation, and thus, over and above the immediate allegorical meaning its author may have intended, represents the process of allegory itself: it is an allegory of allegory.

Other kinds of action also lend themselves to representing allegorical interpretation: the anatomization of a body or dismantling of a building, for instance, or the following of an earlier, enigmatic scene by a later scene that seems to restate the terms of the earlier scene in clearer, more differentiated form. In *The Scarlet Letter*, for example, the discovery of a letter and scroll on the second floor of a customs house presents metaphorically the discovery of a higher level of signification in the history of a culture. The three scaffold scenes successively reveal the natures of the characters involved in them. More strikingly, Dimmesdale's turn away from a text (the Bible of his ministry) and toward a body (Hester's) constitutes his decisive moment, a moment completed only by his discovery of a writing on a body—his own. Another image of murderous writing on a body is the basis of Kafka's "The Penal Colony." Both these

28. Cf. the *peripeteia* de Man detects in the narrative of Rousseau's *La Nouvelle Héloïse* (*Allegories of Reading*, 216).

works give new meaning to the statement that the letter kills. Hence allegory does not achieve a solution to the crisis that engenders it, for the reinscription of the old text on the living body can destroy life just as much as it disrupts the literal sense of the action. What allegory does achieve is the birth of significance and thereby the reclaiming of the past for the future.

The distinction between allegory and allegoresis, or the similar distinction in Dante's *Convivio* between the allegory of poets and the allegory of theologians, is useful but does not mark off two fundamentally different forms. In allegory fictional creation is implicitly united with interpretation, because allegory is a mode of writing that must invent fictions in order to read (as with Philo's interpretation of Cain's wife) or must read in order to continue fictional action (as with Dante's thresholds). Similarly, the important distinction between the timeless, "vertical" allegory on several levels—the cosmos, virtues, etc.—invented by the Hellenists, and the historical, "horizontal" allegory of Judaeo-Christian figural typology implies not two completely separate species so much as the two coordinates of all allegory. Allegory is essentially about the relation of the timely to the timeless, the attempt to see earthly actions in the light of some heavenly paradigm. Though one or the other may be suppressed, neither history nor the Idea can be entirely absent from allegory.

All facets of allegory have a common point of origin, regardless of how that origin may be obscured. Political allegory, satirical allegory, and "personal" allegory all accomplish their essential troping by viewing their sad or ridiculous procession of events in the often ironic or condemnatory light of a heavenly paradigm. Since Christianity, this paradigm has been preeminently sacred history and, implied in it, the community as chosen people. "Personal" allegory can never be solely personal, since the motives for writing in that genre, like the motives for writing secret political allegory, stem from a desire to indict society or a political regime for being the opposite of what it ought to be—Utopia or the *Civitas Dei*.

Finally, allegory is not an honorific term. Benjamin's study of the baroque allegorical devices that were so repulsive to neoclassical tastes shows them to be the expression of a frightening discovery by a whole culture. In his interpretation, the deadness, mechanical-ness, and lack of grace in these emblems reveal the dominance of three agents in the world of seventeenth-century Germany: politi-cal and mercantile force, alienation from nature, and death. In our time, of course, the pure strangeness of baroque allegory lends it a grotesque charm. But whether its excesses be extolled or con-demned, as allegory it cannot be completely dismissed. For even "bad" allegory (by whatever aesthetic standards it is judged) is in the final analysis not wholly "untrue," since its mere existence is a sign that a culture has attained a critical self-scrutiny—a coming to awareness of the current absence of community, or of the virtues, or of the progress of the soul, however murky that awareness may be. This crisis surfaces with its greatest force yet in the epoch of Melville.

II

~~~~

THE ROMANTIC CRISIS
OF ALLEGORY

ALLEGORY IS a device for bonding together opposite and contradictory aspects of a functioning society—aspects too widely separated for the immediate and delightful conjunction that paradox implicitly effects within the individual. A graver disjunction in society itself is the matter of concern for allegory. That Melville was aware of a misalignment of the Western social order is evident in a passage in *Pierre*, written within a few months after the completion of *Moby-Dick*. In it he makes explicit the contradiction between text and culture that produced the most serious crisis of his day:

> Sooner or later in this life, the earnest, or enthusiastic youth comes to know, and more or less appreciate this startling solecism:—That while, as the grand condition of acceptance to God, Christianity calls upon all men to renounce this world; yet by all odds the most Mammonish part of this world—Europe and America—are owned by none but professed Christian nations, who glory in the owning, and seem to have some reason therefor.
>
> This solecism once vividly and practically apparent; then comes the earnest reperusal of the Gospels: the intense self-absorption into the greatest real miracle of all religions, the Sermon on the Mount.[1]

Although these lines issue from a narrator admittedly at some distance from Melville himself—it has been proposed that the narrator

1. Herman Melville, *Pierre, or The Ambiguities*, ed. Harrison Hayford, Hershel Parker, and Thomas Tanselle (Evanston, Ill., 1971), 207. Hereinafter cited as *Pierre* in the text.

is Pierre—they nonetheless carry serious weight in their presentation of the problem that profoundly troubled the mid-nineteenth century: the chasm between Christian principles and bourgeois social action.[2] In roughly the same years (1843–1855) that embraced the composition of Melville's major novels, Søren Kierkegaard was firing off his attacks on "the blinding illusion of Christendom" and on "geographical Christianity."[3] For him, as Karl Löwith points out, "true Christianity is nothing more than following Christ, an absolute renunciation of the entire world." Hence, Kierkegaard can maintain, "the extension of modern Christendom has done away with Christianity."[4]

What Kierkegaard is warring against is precisely the reasoned accommodation defended in Melville's *Pierre* by Reverend Falsgrave and by Plinlimmon in his pamphlet. The unyielding anti-worldliness of Kierkegaard's position causes him to renounce the quest for a balanced normalcy in an age which, to his view, had lost all sense of correspondence between real and ideal, between individual and common good, and—most fundamentally—between signifier and signified. Melville condemns the falsity with equal vigor, but by placing the argument in a fictional satire of worldly wise clergy and of innocent youth, he encompasses the human condition without rejecting it.

A crisis of language lies at the heart of the issue. Language is the medium wherein a people most fully asserts its actual unity. At the same time, language bears referential traces to the ideal unity, or community, envisioned in the commonly held patriarchal text. For Kierkegaard, a violation of language reflects a sin against truth. When well-endowed and thoroughly respected bishops are eulogized as being "witnesses to the truth"—using the same term applied to the early Christian martyrs (*martyros* = witness)—then Kierkegaard has to protest that the signifier no longer brings to

2. Raymond J. Nelson, "The Art of Herman Melville: The Author of *Pierre*," *Yale Review*, LIX (Winter, 1970), 197–214.

3. Søren Kierkegaard, quoted by Howard A. Johnson, "Introduction," in Walter Lowrie (trans.), *Kierkegaard's Attack upon "Christendom," 1854–1855* (2nd ed.; Princeton, 1968), xxiii.

4. Karl Löwith, *From Hegel to Nietzsche: The Revolution in Nineteenth-Century Thought*, trans. David E. Green (New York, 1964), 159–60.

mind anything like its signification in the New Testament: "Now what I argued against was the linguistic solecism of calling what we mean by priests, deans, bishops, 'witnesses' or 'witnesses to the truth'; it was against this linguistic usage I protested, because it is blasphemous, sacrilegious."[5] "Solecism" seems an ironic understatement, for Kierkegaard goes on to inveigh against the hypocrisy of an entire bourgeois civilization on the basis of this mere error in linguistic usage. Yet his use of the term is also quite serious, for his attack is more concerned with honesty than with reform. Kierkegaard sees that Christianity's signifiers have become petrified.

Melville's satire in *Pierre*, similarly, demonstrates no wish to put things right by ridiculing the wrong. The same term *solecism* appears in the passage I have just quoted, used with the same combination of irony and serious intent. Melville further undercuts the gravity of the crisis he describes by making the person who discovers it the "earnest, or enthusiastic youth," a naïve and self-occupied version of the seeker of truth or of the good (both *earnest* and *enthusiastic* had gained pejorative connotations in Melville's time). Yet once the center of orthodoxy iself is seen to be the position most false (as it is when Kierkegaard calls the clergy's use of language "blasphemous"), then a central nonironic point of view no longer exists, and one has to be somewhat eccentric in order to see the aberration of a world gone radically astray. Accordingly, a program for revolution or reform is not the answer, since it would proclaim a new center around which eventually a new security would develop. For both Melville and Kierkegaard, security itself is the enemy. To undermine the complacency of the bourgeois world one must de-center all points of view; and if the message one proclaims can be seen equally well as either a somewhat foolish misunderstanding or the central intellectual crisis of the epoch, that is the risk one must—and wants to—take.

Against this backdrop of misdirections one can discern in the earnest youth's discovery the outlines of the cultural situation that produces allegory. As in the Platonic model of unchaining and ascent from the cave, this critical moment is structured in a series of

5. Lowrie (trans.), *Kierkegaard's Attack upon "Christendom,"* 23.

turns. The first turn is a recognition of the discrepancy between the biblical and social meanings of Christianity (Europe and America "the most Mammonish part of the world" and yet "professed Christian nations"). The second turn is an unmediated gaze at the origin-text, an attempt to read it by native powers and force of will alone ("earnest reperusal" and "intense self-absorption"), by means of a direct encounter with a source of power that should have remained somehow veiled or mediated. In this turn to scripture, the result is less a petrification—as it is when Pierre directly confronts Isabel's revelation of kinship—than a fascination with, one might even say a fixation upon, the principles of the text. This turn produces a total attunement to the message of the Sermon on the Mount.

We come here to something quite close to Melville's heart. By all indications Melville took the Sermon on the Mount to be the very core of spiritual truth. One recalls his joyful remark in a letter to Evert Duyckinck on discovering Shakespeare belatedly—"Ah, he's full of sermons-on-the-mount, and gentle, aye, almost as Jesus."[6] The succinct reversals of the Beatitudes—"Blessed be ye poor: for yours is the kingdom of God"; "blessed are ye that weep now: for ye shall laugh" (Lk. 6:20, 21)—stand at the origin of an Ishmael that could extol a sub-sub-librarian. These words, continues the passage in *Pierre*, "embody all the love of the Past, and all the love which could be imagined in any conceivable Future" (*Pierre*, 207). Yet for all the purity of the Sermon on the Mount, the "enthusiastic heart" draws from its reading a dangerously uncritical notion of its intent: "Such emotions as that Sermon raises in the enthusiastic heart; such emotions all youthful hearts refuse to ascribe to humanity as their origin. This is of God! cries the heart, and in that cry ceases all inquisition" (*Pierre*, 207–208). This description is a kind of caricature of what the interpretation of a text has become after the loss of a coherent intellectual tradition. No longer the insertion of oneself into a community of discourse that spans centuries, it is now a solitary encounter that allows one's own emotional experiences alone to be a privileged source of meaning.

The third and fourth turns compound the error of the first two:

6. Herman Melville to Evert Duyckinck, February 24, 1849, in Merrell R. Davis and William H. Gilman (eds.), *The Letters of Herman Melville* (New Haven, 1960), 77.

Now, with this fresh-read sermon in his soul, the youth again gazes abroad upon the world. Instantly, in aggravation of the former solecism, an overpowering sense of the world's downright positive falsity comes over him; the world seems to lie saturated and soaking with lies. . . . But again he refers to his Bible, and there he reads most explicitly, that this world is unconditionally depraved and accursed; and that at all hazards men must come out of it. But why come out of it, if it be a True World and not a Lying World? Assuredly, then, this world is a lie.

Hereupon then in the soul of the enthusiast youth two armies come to the shock; and unless he prove recreant, or unless he prove gullible, or unless he can find the talismanic secret, to reconcile this world with his own soul, then there is no peace for him in this life. (*Pierre*, 208)

For all his turns, the earnest youth makes one too few. His allegiance to the true world that the scriptures represent, a world of unquestioned authority and literal meaning, chains him to inaction and finally, as with Pierre in his allegiance to paternal truth, leads him to self-annihilation. The allegorist swerves away from this fate by making one further turn. Although in Melville's time he cannot escape knowing that "this world is a lie," he nonetheless can project a move to embrace the world as though it were a body, even if it lies "saturated and soaking with lies," whether out of love for the world or (like Dante embracing Virgil) out of sheer instinct for survival. In Melville's age the romantic hopes of historical synthesis began to disintegrate visibly, and, for the poets who saw this decay, a desperate cohesion of high love and low instinct may have seemed the only recourse (although the grotesqueness of that partnership was publicly rejected). No better example for this attitude does the age provide than in a work appearing six years after *Moby-Dick*—and equally misunderstood—*Les Fleurs du mal*, in which Baudelaire's persona embraces his whore in full awareness of their perdition.[7]

Because the characters in *Pierre* refuse to embrace an imperfect world, the novel poses all the more sharply the nineteenth-century predicament of Biblical interpretation. Pierre places himself apart

7. See Charles Baudelaire, "Au Lecteur," *Oeuvres complètes*, ed. Claude Pichois, Bibliothèque de la Pléiade (2 vols.; Paris, 1975), I, 5. This edition hereinafter cited as "Pléiade."

from the official carriers of the tradition because he has seen that, far from truly representing the virtue they profess, they in fact oppose and suppress it. The pamphlet of Plotinus Plinlimmon is a sardonic response to that recognition. It begins with the categories of "chronometricals" and "horologicals"—the absolute standard of the true versus its earthly approximation—thus establishing the Platonic dichotomy that has always been preliminary to the human attempt to make this flawed world more like its flawless counterpart. But here the argument veers in the opposite direction. The clock-metaphoric categories allow Plinlimmon to argue that just as Greenwich time is wrong in other meridians of the globe, so absolute "chronometrical" virtue in this world is both foolish and disastrous, and one should be satisfied with "horological" virtue, accommodated to creaturely needs. Furthermore, the entire history of Western civilization has shown chronometrical truth to be "false," for "the only great original moral doctrine of Christianity (*i.e.*, the chronometrical gratuitous return of good for evil . . .) has been found (horologically) a false one; because after 1800 years' inculcation from tens of thousands of pulpits, it has proved entirely impracticable" (*Pierre*, 215). Plinlimmon's analysis of the historical situation bears roughly the same relation to Melville's view that the author's viewpoint in "A Modest Proposal" bears to Swift's: the proposed solution is sardonic, but the problem described is genuine.

Allegory is implicit in the structure of this recognition that the two worlds of Christianity and Christendom are separate and opposed. Pierre's and the enthusiastic youth's refusals to turn to the world despite its corruption determine their destiny and mark their interpretive practice as a refusal of allegory. However, they still remain within an allegorically structured world, wherein distance from the ideal is the primary fact. *Pierre* is thus an allegory of the refusal of allegory, and of the disastrous consequences of that refusal. More than a tour de force, as this formulation might suggest, it is Melville's representation of the modern mind, nurtured in a tradition of Protestant appeal to the literal text but discovering that that text cannot be found written anywhere on the living body of the world.

Furthermore, *Pierre*'s narrator is anxious to refute any notion that

37

this dilemma can be solved by a radical rejection of either the world or the heavens. He refers to Plato, Spinoza, and Goethe as belonging to a "guild of self-impostors" who claim to have found the "talismanic secret" reconciling the soul and the world. This is a curious list, since Plato's turn away from the world's dark cave exactly opposes Spinoza's and Goethe's enthusiastic embraces of this world. But placing them together in this way serves to emphasize that they all propose a false solution to the tension between world and soul. "That profound Silence," the narrator continues, "that only Voice of our God, which I before spoke of; from that divine thing without a name, those impostor philosophers pretend somehow to have got an answer; which is absurd, as though they should say they had got water out of stone; for how can a man get a Voice out of Silence?" (*Pierre*, 208).

As the narrator poses it, the solution to the youth's dilemma seems to lie only in the realm of miracle, furthermore a miracle not even acknowledged as such but considered simply as an impossibility. The last words of this passage deliberately recall other crises of the impossible. The water from the rock, of course, denotes a historic moment in the Exodus, Moses' miraculous refreshment of his people at God's command. (The sacred-historical character of this event becomes explicit in I Cor. 10:4, when Paul adds, "and that Rock was Christ.") The tormented soul can be rescued only at moments such as this, and as the narrator has already stated at the beginning of the chapter (Book 14, "The Journey and the Pamphlet"), "All profound things, and emotions of things are preceded and attended by Silence" (*Pierre*, 204). Silence is a gap in the world of discourse, which is the world of secular temporality and understanding; hence the impossible and the miraculous can happen in this gap: "Yes, in silence the child Christ was born into the world" (*Pierre*, 204). But miracles cannot happen in a world accessible to discourse, where their mere suggestion is "absurd." Furthermore, the silence as described here is also a gap in which the miraculous might not happen: it may be simply a pure absence, an abyss: "Silence is at once the most harmless and the most awful thing in all nature. It speaks of the Reserved Forces of Fate. Silence is the only Voice of our God" (*Pierre*, 204).

38

With this paradox the earnest youth's question is given its final assessment: there may be a "salvation" from it; there cannot be a "solution" to it. The "Voice out of Silence" admits of no logical or discursive answer. Its overtones of the sublime silent God of the Old Testament challenge and intimidate any purely discursive thought. A passage in Job that Melville has elsewhere shown he knew quite well dramatically depicts this shattering encounter with the numinous: "In thoughts from the visions of the night, when deep sleep falleth on men, Fear came upon me, and trembling, which made all my bones to shake. Then a spirit passed before my face; the hair of my flesh stood up; It stood still, but I could not discern the form thereof: an image was before mine eyes, there was silence, and I heard a voice, saying, Shall mortal man be more just than God? Shall a man be more pure than his maker?" (Job 4:13–17).

The first phrase of this passage appears in Chapter 94 of *Moby-Dick*, given a comic joy instead of fear and trembling: "In thoughts of the visions of the night, I saw long rows of angels in paradise, each with his hands in a jar of spermaceti."[8] The entire encounter, however, strongly resembles Ishmael's childhood memory recalled in Chapter 4, "The Counterpane," when, banished to his bed by an unforgiving stepmother, he wakes in the night and "nothing was to be seen, and nothing was to be heard; but a supernatural hand seemed placed in mine" and "the nameless, unimaginable, silent form or phantom" seems seated at his bedside (p. 33).

Was this "form or phantom" benevolent—the hand placed in his—or malevolent—the "horrid spell" he goes on to say he felt at the time? The supernatural experience described here seems to have features of both good and evil and finally to transcend both categories, like the God in Job, who after long silence finally reveals himself to Job as beyond his conceptions of right and wrong. It is

---

8. Herman Melville, *Moby-Dick*, ed. Harrison Hayford and Hershel Parker (New York, 1967), 349. Page numbers in parentheses in the text refer to this edition.

Hayford and Parker print the phrase as "In visions of the night" because, failing to recognize the biblical echo, they suppose Melville changes the phrase without deleting his first version of the phrase. Parker has since acknowledged the error: see Hershel Parker, "Melville," in James Woodress (ed.), *American Literary Scholarship: An Annual, 1975* (Durham, N. C., 1977), 61.

only in such "impossible" experiences that some deliverance from the riddle of Christ versus Christendom, text versus culture, or chronometer versus horologe can be seen. In determinable experience, and in language, they remain at odds.

Here as elsewhere Melville shows the signature of the allegorist by using devious strategies to reintroduce the crisis-text in a way that will circumvent the impossibility of reading it in a contemporary setting. Here it is first of all disguised in the form of an unacknowledged allusion, and, in addition, it undergoes a metalepsis in that the problem of a New Testament passage (the Sermon on the Mount) is resolved by passages from the Old Testament (Exodus and Job). The earlier text thus denies the superiority of the later text. Both metalepsis and prolepsis can introduce the perspective of allegory because they subvert the monolithic authority of a text and make it only one member in a chain of texts separated by time and related by mutual reference. They thus introduce the perspective of history and especially of sacred or legendary history. Here the Old Testament allusions undermine both the primacy of the New Testament and the originality of the earnest youth's religious crisis by suggesting an instance of crisis earlier than the Gospels and by presenting a more ambiguous and all-encompassing version of religious experience.

This passage presents the central features of the situation for allegory in Melville's century. First of all, the arena for the crisis has shifted from the public discourse of a society to private experience. The text that has become unreadable is the Bible, and preeminently the New Testament, seen in the light of the entire Western secular tradition that has proceeded since that text first attained its central position in the West. The contradictions between text and tradition engender a crisis powerful enough to destroy the solitary subject, exemplified here by Pierre, who remains under the spell of a desire for nothing less than the Absolute but who can never move beyond the wall separating the self from the rest of the world. And, finally, the solution to the Romantic impasse is phrased in terms of an impossibility that is also a hidden reintroduction of the origin-text ("how can a man get a Voice out of Silence?")—but disguised, freed from the burden of its privileged status.

Re-allegorizing the Bible

Within the orbit of allegory as it functions in culture, Romanticism can be seen as the beginning of a general literary awareness of unreadability, not only as a local problem pertaining to a specific text but as an intrinsic problem in texts and in culture. Any text that comes to grips with issues of belief and commitment must demand a leap of certainty whose base it can neither supply nor invoke.[9] Often the locus of this crisis was the Bible, and quite often poets found they could not place the kind of trust in scripture that Melville's earnest youth does. The crisis of biblical interpretation brought on by the Enlightenment called the factuality and unity of sacred scripture into question, challenging its claims for a self-consistent morality. Herder led the surge of Romantic desire to discover a higher meaning at which a unity would again exist; but the route of medieval allegory, based on a theory of analogy, was no longer possible.

Instead, a more historical task for hermeneutics emerged: to discover the mythic level of meaning in Judaic culture, which would then stand as an exemplum to contemporary reality. Recent studies of hermeneutics have reinforced our realization that the Bible has generally been the text around which each epoch has formed its art of interpretation.[10] Although many Romantics wanted to discover analogical links between the Bible and contemporary reality, forming a continuous, progressive line of history, to others the continuity of that relation became the central issue—a problem which it became the task of history itself to solve.[11]

William Blake's use of the term *allegory* in his letters reflects an acute awareness of this ironic condition. For the established churches, he insists, "God is only an Allegory of Kings & nothing Else. . . . God is the Ghost of the Priest & King, who Exist, whereas God exists not except from their Effluvia."[12] In Blake, "allegory"

9. See Paul de Man's analysis of Rousseau's "Profession de foi du vicaire savoyard" in *Allegories of Reading*, 221–45.
10. See the studies of Hans W. Frei, *The Eclipse of Biblical Narrative: A Study in Eighteenth and Nineteenth Century Hermeneutics* (New Haven, 1974), and Gadamer, *Truth and Method.*
11. M. H. Abrams traces the line of Romantic belief in the continuity of history in *Natural Supernaturalism: Tradition and Revolution in Romantic Literature* (New York, 1971).
12. William Blake, marginal note on Thornton's *A New Translation of the Lord's Prayer,*

bears this stamp of officialdom, where all is reversed and the spirit is only an allegory of the letter. His vigorous repudiations of allegory in "A Vision of the Last Judgment" continue this line of thought: "Fable or Allegory are a totally distinct & inferior kind of Poetry. Vision or Imagination is a Representation of what Eternally Exists, Really & Unchangeably. Fable or Allegory is Form'd by the daughters of Memory. Imagination is surrounded by the daughters of Inspiration, who in the aggregate are call'd Jerusalem. . . . The Hebrew Bible & the Gospel of Jesus are not Allegory, but Eternal Vision or Imagination of All that Exists."[13] Blake rejects the element of allegory that Benjamin has called "routine," its portrayal of the world as a collection of familiar emblems, revealing the mundaneness and *vanitas vanitatum* of the world but virtually destroying any possibility of new inspiration. Blake's insistence that the Bible is "vision," on the other hand, already reestablishes a connection to the divine world as something that exists in the Idea, having constantly to be adequately imagined, and susceptible only to "Representation" in poetry, not to a direct conveying of experience as the Romantic symbol claims to do.

"Vision" thus becomes Blake's name for reading the Bible as *true* allegory: "Allegory addressed to the Intellectual powers, while it is altogether hidden from the Corporeal Understanding, is My Definition of the Most Sublime Poetry; it is also somewhat in the same manner defin'd by Plato."[14] Certainly his reading does not give the Bible a historical connection to the present in any continuous way —it is no blueprint for *Universalgeschichte*, marking the progress in human civilization. Read as Vision, rather, it reverses the signifier: signified relation of traditional allegories (in which the figures in the text signify the outside world) and becomes the truth of which the historical world is only the allegory. The Bible contains the design of spiritual history, a design reflected in the present epoch only by its continual failure to be drawn. In the same letter in

in Geoffrey Keynes (ed.), *The Writings of William Blake* (3 vols.; London, 1925), III, 387–88. Cf. Northrop Frye, *Fearful Symmetry: A Study of William Blake* (Princeton, 1947), 62.

13. William Blake, "A Vision of the Last Judgment," in David Erdman (ed.), *The Poetry and Prose of William Blake* (rev. ed.; Garden City, N.Y., 1970), 544.

14. William Blake to Thomas Butts, July 6, 1803, in Geoffrey Keynes (ed.), *The Letters of William Blake* (Cambridge, Mass., 1968), 69.

which he redefines sublime poetry as "Allegory addressed to the Intellectual powers," Blake sets himself the task of a poetry which will reveal the biblical Vision, "to speak to future generations by a *Sublime Allegory.*"

One critic explains the Blakean distinction between allegory and vision in this way: "Memory records and recalls unredeemable time; that is, memory *is* unredeemable—time past. . . . Vision, on the other hand, records redeemed time; that is, vision *is* redeemed time —eternal time."[15] The aim of redeeming the time unites itself with that recovery of lost tradition which Benjamin in our century saw as the task of history writing, made possible by allegorical contemplation. Blake's sublime allegory is thus a radical appropriation of tradition, but it is tradition transfigured, made into the object of visionary experience.

Coleridge presents a more moderate stance toward the visionary potential of the Bible. His remarks on biblical interpretation attempt a synthesis of the various movements of his time, to reconcile, if possible, the new notions of the Bible as historical myth and poetry with the Christian sense of its primacy as an inspired text for all times. Basil Willey presents Coleridge's attack on the fundamentalist literalism of his church in terms of the Pauline categories of letter and spirit, stone and flesh. For Coleridge, Willey summarizes, the Bible "must be approached as a receptacle of living truths, and not as a dead letter"; the doctrine of verbal inspiration "'petrifies' the whole body of sacred literature, and 'turns at once into a colossal Memnon's head, a hollow passage for a voice,' that which is in truth a living, breathing organism."[16]

For Coleridge, Blake, and increasingly for all poets since Robert Lowth's study of the Bible (*De sacra poesi Hebraeorum*, 1753) on the one hand and the Enlightenment challenges to the factual and authorial consistency of the Bible on the other, belief in the scriptures came to hinge on their power for the imagination. On that score Coleridge learned much from Herder's mythopoeic study of the Bi-

15. Edward J. Rose, "Los, Pilgrim of Eternity," in Stuart Curran and Joseph Anthony Wittreich (eds.), *Blake's Sublime Allegory: Essays on "The Four Zoas," "Milton," "Jerusalem"* (Madison, Wis., 1973), 99.
16. Basil Willey, *Nineteenth Century Studies: Coleridge to Matthew Arnold* (New York, 1949), 38–44.

ble, but he had to conclude that Herder fell far short of restoring the power of the scriptures to speak to the present day. The notion of *Einfühlung*, a foundation stone of historicism, placed great importance on a vivid, synthesizing imagination and a rich, living culture in re-creating the compositional milieu of the text. The price of this vividness was the loss of any ability of the text to refer to concerns of the present. Coleridge objects:

> How can Herder have the effrontery to assert that there is no Tone of ALLEGORY in the Tree of *Life*, and the Tree of the Knowledge of Good and Evil—& a talking Serpent—&c. &c. If these do not possess all the marks of Eastern Allegory, of allegory indeed in genere, what does? And why should not Moses introduce historical Persons in an allegory, as well as the Author of the Book of Job?—History was for instruction—no such cold Divisions then existed, as *matter of fact* Chronicles, & general Gleanings of the Past, such as those of Herodotus.[17]

Maintaining the claim of the Mosaic authorship in order to assert the poetic intention, power, and unity of the Old Testament, Coleridge here goes beyond Herder's construction of myth as a primarily intracultural set of data that cannot speak directly to us but must be seen only within the general frame of its own historical epoch.[18] By espousing an allegorical intention on the author's part—from just the same evidence that had led Philo to the same conclusion—Coleridge is able to argue that the purpose of history goes beyond mere recording and is in fact antithetical to data collecting. The task of history writing is not to make "cold Divisions" but to unify, to indicate transcendent historical patterns as well as to record the past. Coleridge's program would restore the Bible to the modern reader as a potent text for the imagination.

However, the interpretation of the Bible could no longer be the collective act of an entire people, accomplished by a systematic allegory to which all assent. Its power of living significance could op-

17. Samuel Taylor Coleridge, marginal note on Herder's *Briefe, das Studium der Theologie betreffend*, quoted in Elinor S. Shaffer, *"Kubla Khan" and "The Fall of Jerusalem": The Mythological School in Biblical Criticism and Secular Literature, 1770–1880* (Cambridge, 1975), 134–35.
18. See Frei, *Eclipse of Biblical Narrative*, 183–201, on Herder.

erate only if the individual reader were to bring to bear on it all his interpretive ability, his knowledge of poetry, and his experience from life. Coleridge argues in *Confessions of an Inquiring Spirit* that "as much of reality, as much of objective truth, as the Scriptures communicate to the subjective experiences of the Deliverer, so much of present life, of living and effective import, do these experiences give to the letter of these Scriptures."[19] Life and text are to exist in mutual interaction. A disjunction or suspension between the two would be intolerable to him: "Is the grace of God so confined,—are the evidences of the present and actuating Spirit so dim and doubtful,— that to be assured of the same we must first take for granted that all the life and co-agency of our humanity is miraculously suspended?"

Coleridge wanted to bridge the disjunction which he felt to exist in the traditional allegorical reading of scripture, a "suspension" of continuous standards between religious language and social language that increasingly turned into hypocrisy between religious life and social life. If the claims of the spirit are seen to operate only on a special, isolated group of actions unconnected to most of life, or if they are interpreted only in a special way that might actually reverse their professed meaning in practice, then the result is the crisis world of Plinlimmon's pamphlet. Coleridge's hope was to prevent that crisis.

Coleridge enunciates his famous definition of the symbol precisely as a response to this need. The title of the essay in which this appears, *The Statesman's Manual*, refers to the Bible and indicates the breadth of meaning he believes could be possible in reading Scripture. He begins by reflecting that "it is among the miseries of the present age that it recognizes no medium between *Literal* and *Metaphorical*. Faith is either to be buried in the dead letter, or its name and honors usurped by a counterfeit product of the mechanical understanding, which in the blindness of self-complacency confounds SYMBOLS with ALLEGORIES."[20] There follows the definition of symbol as something characterized by "the translucence of

---

19. Samuel Taylor Coleridge, *Confessions of an Inquiring Spirit*, ed. H. StJ. Hart (Stanford, 1957), 70.

20. Samuel Taylor Coleridge, *The Statesman's Manual*, in *Lay Sermons*, ed. R. J. White (Princeton, 1972), Vol. VI of 16 vols. projected, *Collected Works*, ed. Kathleen Coburn, 30.

the Eternal through and in the Temporal" and by its existence "as a living part of that Unity, of which it is the representative." But the beginning of the paragraph first locates the place that symbol is to fill, a "medium between" the dead letter and the mechanical understanding, a bridge between mere designation and a priori imposition of universals. The symbol, textually considered, is the place where authoritative precedent and principle can meet and interact with the gleanings of lived experience.

Elinor Shaffer has paralleled Coleridge to Origen in defending the coherence of the Bible against charges of barbarism.[21] Like Philo, Origen's mentor, Coleridge was passionately concerned to preserve the centrality of his society's chief religious text, but to do so by liberalizing its sense so that it could have important ethical and practical significance in the present. Yet if Coleridge is a mediator of interpretations like Philo and Origen, he is so not in the service of a mode of interpretation that abstracts textual meaning out of a temporal, historical realm and into a realm of pure timeless principles. True to his age, he must make present temporal experience the focus of the search for meaning. Insisting that scripture has a "symbolic" import that is fully temporal, that is, is completed by the wealth of experiences we as readers bring to it, Coleridge smoothes over the abyss between text and life. In the same movement, however, he locates a break within experience, so that it no longer is purely and simply itself, unambiguously possessing its own sense; indeed, it may now be called directly into question by a text. De Man has pointed out the interpretive implications of the term *translucence*: in Coleridge's definition, "symbol and allegory alike now have a common origin beyond the world of matter. The reference, in both cases, to a transcendental source, is now more important than the kind of relationship that exists between the reflection and its source."[22]

These two sets of responses to scripture and allegory by two epoch-making poets represent limit-cases, extremes in opposite directions. Certainly Blake would disclaim for himself anything re-

---

21. Shaffer, *"Kubla Kahn" and "The Fall of Jerusalem,"* 136.
22. Paul de Man, "The Rhetoric of Temporality," in Charles S. Singleton (ed.), *Interpretation: Theory and Practice* (Baltimore, 1969), 177.

motely like Coleridge's intention of interpreting the Bible as the most perfect manual for statesmen—the Bible for Blake was, as vision, the triumphant dethroning of earthly kings and rulers. Coleridge is more concerned with hermeneutic application; hence it is not so much that the two poets controvert each other as that they take up the Bible at opposite ends: Blake at a transcendent point of origin and Coleridge at the near end where the wisdom of the text must decant into everyday understanding. Both are fundamentally Protestant modes of reading—the apocalyptic view of scripture as direct revelation, without need of a mediating zone of exegetes, and the concern (in lieu of breviary and confessional) to make scripture a guidebook that can direct every action in life. The two concerns become the two features that allegory must assume in order to live on into the nineteenth century. It must be *visionary*, transfiguring reality into a moment in the face of the heavenly Ideas. (One of Friedrich Schlegel's fragments remarks that a spiritual man is one for whom "everything visible has only the truth of an allegory."[23] It is the world, not the text only, which now must become allegorical.) And it must be *experienced*: Coleridge's project of harmonizing the Bible with contemporary understanding depends on drawing meanings out of one's store of lived experience, refusing to base meanings any longer on a special store of intellectual commentary.

Paradoxically, Coleridge's description of the symbol helps account for the possibility of a reformulated mode of allegory in the Romantic age as a mode centered on private experience rather than transcendent system. Because the new definition of symbol moved the locus of meaning out of a purely discursive context and into the sphere of individual life, the method of signification for allegory could no longer remain based in interpretive tradition. It had to shift to a temporal experience that could confront a person at certain moments and in certain places where meaning would appear, not in an image of fullness but as a fragment. Sacred tradition, once thought to be a seamless garment forming the clothing of being, could now appear as only a few tatters here and there, calling to

23. Friedrich Schlegel, "Ideen," in Ernst Behler (ed.), *Kritische Friedrich-Schlegel-Ausgabe* (35 vols projected; Munich, 1955–), II, 256. Hereinafter cited as *Kritische Ausgabe*.

mind both a former richness and one's present poverty. In his stroll through the streets of Paris, for instance, Baudelaire's *flâneur* experiences "local" (rather than "global") allegories. In a kind of obverse of the Wordsworthian "spots of time," he suddenly intuits not a participation of the self in being but an unbridgeable chasm of separation. Whereas the Romantic symbol, the expressive form chosen by Goethe in opposition to allegory, turns to inner experience, sealing off all divisive influences, in an attempt to allow the self to commune effortlessly with the divine, allegory reveals within the heart of this interiority a "silence" which, though it may be "the only Voice of our God," may not be the voice one seeks.

Two Test Cases: The City and Nature

The place of experiencing allegory moved from the throne room and the dungeon in the seventeenth century to the city in the nineteenth, where everyman in his everyday existence could fleetingly perceive those secrets of state and church that before were permitted only to the hero. By the time of Balzac and Poe, the city was no longer the place of civilization's future, where utopian plans could be projected in limitless potency. It had become a landscape to be seen in all its actual squalor, in a harsh, if implicit, comparison to the ideal landscape. Furthermore, as Peter Brooks insists, the description of the city was not destined to remain at a level of merely "registering" impressions: "It is here that we most feel the continuing force of the ethical motives behind Rousseau's pastoral—the very premise of a Balzacian or Baudelairean cityscape is the effort to move through and beyond phenomenology to total moral significance, to a vision of the landscape as an ethical framework and context for human life." Following Benjamin's work, Brooks notes that Baudelaire's poetry especially "makes the cityscape figure a drama of loss and exile," an allegory in which "the very presence of the city comes to figure absence, the destruction of what it replaces, the loss of home that it has masked with its constructions." [24]

This way of seeing was not confined to Paris but was a possibility for any city touched by the Western idea of the metropolis. Donald

24. Peter Brooks, "Romantic Antipastoral and Urban Allegories," *Yale Review*, LXIV (Autumn, 1974), 20, 23.

Fanger observes that Gogol's panoramic stories of Petersburg see only a "negative unity" in the city, but that "to perceive the negative image, one must believe in the possibility, constantly betrayed, of a positive one."[25] Andrey Bely once remarked of Gogol's characters that "the overthrown images of romanticism turned, as it were, inside out, overflow his works."[26] It is this "romanticism turned inside out" that forms the basis of rejuvenation for a discredited mode of literary representation—allegory—and allows it to attain, in Gogol, Baudelaire, Balzac, Dickens, Poe, and the Melville of *Pierre* and the urban stories, a remarkably contemporary and concrete realization.

The city becomes the place where the soul of a people can be seen materialized, but only as an immense corpse sprawled across the landscape. The myth of the city always reveals the fate of the "secret life" of the city, a life identified at once with a supposed soul or "mighty heart" (Wordsworth) and with the common people, the forgotten and misused people who built the city.[27] But neither can the city remain at the level of myth. Since it wears the scars of its history for all to see, it initiates its own explication and draws the contemplative citydweller into a reverie of loss. Benjamin wrote that the baroque allegory presented "history as a petrified primordial landscape"; its form for this melancholy revelation was the ruin. As the nineteenth-century city came to be seen not as a construction project but as a ruin, as Paris appears in Baudelaire's "Le Cygne," all of Western history began to fall under that same judgment and to appear as one long *Trauerspiel* of destruction and loss:

> Paris change! mais rien dans ma mélancolie
> N'a bougé! palais neufs, échafaudages, blocs,
> Vieux faubourgs, tout pour moi devient allégorie,
> Et mes chers souvenirs sont plus lourds que des rocs.[28]

> Paris changes! but nothing in my melancholy has
> stirred! new palaces, scaffoldings, blocks, old

---

25. Donald Fanger, *Dostoevsky and Romantic Realism: A Study of Dostoevsky in Relation to Balzac, Dickens, and Gogol* (Chicago, 1965), 109.

26. Quoted in Fanger, *Dostoevsky and Romantic Realism*, 114.

27. See the discussion of the "myth of Petersburg" portrayed by Pushkin in *The Bronze Horseman*, Fanger, *Dostoevsky and Romantic Realism*, 104.

28. Charles Baudelaire, "Le Cygne," Pléiade, I, 86.

suburbs, have all become an allegory for me, and
my dear memories are heavier than rocks.

The emerging modern city seemed designed to bring out all the
negative features of allegory: fixation on the past and on the errors
and villainies of history, distance from a state of nature as well
as from human community, the replacement of living with dead
forms, the repetitious familiarity of the conventions of allegorical
expression. Yet the distance of sign from significance in allegory can
also be cause for wonder and erotic pursuit, as Dante's *Paradiso* and
all allegories of vision show. In those the features are reversed and
allegory points toward a future of transfigured glory; its signature is a
hope no longer desperate but premised on a faith in a manifest and
radiant, even if mysterious or unattainable, body.

The German Romantics found this body in the forms of nature.
In a paradox crucial to the age, nature came to occupy center stage
not because of its exemplary simplicity but because of its challenging complexity, not because of its unshakable reality and "there"-
ness but because of its ambiguities and the absence of a definitive
interpretation of it. In the late eighteenth century J. G. Hamann
revived the medieval Christian notion of the world as God's second
text of revelation: "The Book of Nature is no other than ciphers,
hidden signs, which require that same key that unlocks Holy Scripture."[29] Alternatively, many writers used the ancient mystery-cult
trope that saw the world as a set of hieroglyphic signs constituting
God's writing in the world.[30] In either image, the world seen as a
text figures both the presence and the absence of divinity: the signs
testify to a higher power that has intentionally composed them, but
they also indicate the inability of that power to manifest itself directly or leave an unambiguous message. Hamann is aware of both
the disorder and the promise of order implied in nature: "Wherever
the guilt may lie (outside or inside us): in nature we have nothing
but a confusion of verses and *disiecti membra poetae* left to our dis-

29. Johann Georg Hamann, "Über die Auslegung der heiligen Schrift," in *Sämtliche
Werke*, ed. Josef Nadler (6 vols.; Vienna, 1949–57), I, 308. This edition hereinafter cited as
Sämtliche Werke. Cf. Abrams' discussion of this passage, *Natural Supernaturalism*, 402–403.
30. Liselotte Dieckmann, *Hieroglyphics: The History of a Literary Symbol* (St. Louis,
1970).

posal. To collect these [fragments] is the scholar's part; to interpret them, the philosopher's part; to imitate them—or yet bolder!—to set them right, the poet's part." [31]

Novalis describes this sense as a kind of phenomenological discovery: nature is experienced as not being simply natural, nor simply fallen in sin from a preternatural state, but as both more and less than natural: it is enchanted by signs. *Die Lehrlinge zu Sais* (1799) begins with this sense:

> Men walk various paths. Whoever pursues and compares them will see wondrous figures arise: figures that seem to belong to that great cryptology [*Chiffernschrift*] that can be glimpsed everywhere, on wings, eggshells, in clouds, in snow, in crystals and in rock formations, on freezing waters, inside and outside mountains, plants, animals, people, in the lights of the heavens, on sheets of pitch and glass that have been touched and smoothed, in filings around the magnet and strange conjunctures of chance. In them one divines the key to this magic writing [*Wunderschrift*], its grammar [*Sprachlehre*], but the divination refuses to be arranged according to any fixed forms and seems not to result in any higher key. An alkahest seems to have been poured out over the senses of men. Only momentarily do their wishes, their thoughts condense [*sich verdichten*]. Thus arise their divinations, but after a short while everything swims before their view again as before. [32]

This "divination" [*Ahndung*] is a momentary [*augenblicklich*] experience of condensation—Novalis preserves the etymological link to poetry [*Dichtung*] in *verdichten*. It is a pregnant moment of the kind to which the proponents of the Romantic symbol frequently attest. For Novalis, however, this condensation is not itself a communication of being but only a foreshadowing of the final revelation of a "higher key" which will unify all things. In the subsequent action in *Die Lehrlinge* the questing protagonist falls asleep and dreams he has completed the quest to unveil the mysterious face of Isis only to find there the face of his own beloved or, as in an earlier draft of the

31. Johann Georg Hamann, "Aesthetica in nuce," *Sämtliche Werke*, II, 199.
32. Novalis, *Die Lehrlinge zu Sais*, in Paul Kluckhohn and Richard Samuel (eds.), *Novalis Schriften* (4 vols.; Stuttgart, 1960–75), I, 79.

dream passage, his own face. Yet the narrative ends shortly after this point. Novalis, the poet of longing, differs significantly from the poets of adequate symbolic expression from Schiller to Joyce because he makes the moment of unification projected rather than present and makes it an intellectual, semiotic-linguistic moment as well as an emotional one.

The allegory of nature thus takes on the form of a discovery of writing on the body of nature and a quest to decipher that writing, a quest in which intellect and the passions are interblended. The quest motif is indigenous to the "allegory of love," as C. S. Lewis has shown;[33] and, as it becomes a task for the imagination, it ties in with another conviction felt deeply throughout the literary world after neoclassicism: the ardent desire for a new poetry based somehow on no mythological material of the past but on nature itself. Wilhelm von Humboldt envisioned something like a new Hesiod: "But what we miss even yet is a poet who . . . truly weds the formless mass to the developmental urge; one who, forever giving up dull description of any sort, will introduce us instead to the battle and the reconciliation of these creative energies themselves. . . . His main contribution would be the enrichment of our least fertile genre, that of didactic poetry, with some hitherto unknown models."[34] Thus, while turning directly to the things themselves, this poetry would still retain the ethical intention of allegorical poetry.

Friedrich Schlegel puts this desire most clearly in his critical landmark, the *Dialogue on Poetry* (1799). Ludovico, one of the Socratic characters in this fictionalized discussion, delivers a "talk on mythology" beginning with the theme that poetry is losing its vital energy, having long since lost a mythological ground out of which a poetic symbology could develop. Ludovico insists that a new mythology is needed, not, however, to be derived from "what was most immediate and vital in the sensuous world," as was the old mythology, but to arise out of "Idealism"—a term Schlegel uses to describe the new method of physics in his day, "idealist" because it observes

33. C. S. Lewis, *The Allegory of Love: A Study in Medieval Tradition* (London, 1936).
34. Wilhelm von Humboldt, *Cantabrica*, as translated in Marianne Cowan (ed.), *Humanist Without Portfolio: An Anthology of the Writings of Wilhelm von Humboldt* (Detroit, 1963), 117.

phenomena through what the twentieth-century historian of science Thomas Kuhn has called paradigms. By virtue of this rigor, he continues, "there must and will arise from the matrix of idealism a new and equally infinite realism, and idealism will not only by analogy of its genesis be an example of the new mythology, but it will indirectly become its very source." The new mythology would therefore not truly be myth, but rather, one supposes, a kind of allegorical expression of natural laws. For Schlegel there is never any question of a poetic mode that would provide direct access to the truth of nature. His character Ludovico evidently assumes that mythology is a consciously produced cultural artifact and so does not distinguish rigidly between the older mythology and the kind he is proposing. After all, he asks, "what is any beautiful mythology, other than the hieroglyphic expression of surrounding nature in [a] transfigured form of imagination and love?" Yet "hieroglyph" hardly seems correct here, for it is the human imagination and not some source from on high that does the encoding in a purely artifactual mythology. It is rather that nature itself is already hieroglyphic, and that the coded systems of artifacts are only allegorical expressions of this original codedness in nature. Under the pressure of discussion after his talk, Ludovico rephrases his claim to fit more closely the viewpoint that has been implicit all along, and his words provide a guidepost for the Romantics' reappraisal of allegory:

Lothario: All the sacred plays of art are only remote imitations of the infinite play of the universe, the work of art that is eternally forming itself.

Ludovico: In other words: all beauty is allegory. That which is highest, because it is inexpressible, can be said only allegorically.[35]

Yet even nature in this sublime sense is not the final basis for a new poetry. Lothario goes on to criticize Ludovico "for seeming to mention physics so exclusively, since in fact he tacitly based every-

35. Friedrich Schlegel, "Gespräch über die Poesie," in Behler (ed.), *Kritische Ausgabe*, II, 312, 318, 323. Translations are taken, with some changes, from Friedrich Schlegel, *Dialogue on Poetry and Literary Aphorisms*, ed. Ernst Behler and Roman Struc (University Park, Pa., 1968), 81–90.

thing on history, which, as much as physics, should be the real source of his mythology."[36] In this brief remark Lothario exposes Ludovico's hidden omission: mythology is primarily about human beings in relation to nature; hence it cannot escape being historical. This is a point brought out by Jürgen Habermas in refuting the twentieth-century illusion of a possible "atomic poetry": the information of the natural sciences "can only attain significance through the detour marked by the practical results of technical progress."[37] Nature, and natural science, can thus enter into poetry only insofar as they become historical.

The Romantic poets' judgment on history in relation to nature, however, is the very opposite of one that sees technical implementation as progress. Nature was to Wordsworth, in Harold Bloom's words, "the hard, phenomenal otherness that opposes itself to all we have made and marred."[38] It plays the adversary to human fantasies of domination. As a last testament of Eden, however, nature becomes increasingly allegorical the more it is marked by human destruction. Thus the final Romantic vision of nature sees its originary hieroglyphic markings mixed and disfigured with scars that themselves become part of a text, telling the history of nature.

In America, Emerson, to whom Melville like most other writers of his day looked for guidance, had absorbed the more optimistic side of these currents and espoused an aesthetic akin to Goethe's. For him the immediate apprehension, whether of beauty or of divine inspiration, took precedence over analysis. When he writes that the fable is a genre that "has in it somewhat divine . . . . [coming] from thought above the will of the writer" and emanating from "his constitution and not from his too active intention,"[39] he applies to a narrative form the attributes Coleridge assigned to the instantaneous revelation of the symbol. His derogation of conscious

36. Schlegel, "Gespräch über die Poesie," 324.

37. Jürgen Habermas, *Toward a Rational Society: Student Protest, Science, and Politics*, trans. Jeremy J. Shapiro (Boston, 1970), 52.

38. Harold Bloom, *The Visionary Company: A Reading of English Romantic Poetry* (rev. ed.; Ithaca, N.Y., 1971), xv.

39. Ralph Waldo Emerson, "Compensation," *Essays, First Series*, ed. Alfred R. Ferguson and Jean Ferguson Carr (Cambridge, Mass., 1979), Vol. II of *Collected Works*, ed. A. R. Ferguson, 63.

authorial intention implies a mistrust of allegory, but like Blake and Coleridge he distinguished between mere conventional allegory and an allegory of a higher kind. He writes in his journal, "I like that poetry which without aiming to be allegorical, is so. Which sticking close to its subject & that perhaps trivial can yet be applied to the life of man & the government of God & be found to hold."[40]

It is this unintentional allegoricalness that Emerson deems worthy of constant contemplation. For him allegory has great value if it indicates some prior unity of appearance and meaning. Another journal entry asks, "Will any say that the Meaning of the world is exhausted when he sees the allegory of a single natural process?"[41] In chapter 4 of *Nature*, Emerson characterizes man as continually stumbling onto glimpses of the transcendent in the natural world and in language. Words contain hidden truth in their etymological origins—"words are signs of natural facts"; but beyond that relation lies a further allegorical dimension in which "the world is emblematic": nature is an image of spirit.[42]

The possibility of language thus depends on a relation between nature and spirit that is significative, and that can be termed allegorical insofar as nature is structured not simply for its own ends but to signify another, higher structure. Nature's mediating role is characterized in terms of language: "Thus is nature an interpreter, by whose means man converses with his fellow men" (*Nature*, 20). Furthermore, language itself is allegorical: "Good writing and brilliant discourse are perpetual allegories," because in the mind of the person conversing "always a material image, more or less luminous, arises . . . which furnishes the vestment of the thought" (*Nature*, 20). Beneath all Emerson's comments, however, lies a faith in the ultimate connectedness of nature and spirit. Hence if nature is a text, it is a text that is finally completely knowable: "A life in harmony with nature," he asserts, "the love of truth and of virtue, will

40. Ralph Waldo Emerson, *Journals and Miscellaneous Notebooks*, ed. William H. Gilman *et al.* (16 vols. projected; Cambridge, Mass., 1960–), V, 88.

41. *Ibid.*, V, 185.

42. Ralph Waldo Emerson, *Nature*, in *Nature, Addresses, and Lectures*, ed. Robert E. Spiller and Alfred R. Ferguson (Cambridge, Mass., 1971), Vol. I of *Collected Works*, 17, 21. Hereinafter cited as *Nature* in the text.

purge the eyes to understand her text. By degrees we may come to know the primitive sense of the permanent objects of nature, so that the world shall be to us an open book, and every form significant of its hidden life and final cause" (*Nature*, 23). In Emerson what is strikingly like allegory as opposed to Romantic Symbolism is his sense that nature exists not in or for itself but for spirit. Thus nature always has a didactic function rendering it potentially a "perpetual allegory."

Earlier in *Nature*, Emerson introduces the image of the stars as a paradigm of the way in which nature holds significance: "The stars awake a certain reverence, because though always present, they are always inaccessible: but all natural objects make a kindred impression, when the mind is open to their influence" (*Nature*, 9). It is nature's quality of being always inaccessible that links Emerson's thought on signification to allegory rather than to symbol. Even though he rejects a reliance on tradition and places his faith in the power of immediacy to reveal the truth, he knows that such moments of vision are rare. *Experience* is a word of supreme importance for Emerson, but in his statements it has a core of absence, a reference to something else never entirely defined, a continual deferral of completeness clearly opposing the supposition of a leap into totality. In the Introduction to *Nature* this absence is intimated: "Every man's condition is a solution in hieroglyphic to those inquiries he would put. He acts it as life, before he apprehends it as truth" (*Nature*, 7). The distance between unconscious action and conscious apprehension of truth does not appear to concern him in this 1836 essay, but it is in fact what constitutes one's life history as a record of errors and griefs. The negative implications of this distance for the life of the mind unfold in "Experience" (1844), where the allegorical "lords of life" (Illusion, Temperament, Succession, Surface, Surprise, Reality, Subjectiveness) combine to allow man very little opportunity for vision.

Recent studies have pointed out the widespread employment of the concept of hieroglyph as model and as metaphor among writers of the American Renaissance.[43] In *Walden*, Thoreau, like Emerson,

43. See William J. Scheick, *The Slender Human Word: Emerson's Artistry in Prose* (Knoxville, Tenn., 1978), and John T. Irwin, "The Symbol of the Hieroglyphics in the American

implies that the hieroglyphics of nature can ultimately be discovered. By contrast, indecipherability is the main quality of the mysterious hieroglyphical configurations in Poe's *Arthur Gordon Pym*; of *The Scarlet Letter*'s "living hieroglyph," Pearl; and in *Moby-Dick* of the hieroglyphics of Ahab's brow, the surface of the whale's body, and Queequeg's tattoos. Melville uses the term to indicate both a sign system, intentionally codified and self-coherent, and an utter enigma to those who attempt to read it. The whale's markings resemble those on the pyramids and the banks of the upper Mississippi, and "like those mystic rocks, too, the mystic-marked whale remains undecipherable" (p. 260).

Melville's understanding of the term *allegory* was bifurcated much like Blake's, Coleridge's, and Emerson's. A passage in Chapter 45 of *Moby-Dick* has frequently been cited in support of a nonallegorical reading of his whaling epic, for there Ishmael makes his stand against seeing the great white whale as "a hideous and intolerable allegory." On the contrary, he assures us that the whale is real, as are all the procedures of whaling so painstakingly described in his narrative. However, not to recognize that the adjectives "hideous and intolerable" define only a *kind* of allegory without literal substance is to overextend Ishmael's terms. F. O. Matthiessen pointed out years ago, moreover, that the "jaunty" tone of the passage must be taken into account; that is, Ishmael is bearding the American novel-reader, who would condemn out of hand anything smacking of metaphysics.[44] Nonetheless, the sense of the passage is that Melville did not want the literal level of his work to be ignored. To take the whale hunt as the two-dimensional map of an ideology would be indeed hideous and intolerable. The facts of the ocean and of whaling presented him with a unique poetic opportunity. Here was something stamped with the veracity of reality, but so unfamiliar and mysterious to most land-dwelling readers that without any distorting effects it already seemed a mythic and suggestive

---

Renaissance," *American Quarterly*, XXVI (1974), 103–26. Irwin's more wide-ranging and ambitious study, *American Hieroglyphics: The Symbol of the Egyptian Hieroglyphics in the American Renaissance* (New Haven, 1980), explores the theories of signification and language implicit in American writers' treatment of hieroglyphics.

44. F. O. Matthiessen, *American Renaissance: Art and Expression in the Age of Emerson and Whitman* (New York, 1941), 250–52.

world. Like Blake's poem of Vision, and like Dante's "Vision" (the *Commedia*'s title in Cary's translation read by Melville), *Moby-Dick* presents a world that is not a pale reflection of reality but an unveiled vision of the true realm, of which our mundane historical world is only an allegory.

A letter written in response to Hawthorne's evidently favorable reading of *Moby-Dick* uses the term allegory in two separate but related senses. Melville thanks his literary friend while at the same time intimating his foreknowledge that the book will not be received well by the public:

> Not one man in five cycles, who is wise, will expect appreciative recognition from his fellows, or any one of them. Appreciation! Recognition! Is love appreciated? Why, ever since Adam, who has got to the meaning of this great allegory—the world? Then we pygmies must be content to have our paper allegories but ill comprehended. I say your appreciation is my glorious gratuity.[45]

The interesting thing here is not only that Melville falls thoroughly within this Romantic conception of the world as something both meant to be deciphered and finally undecipherable. In implying that his own work is only a "paper allegory," he shows more deprecation than the poets of vision about the bridging or deciphering power of his own imaginative product. Extended logically, this comment shows Melville's awareness that *Moby-Dick* is an allegory of an allegory.

Melville's great epic moves between two focal points of Romantic allegory, the exilic allegory of the city and the quest allegory of nature. Both elements run throughout his work and appear strikingly isolated in two of the three novels he wrote in the three years preceding *Moby-Dick*: *Mardi* and *Redburn*. It remains for *Moby-Dick* to trope the conventional romantic sense of urban life as an exile from the garden, turning it around to make nature itself an exile from the true city, whose official charter the actual city bears but has betrayed. The sea is a world of unofficial, unsanctioned action where

45. Herman Melville to Nathaniel Hawthorne, November 17, 1851, in Davis and Gilman (eds.), *Letters of Melville*, 141–42.

no orthodoxy has control; and it is resorted to precisely because the typology of Western culture has become in its official status a dry husk, its forms still invoked by the manipulators of power and its inner emptiness exposed by relentless literalists of nature and history—the Bacons, Newtons, and Voltaires whom Blake despised. *Moby-Dick* envisions the natural world as a world of "for ever exiled waters" (p. 165), in which the quest for an adequate city is recognized as defeated from the start. Yet it is an exile in which the image of men in peace with other men and with nature can fleetingly be glimpsed as signs amidst the general action of unremitting war.

III

~~~~

FROM CENOTAPH TO SEA:
THE TURN

(*Moby-Dick*, Chapters 1–23)

IT IS OF the very character of *Moby-Dick* as allegory that it begin retrospectively, long after the disastrous whale hunt is past, when the sole survivor of the *Pequod* has had sufficient time to meditate on and interpret his mysterious and overwhelming experience.[1] Even in passage Ishmael the seafarer tends to be instantaneously reflective, to be the reader of a text still in the making. The gap that lies between the two Ishmaels, however, is absolute. And that gap is indicated at the very outset by the traces of his study, his laborious attempt, in going through "the long Vaticans and street-stalls of the earth, picking up whatever random allusions to whales he could anyways find in any book," to transform himself into an adequate scholiast.

Two laborious passages, both supplied with prefaces—the Etymology and Extracts—stand between the reader and the beginning of the narrative. The Ishmael of the novel whom we are to meet later is already present in the tonality of these prefaces—ironic, jaunty, whimsical, morosely defiant. "Give it up, Sub-Subs!" he en-

---

1. On the narrative structure of *Moby-Dick*, see Franz Stanzel, *Narrative Situations in the Novel*, trans. James P. Pusack (Bloomington, Ind., 1971), 70–91. On the narrator's states of mind, see William B. Dillingham, "The Narrator of *Moby-Dick*," *English Studies*, XLIX (February, 1968), 20–29.

The best defense of *Moby-Dick's* narrative discontinuities is Wolfgang Kayser's: "It would be entirely wrong to designate this shift of perspectives as a technical error and to explain it—it has been tried—as a result of different conceptions and stages of work. Melville published his work in this form, and he was right in doing so. The first-person narrator of a novel is, here just as everywhere else, in no way the rectilinear continuation of the narrated figure." *Die Vortragsreise: Studien zur Literatur* (Bern, 1958), 97, my translation.

joins those who belong to "that hopeless, sallow tribe which no wine of this world will ever warm," the Ishmaels of the world, among whom he numbers both author and reader. But he promises a future inversion of things, for the meek who have gone before are "clearing out" the archangels from the "seven-storied heavens" to make a place for the lowly of the earth. It is this inversion that the entire novel depicts, a movement in which an Ishmael of the world becomes an Isaac, so to speak, and is incorporated into the main line of human history. This "wicked book," as Melville referred to it, is a depiction of the outcasts inheriting the earth and, allegorically, of an older text being "found," recovered as only allegory can recover a lost truth in an age of decline.

Entering the Book

Cesare Pavese has observed that the Etymology and Extracts form an especially effective beginning to *Moby-Dick* because they "serve to bring the reader to that level of universality, to accustom him to that secularized atmosphere of learned discussion, which will be the structural basis . . . of all the future chapters."[2] The prefatory material as a whole distances the reader from the action, bringing out an acute awareness that one is entering a world of reading and "learned discussion" rather than being caught up immediately in character and action. There is of course something epic about the Etymology and Extracts, for their very size and scope tend to magnify the stature of whales and whaling in the history of human regard. Yet here is an epic that does not begin *in medias res*, but immediately transforms the *res* into *signa*. Ishmael, often seen as a Yankee fabulist or homegrown oral bard, is really first and foremost a writer; few opening pages present as unmistakably as these a dismantling of the presence of the narrator's voice.

When seen in sequence with the title-page epigraph from Milton (appearing only in the English edition) and the dedication to Hawthorne, "in token to my admiration for his genius" (p. xiv), the prefaces reveal an epic purpose that is not an actor-hero's but an author's quest for epic writing and books. The tension between epic

2. Cesare Pavese, *American Literature: Essays and Opinions*, trans. Edwin Fussell (Berkeley, 1970), 73–74.

venture and allegorical commentary is what defines the structure of the entire narrative to come. The imagination of Ishmael as researcher and retrospective narrator has fully shaped the presentation of these beginning pages; even before he is presented as a character the sensitive and ironic structure of his mind is given in advance, though without being denominated as such. One knows from these opening pages that the whale, the "grand hooded phantom" around which the book moves, is an "overwhelming Idea," something to be aimed at but never entirely to be captured in writing.

Melville's "poetics of quotation" in these introductory sections provides two bodies of textual juxtapositions, left uncommented upon, in which one can discern some order and see some foreshadowing of things to come in the narrative.[3] In the indeterminacy of this assemblage of quotations Melville structures the entire work implicitly as a commentary-by-narrative on these passages, one that will aim at making all their diverse aspects cohere, at filling in their gaps. The transformation of narrative into commentary is the work of what Maureen Quilligan calls a "threshold text," the emblem occurring near the beginning of most allegories that transforms the subsequent action into explication of a text.[4] (In this discovery she continues the thought of Edwin Honig, who first wrote of "threshold symbols" in allegory as presenting a "fearful indeterminacy" which the following story is committed to making explicit.)[5] The threshold text goes against the grain of the romantic and novelistic ideal of "lived" experience by transforming it in advance into a series of fragmentary discourses to be interpreted. It is the whale, of course, that needs interpretation and that will never

3. Hermann Meyer maintains in *The Poetics of Quotation in the European Novel*, trans. Theodore and Yetta Ziolkowski (Princeton, 1968), that "the charm of the quotation emanates from a unique tension between assimilation and dissimilation . . . permitting another world to radiate into the self-contained world of the novel" (6). By quoting from the Bible, world literature, and factual narratives, Melville is buying an option for his own text to expand into the realm of sacred psalm, epic, learned discourse, eyewitness account, etc., while at the same time disestablishing his piety toward *auctores* by interpolating bogus and irrelevant quotations (cf. the "tradition of willfulness" in quoting, 10).

4. Maureen Quilligan, *The Language of Allegory: Defining the Genre* (Ithaca, N.Y., 1979), 51–64.

5. Honig, *Dark Conceit*, 71–78.

be entirely interpreted even by "veritable gospel cetology." But the structuring of the enterprise as philosophical, at a level henceforth concurrent with the action, is the particular accomplishment of the book's beginnings.

The very presentation of all this material without a running, unifying explanation—the absence, that is, of narrative at this stage—serves to posit a hope in the existence of a perfect gloss on all these texts. But at the same time that these passages introduce the idea of cetology as a project, their arbitrariness, oddness, and sometimes facetiousness suggest that no rational unification of aspects could possibly be devised.[6] At the same time that they point to a future understanding of the whale, they cut away the possibility of that understanding at a discursive level. "Real" knowledge, available for possession by the investigator, is henceforth impossible, and the only understanding of the mysteries of the whale must be an allegorical kind, one that takes the form of a learned inquiry but does so only as a self-mocking allegory of the quest for wisdom. The misspellings of the word for *whale* in Greek, Hebrew, and Anglo-Saxon, and the fictionalized "Feegee" and "Erromangoan" word—skewings of language as in Jean Paul or Carlyle—achieve this facetious seriousness by exposing their hoax only to those who know or have researched those languages.[7] In sum, the discontinuities within and between entries indicate a posited but infinitely distant total understanding.

As philological examinations of a text, the Etymology examines the grammar of the whale, the Extracts its rhetoric. The Etymology uncovers temporality in tracing the progress of a word. The names of the whale come to represent the epochs of human history, beginning with the Hebrew and plunging on through the Greek and Latin, westward in time as well as space, to end with the Fiji and New Hebrides Islands just east of Australia, where Western history is finally left behind. This brief list provides in miniature a kind of universal history. The overall sense, however, is the failure of all

6. See Rodolphe Gasché, "The Scene of Writing: A Deferred Outset," *Glyph*, I (1977), 150–71.

7. On Melville and Jean Paul (known partly through Carlyle), see Matthiessen, *American Renaissance*, 120n, 385n.

languages to denominate the whale successfully. The diversity of names suggests the continual omission of something essential, as the curious excerpt from Hakluyt indicates: "While you take in hand to school others, and to teach them by what name a whale-fish is to be called in our tongue, leaving out, through ignorance, the letter H, which almost alone maketh up the significance of the word, you deliver that which is not true" (p. 1). In this perspective each successive epoch has been brought about by the failure of the previous one to capture the whale's nature completely in a name. Naming the whale becomes a quest for the letter *H*, a letter that signifies signification if the Hakluyt quotation is to make sense.[8]

The two dictionary entries after Hakluyt's comment seem to stretch this enigma of the letter (and the name) further by setting up a dialectic of names. Webster's Dictionary derives *whale* from *hvalt*, preserving the *H* and meaning arched or vaulted and hence "high"; Richardson's Dictionary cites *Walw-ian*, leaving out the *H* and meaning to roll or wallow, hence "low." (Furthermore, *wal* is the Dutch or "Low-Land" name for the whale.) The difference between these two derivations may signify the opposite aspects of the whale, its grandeur as an object of contemplation, as something that gloriously signifies—and for "arch" see the whale's skeleton in "A Bower in the Arsacides" (Chap. 102)—and its terror and deadliness when subjected to the hunt as an object to be possessed, and as the avatar of whiteness—pure nonsignification. Like the letter *H*, which is a pure signifier here—a signifier of signification—the difference between the two etymologies is pure difference, signifying nothing so much as an unresolved something at the heart of Ishmael's knowledge about the whale.

The prefatory collections are dominated by two nameless figures who seem emblematically to represent the spirit of allegory. At the gateway to *Moby-Dick* stands the figure of "a late consumptive usher to a grammar school"—a guardian like the doorkeepers of the *In-*

---

8. In a curious parallel, J. G. Hamann wrote in 1773, against German modernizing orthographers, a "self-defense" of the letter H as the palpable and forgotten sign of the spirit. For a translation, see Ronald Gregor Smith, *J. G. Hamann, 1730–1788: A Study in Christian Existence* (New York, 1960), 201–206.

ferno and *Purgatorio*, for he is a keeper of books, dusting them with his queer handkerchief decorated with a pastiche of flags. The usher is a strangely ethereal presence at this threshold between reality and textuality; not only is he obsessed with death, he actually *is* dead, having died of consumption, apparently, between the time of the narrative and the time of its frame. Hence he does not speak at all but has only left behind written notes. "Threadbare in coat, heart, body, and brain," he seems to present the very spirit of privation. The books that "somehow mildly reminded him of his mortality" remind us, with the old gesture *memento mori*, of the opposition of vitality and intellectuality. Books that gather dust serve as a sign, like a baroque emblem, reminding us that we too shall be dust. This emblematic procedure typifies Melville's art.

The sub-sub-librarian, supplier of the Extracts, is another gate-keeper, and his comic title makes the reader acutely aware of the mediative chain through which books are able to exist at all. A commentator on commentaries, the sub-sub emblematizes the dry and humble action of transmission of knowledge from text to text that constitutes the mechanics of culture. The "poor devil of a sub-sub" is an underworld figure, a kind of Charon leading into the bowels of the library. He has hollowed out his life in the service of books and in the odd pursuit of references to whales in books, conflating "sacred or profane" indifferently. The obsessive pursuit of this patchwork gospel makes him, like the usher, into a detached creature of the book world, palely cerebral: "Thou belongest to that hopeless, sallow tribe which no wine of this world will ever warm; and for whom even pale Sherry would be too rosy-strong" (p. 2).

Unconsecrated by earthly wine, however, he is paradoxically sanctified by his pursuit, and he is assured that "your friends who have gone before are clearing out the seven-storied heavens, and making refugees of long-pampered Gabriel, Michael, and Raphael, against your coming. Here ye strike but splintered hearts together —there ye shall strike unsplinterable glasses!" (p. 2). This sudden prolepsis anticipates the sub-sub's transfiguration from despondency to exaltation. In it the inversion of the heavenly hierarchy, play-fully illustrating that "the last shall be first," is paired with the seriously intended image of convivial drinking, expression of a fullness of spirit which is dreamed as his reward. The "here—there" pairing echoes St. Paul's antithesis: "For now we see through a glass, darkly; but then face to face" (I Cor. 13 : 12). And the image of the fragmented heart made whole completes the "miraculous" effect of this ending.

The allegorical structure of Ishmael's world is clearly indicated in these prefaces. In the usher, the sub-sub, and the texts themselves, the procedure is to go patiently about a humble task of collecting, without even a hint of synthesizing the data, without attention to the "meaning" of the signifiers one is collecting, as if by emphasizing the very impoverishment of one's enterprise the fulfillment of an impossible yearning could be evoked. The sub-sub anticipates in bibliophilic form Ishmael's quest. In their relation, however, quester and scholar are strikingly reversed: Ishmael declares, "So fare thee well, poor devil of a sub-sub, whose commentator I am." Ishmael, *servus servorum*, thus plays the even more subsidiary role of narrator and retrospective mind of the entire book. In the "Cetology" chapter he will refer to the book he is writing as "but the draught of a draught." Only after the book has been exposed as being impossible to write can it truly begin.

Ishmael as Allegorist

Ishmael establishes himself at the beginning of *Moby-Dick* as a potential Baudelairean *flâneur*, an alienated cultural misfit who strolls about the city seeking flashes of revelation in a secular landscape. This type of character was in the air at the time; Melville must certainly have picked up reinforcement of his perception of such a character from Baudelaire's own constant reference, Poe. Especially in "The Man of the Crowd" and other stories, Poe portrayed the urban setting as dreary, enervating, and unnaturally stimulating—the perfect place for an imagination cut free from the oppressive norms of "nature" to emerge.[9]

9. Walter Benjamin writes on Baudelaire and Poe's "The Man of the Crowd" in "On Some Motifs in Baudelaire" and in "The Paris of the Second Empire in Baudelaire," *Charles Baudelaire: A Lyric Poet in the Era of High Capitalism*, trans. Harry Zohn (London, 1973), 48–54, 126–35.

Melville was constantly aware of the phenomenon of absence in the city; in *Redburn* he speaks of the London discovered by his young American hero as the City of Dis (prophetically anticipating its Dantesque transformation by Eliot). He was to develop this city-displaced figure in tragic fullness in *Pierre* and "Bartleby," in which it becomes clear that Melville's vision of the imagination in the city sharply diverges from Baudelaire's and the European view in general. The *flâneur* is driven to melancholy, not to despair, by the economic hardships and impersonal coldness of the city; he does not become irreversibly bitter. For Pierre and Bartleby, by contrast, allegory fails, or has immemorially failed, because of the absolute failure of signs to signify.

The collapse of meaning, then, is the fate of Melville's characters who become or remain city dwellers. But Ishmael instinctively knows to avoid this end: like a true Romantic version of Dante, he tropes the petrifying text of the city by turning away from it to the sea—the world of primal nature and of imagination. He remarks, seemingly casually, that ocean-going "is a way I have of driving off the spleen," the same spleen Baudelaire saw as the dominant mood induced by Parisian life. The urban kind of allegory, then, is not for Ishmael; he is not content, like the European intellectual, to celebrate and mourn the ashes of a vanished culture that once opened its arms to the heavens.

The fourth sentence of *Moby-Dick* ironically mimics the melancholy stance of allegory only to turn from it decisively at the end:

> Whenever I find myself growing grim about the mouth; whenever it is a damp, drizzly November in my soul; whenever I find myself involuntarily pausing before coffin warehouses, and bringing up the rear of every funeral I meet; and especially whenever my hypos get such an upper hand of me, that it requires a strong moral principle to prevent me from deliberately stepping into the street, and methodically knocking people's hats off—then, I account it high time to get to sea as soon as I can. (p. 12)

The "coffin warehouses" of New York are a perfect baroque *Trauerspiel* image, reduplicating a typical seventeenth-century excursus of the kind cited by Benjamin—Christoph Männling calling "die

Welt . . . einen allgemeinen Kauffladen/ eine Zollbude des Todes"
(the world a general store, a customs-house of death) in which "das
Grab aber das versiegelte Gewand und Kauff-Hauss" (the grave [is]
the bonded drapers' hall and ware house).[10] Besides the kinship to
baroque allegory, Ishmael's words here are structured syntactically
with the unmistakable stamp of the allegorist, who has begun to
experience all events only as typical instances of a repeated series
and who therefore distances himself from immediate experience in
order to draw significance from it. (The same effect can be found
in Baudelaire's "spleen" sonnet "Quand le ciel bas et lourd pèse
comme un couvercle/ Sur l'esprit.") The long sequence of depen-
dent clauses reduces the impact of any single clause; the repeated
temporal adverb stresses the inexorable flow of time in an immutable series; and the generalizing note of "when*ever*" further stresses
the reduction of unique temporal moments to mere scenes in a
long-run allegorical drama, a play of mourning, a *Trauerspiel.*[11]

But just at the end of this series, just when it has begun to seem
interminable as well as unchangeable, Melville veers off sharply.
His melancholy would not spur him to passive, receptive contemplation but to destructive and self-destructive action—his "stepping into the street and knocking people's hats off" seems to anticipate the end of *Pierre* on the streets of New York. Ishmael cannot
take comfort in the inevitability of allegorical decline and internal-
ization, as Baudelaire does when the depressing sights in the urban
landscape become significant in his soul. Walter Benjamin called
Baudelaire the most complete (and the last) inheritor of baroque
allegory, the melancholy allegory of the *Trauerspiel.*[12] But Melville
signals a new career for allegory, making a paradoxical turn away
from an allegorical tradition that has become Medusan. Making the
saving turn away from a petrifying text, reenacting metaphorically
the saving allegory of Dante, he rejects, in doing so, the very thing

10. Quoted in Benjamin, *Origin of German Tragic Drama,* 159.
11. Cf., however, Harrison Hayford's deflative reading of this sentence in "'Loomings':
Yarns and Figures in the Fabric," in Robert J. DeMott and Sanford E. Marovitz (eds.), *Artful
Thunder: Versions of the Romantic Tradition in American Literature, in Honor of Howard P. Vincent* (Kent, Ohio, 1975), 131.
12. Walter Benjamin identifies Baudelaire as the last great inheritor of baroque allegory
in "Zentralpark," *Gesammelte Schriften,* Vol. I, Pt. 2, pp. 659, 671, 676, 681, 684, 690.

that allegorical tradition has become in his time. Ishmael's story is thus both an allegory against allegory and an allegory of allegory; he forges for our age the possibility of reuniting with a tradition by first reacting against it.

If this pattern seems revolutionary, revisionary, Luciferian, Hegelian, or Faustian, and hence a mere assimilation of Ishmael to the quite familiar type of the Romantic hero, one must emphasize the differences between the two figures. The peculiar path of Ishmael's journey leads him to two kinds of crucial moments: one in which he is forced to acknowledge the illusoriness of a quest for an autonomous act of imagination (as in his chapter on masthead-sitting); and one in which he must acknowledge the presence of an earlier text or tradition in order to perform the unitary act of imagination he has longed for (as in the reminiscence of his first seeing an albatross: though he denies Coleridge's influence—and after Freud, denial hardly negates influence—he must compare himself to Abraham). Gayatri Spivak has stressed the way in which allegorical signification tends to creep back into the most symbolistic Romantic texts and the most anti-traditional modernist texts, deconstructing their projects of creating a new autonomous mode of signification in verbal art.[13] I am arguing the other end of that thesis: if she demonstrates the inescapability of allegory at its "zero point," where it is supposed to have disappeared, I am arguing that Melville's masterwork is already the omega-point of allegory in our epoch; it goes as far as any modern, Western (especially American) work can go in doing what allegories have always set out to do: to save something of value—to save phenomena in the Idea (Plato's and Benjamin's terms); to save culture through interpretation; to save the soul through a changing encounter with the world beyond.

The multiple approaches of *Moby-Dick* present a veritable anatomy of allegory. Melville was making an honest comment when he wrote to Sophia Hawthorne "that the whole book was susceptible of an allegoric construction, & also that *parts* of it were." Our task is to take up the suggestions of the Hawthornes—though undoubtedly in ways far other than they could have conceived—to uncover

13. Gayatri Spivak, "Thoughts on the Principle of Allegory," *Genre*, V (December, 1972), 327–52.

both "the particular subordinate allegories" and "the part-&-parcel allegoricalness of the whole."[14] The progressive phases of *Moby-Dick*, as I intend to show, perform an allegorical contemplation of the combined imperative and impossibility of reuniting those four great broken spheres of the modern world: the community; knowledge; the religious approach to God; history. The community is the first of these contemplative topics, and Ishmael discovers it by its inverse image, the exile.

In the first sentence of his narrative, Ishmael demonstrates the centrality of allegory to his existence as a literary character. He identifies himself only by allusion; from his reference one can gather that he is an outcast, an exile like the original Ishmael.[15] The "real" name of the character behind this literary persona is never to be known; for the duration of his fictional existence he lives in exile in the linguistic sphere also, banished from a proper name and forced to adopt one which is his only allegorically. The sentence accomplishes a double turn on Christian typology, a turn that is the central transformation of Melville's allegory, for it both rejects and re-incorporates the tradition in one stroke. The narrator identifies himself, the book's chief son and the only survivor of its events, with the son of Abraham who was cast out from the main line of sacred history, a first son made definitively second. The narrator's implied rejection of Isaac, the son who is first in sacred history, cannot be seen as the restoration of the first-born son to his supposedly natural primacy, thereby correcting an ancient error. It has to be rather a further displacement of primacy, an unseating of even the original "second" son (Isaac) from his chosen firstness. The reference to Ishmael thus implies an anti-typology, a second typology which in effect asserts the failure of the first. Is Melville's Ishmael, then, a kind of messiah of this subversive history? The original Ishmael would therefore be a foreshadowing *figura* calling for later fulfillment. The paradoxical fulfillment of this already emptied figure, a figure of absence, would have to be a savior who returns and

14. Herman Melville to Sophia Hawthorne, January 8, 1852, in Davis and Gilman (eds.), *Letters of Melville*, 146.
15. On exile in the Jewish tradition and Melville's awareness of it, see Maurice Friedman, *Problematic Rebel: Melville, Dostoievsky, Kafka, Camus* (Chicago, 1970), 81–82.

reappropriates without ever losing his quality of exile and secondariness. The somewhat ironic and arbitrary way he designates himself, of course ("call me," not "I am"), has clear precedent: "Art thou the king of the Jews?" "Thou sayest it."

The tradition of primacy, by contrast, clearly belongs to Ahab, a character with the expansiveness, the command and will of Abraham as well as of the perverse king for whom he is named. But that primacy is easily dispensed with in revisionary history, which has its good as well as bad uses. Not only did the dogs lick his blood when he lay dead, as the naïve Ishmael duly notes (p. 77), but this imagery is incorporated interestingly into Psalm 68, a postexilic hymn wherein Ahab is no longer mentioned by name but is implicitly identified with "the enemy": "The Lord said, I will bring again from Bashan, I will bring my people again from the depths of the sea: That thy foot may be dipped in the blood of thine enemies, and the tongue of thy dogs in the same" (Ps. 68:22–23). It is more than coincidence that the chosen people returning from exile are said to be brought back "from the depths of the sea." Ishmael specifically locates the place of his narrative as "in those for ever exiled waters." One should not lose sight of the fact that Ishmael is in the position, in *Moby-Dick*, of being the revisionary historian.

Ishmael's Language: The Secular-Sacred Disjunction

The impiety of Ishmael's language has often been noted; less frequently is it noted that where he sounds most pious his greatest impieties may hide.[16] And not yet, I think, has it been remarked that often those impieties present him in his most genuine spiritual relation. In Chapter 2, chilled by the wind off the Atlantic, he is reminded of Euroclydon, the "tempestuous wind" that assails St. Paul's ship in Acts 27. Already the context has satiric possibilities —Paul, the apostle of *pneuma*, attacked by a wind that wants to kill

---

16. Lawrance Thompson's study *Melville's Quarrel with God* (Princeton, 1952), though vitiated by a simplistic antitheism, is valuable for exposing Melville's subversive practice of skewing biblical references via Montaigne, Browne, and Bayle. Interestingly, the later, more sophisticated readers of Melville's irony and negativity, such as Edgar A. Dryden, *Melville's Thematics of Form: The Great Art of Telling the Truth* (Baltimore, 1968), John Seelye, *Melville: The Ironic Diagram* (Evanston, Ill., 1969), and Warwick Wadlington, *The Confidence Game in American Literature* (Princeton, 1975), have been less aware of this intertextual complexity.

rather than give life. Ishmael adds a second level of play to this reference by pretending to quote a baroque-style gloss on this passage: "'In judging of that tempestuous wind called Euroclydon,' says an old writer—of whose works I possess the only copy extant" (p. 19). Piling Sternean self-reference upon stylistic parody, he evolves a brief baroque allegory of the body as a house, calling the eyes "that sashless window, where the frost is on both sides, and of which the wight Death is the only glazier."

The antiquated, crabbed, bookish, and thoroughly *schriftlich* character of this excursus is summed up when he denotes the typeface in which this style appears: "old black-letter, thou reasonest well." Then, however, he conflates the parable of Lazarus and Dives with this passage, finding in Lazarus one of the many outcast-figures associated with the line of sacred history. But he makes no mention of Lazarus' final victory in heaven over Dives; in fact, with bitter if somewhat playful irony, his version of Lazarus would rather "yea, ye gods! go down to the fiery pit itself, in order to keep out this frost." Salvation in the afterlife cannot make up for the suffering in this life. The brilliant display of rhetoric—"old Dives, in his red silken wrapper (he had a redder one afterwards)"; "this is more wonderful than that an iceberg should be moored to one of the Moluccas"— makes the tone of this passage all the more difficult to state exactly. The playfulness, however, seems to be progressively overshadowed by a bitter irony aided by allusiveness. Dives lives in an "ice palace made of frozen sighs," recalling Dante's frozen lake Cocytus and making Satan a capitalist who amasses his fortune out of the misery of his workers.

Petrification thus ends this initially spiritual passage. Its movement is in the opposite direction from allegory, deliberately, even perversely, *backward* in the scheme of sacred history—from Acts to gospel, from rescue (of Paul) to denial of rescue (of Lazarus); from spirit (wind) to petrification (frozen sighs), from otherworldly piety ("poor Paul's tossed craft") to worldly resentment and cynicism toward hypocrisy ("being president of a temperance society, he only drinks the tepid tears of orphans").

This regression is abruptly dissolved in a pun: "But no more of this blubbering now, we are going a-whaling," the word *blubbering* serving as a pivot. The whaling world is Ishmael's escape from a killing bitterness at the unforgivable injustices of the human city. His employment-cum-reversal of the New Testament text implies that it does not work any longer; Lazarus would rather go to hell to keep warm than endure freezing to save his soul. One is put in mind of Huck Finn's wishing to be in the bad place if Miss Watson was going to the good place, or Huck's famous declaration later on when he makes a moral but unconventional choice: "'All right, then, I'll *go* to hell.'" Governing the American literary imagination has been a sense that the continuity of this world with the next, a continuity guaranteed by bourgeois Christianity, has been ruptured just as surely as have America's ties with the Old World. For Ishmael the only solution besides a violent end, or an equally killing cynicism, is escape to the whaling world, a place free of the spell of petrification, where the *translatio* into allegory is still possible.

In speaking of life at sea Ishmael is far more tolerant of accompanying inequities, and the perspective of allegory can appear abruptly, somewhat irreverently jostled but genuine. This sudden eternal perspective comes in at moments to justify his abasement on earth:

> What of it, if some old hunks of a sea-captain orders me to get a broom and sweep down the decks? What does that indignity amount to, weighed, I mean, in the scales of the New Testament? Do you think the archangel Gabriel thinks anything the less of me, because I promptly and respectfully obey that old hunks in that particular instance? Who aint a slave? (p. 15)

This last line is usually glossed in the spirit of the lines that follow, culminating in the bleak and cynical view of anti-community as the "universal thump . . . passed round." But the preceding lines recall Gabriel as minion of God, who would hardly be in a position to judge someone harshly for being obedient. Thus in the created world everyone is destined to be mutually subordinate: without losing its note of cynicism, this observation takes on a mystical sublimity as well. Ishmael's remarkable discourse manages to hold both an ironic secularism and a biblical, eschatological perspective in balance and tension with each other. In the next paragraphs the mystical attraction of the sea becomes deflated to the mere reward of "being *paid*," and the enjoyment of "wholesome exercise and pure air," when seen as an alternative to the stale air the "Commodore" must breathe.

The rhetoric of this passage bears still more comment. Ishmael continues:

> For as in this world, head winds are far more prevalent than winds from astern (that is, if you never violate the Pythagorean maxim), so for the most part the Commodore on the quarter-deck gets his atmosphere at second-hand from the sailors on the forecastle. He thinks he breathes it first; but not so. In much the same way do the commonalty lead their leaders in many other things, at the same time that the leaders little suspect it. (p. 15)

Beginning with a "philosophic" (in the sense of proverbial) statement, he then immediately travesties philosophy by equating it with trivial dietary instruction (don't eat beans), punning on "astern," bringing in what Mikhail Bakhtin has called the "bodily lower stratum" to offset and uncrown philosophical abstractness, and hinting that philosophy may be nothing more than *flatus*—the ultimate Rabelaisian deflation.[17] Then, dropping the parenthesis, he constructs a maxim ostensibly on analogy to the original proverb about head-winds but takes the proverb literally rather than in the sense in which it was intended. The infrequency of winds from astern now means not that good fortune is rare but that the Commodore is more likely to breathe air coming from the quarter-deck than directly from the sea (the captain's cabin being the sternmost compartment on a whaling ship). This secondariness of the captain is then formulated into a general principle stating, though in a non-theological way, that the last shall be first. The cynical deflation of captainly ambition turns into a statement that seems grand and mysterious by reason of its vagueness ("In much the same way . . . in many other things"). Indeed, the central procedure of this paragraph, as of much of the first chapters, is de-flation.

17. Mikhail Bakhtin, *Rabelais and His World*, trans. Hélène Iswolsky (Cambridge, Mass., 1968), 368–81.

At this point Ishmael drops his deflative rhetoric altogether and amplifies the strain of the mysterious, while picking up on the theme of "little suspecting" what is taking place. In doing so he enunciates the reason for his narrative.

> But wherefore it was that after having repeatedly smelt the sea as a merchant sailor, I should now take it into my head to go on a whaling voyage; this the invisible police officer of the Fates, who has the constant surveillance of me, and secretly dogs me, and influences me in some unaccountable way—he can better answer than any one else.   (p. 15)

Ishmael's narrative is, as we have said, retrospective; there are always two Ishmaels, as scholars have seen "two Dantes" in the *Commedia*—the writing Ishmael and the acting Ishmael. But the situation is more complicated than Dante's. This passage informs the reader that a difference in knowledge and understanding separates the two Ishmaels—the prior one is characterized by his ignorance. But unlike Dante's orderly presentation, the thoughts of the earlier Ishmael are sometimes given without any diacritical marks such as inverted commas or a parenthetical "I thought" that would separate the comment from the language shaping the narrative. Furthermore, the narrator sometimes adopts the attitude of the earlier Ishmael, duplicating the prior line of action but adding an almost invisible overlay of self-irony. Sometimes the narrator "makes up" an event, relating an action he could not have observed earlier; sometimes he remarks on some fact he could only know in his narratorial perspective, but adopts the attitude of the less experienced Ishmael; and sometimes it is simply impossible to decide which Ishmael is speaking, how deeply the knife of self-irony is cutting.

All this play with temporal perspectives is not merely frivolous (though it is often that): it is the only way Ishmael has of being faithful to the enormous discovery he has made on his voyage that unself-conscious action and overarching design are intimately intermingled, that unknown to us an ultimately saving shape is forming chaotic events toward an invisible end. The Fates were not allowed to have their way with Ishmael. A deity who is not known by name and who is omnipotent, though referred to comically as merely a

75

carrier-out of another's will (but whose?), an "invisible police officer of the Fates who secretly dogs me, and has constant surveillance
of me," is the "unaccountable" cause for the events which have
given Ishmael new life and a not quite articulable understanding of
mystery.

The retrospective narrative that places a double layer on the
narrator-actor confers this double quality on all the events in the
narrative as well. In rough terms, it makes allegory a constant potential, for as the event is acted or uncritically perceived on the first
level, it is available for reflective interpretation at the second level.
And against the notion that allegory can be arbitrary, it must be
stated that an allegory can be convincing only if it gives form to the
relatively unformed. The random allegorizing that takes place in
the medieval *Ovide moralisé*, for instance, is rightly felt to be a sign
of its naïveté. In contrast, medieval biblical exegesis, with its four
levels of interrelated meaning, assumes a mystical understanding of
the outcome of all history, under which all events take their ordered
place.

At the same time Melville the allegorist writes under a counter-
vailing command. Romantic allegory cannot be imposed a priori,
but must be based in immediate experience. So apart from brief
foreshadowings and hints of the total design of the book, Ishmael
must most often present experience in the process of being interpreted in the half-light of its own temporal horizon. Consequently
Ishmael the actor changes in his fundamental attitude as he moves
through the stages of his voyage. The narrator, too, changes, for his
attitude *toward* actor-Ishmael changes as the actor changes. The
irony of his voice in the first few chapters bespeaks two situations of
maximum distance: the knowledge of the narrator is at a maximum
distance from the naïveté of the actor; and the consciousness of Ishmael the actor is at greatest disharmony with his surroundings.

As the surroundings change, and as significant events occur, the
attitudes of actor and narrator change, dividing the narrative into
stages that move from ironic to prophetic allegory. At this point a
diagram, though only approximate, can best indicate these stages.[18]

18. For comparable recent subdividings of *Moby-Dick*, see Herbert G. Eldridge, "Careful
Disorder: The Structure of *Moby-Dick*," *American Literature*, XXXIX (May, 1967), 45–62;

Section	Approximate Extent	Basis of Division	Kind of Allegory Dominant	Object of Allegorical Contemplation
1	Chs. 1–23	Ishmael on land, without experience	ironic	community
2	Chs. 24–48	before encountering whales	diagrammatic	knowledge (as system)
3	Chs. 49–75	after first lowering	Menippean	knowledge (as play)
4	Chs. 76–105	whale examined and revealed in earnest	apocalyptic (anagogic)	religious approach to God
5	Chs. 106– Epilogue	Ahab's pursuit dominant	prophetic	history (eschatology)

The Scene of Petrification

Imagery of obsession and petrification runs through the landlocked chapters of *Moby-Dick*, not leading to the final victory of stasis as in *Pierre*, but as a constant threat to end Ishmael's voyage before it starts. Images such as the city-bound Ishmael mesmerized before coffin warehouses and funerals, the water gazers of Manhattan, and the figure of Narcissus find their reenactment and culmination within Ishmael's experience in the episode in the Whaleman's Chapel.

Entering the chapel, Ishmael immediately comes upon a striking tableau: "I found a small scattered congregation of sailors, and sailors' wives and widows. A muffled silence reigned, only broken at times by the shrieks of the storm. Each silent worshipper seemed purposefully sitting apart from each other, as if each silent grief were insular and incommunicable" (p. 39). The separateness Ishmael sees and feels here presages a deeper separation to be revealed when he ponders the object commanding the regard of these worshippers: "The chaplain

---

Daniel H. Garrison, "Melville's Doubloon and the Shield of Achilles," *Nineteenth-Century Fiction*, XXVI (September, 1971), 171–84; Henry L. Golemba, "The Shape of *Moby-Dick*," *Studies in the Novel*, V (Summer, 1973), 197–210; Paul McCarthy, "Elements of Anatomy in Melville's Fiction," *Studies in the Novel*, VI (Spring, 1974), 38–61.

had not yet arrived; and there these silent islands of men and women sat steadfastly eyeing several marble tablets, with black borders, masoned into the wall on either side the pulpit" (p. 39). The proper term for these marble tablets is cenotaphs, because they commemorate someone whose remains are not interred there. These hold their viewers in a peculiarly numbing and alienating spell. On them the written word is inscribed in *its* fullest differentiation from the spoken word. Carved in stone, the words of these tablets are immutable, and the Pauline connotation of letters on stone tablets, as Melville was undoubtedly aware, suggests a spiritually killing power emanating from them. St. Paul saw the rigidity of codified Mosaic law petrifying the Jews' moral sense; a "thou shalt not" spelled out to the utmost had frozen their ability to interpret reality. In this instance, however, the "thou shalt not" is a declarative, not an imperative, dictum: the widows will never see their husbands again.

Ishmael speculates that this effect is brought on precisely by the fact that the dead for whom these sailors and widows mourn are not interred here. Even in bereavement, he muses, the assertion that the beloved is "there" is a comfort to the mourner, but the absence of any remains takes away even this comfort and induces despair: "What bitter blanks in these black-bordered marbles which cover no ashes! What despair in those immovable inscriptions! What deadly voids and unbidden infidelities in the lines that seem to gnaw upon all Faith, and refuse resurrections to the beings who have placelessly perished without a grave" (p. 41). The black borders emphasize the abyss against which these letters stand out: the border is simply an obituary convention, but behind it stands the awareness that writing in its funereal context is doubly the making-present of an absence. Nor is this absence simply caused by death; rather it is an intensified absence—the very quintessence of loss—expressed by its empty tombs in memory of the men whose bodies are elsewhere.

Furthermore, the origin of these churchgoers' isolation is not grief alone. Closely associated with the act of reading, their solitariness can be seen as located *in* the act of reading. The letters of the cenotaphs project a strange power. Given that there is no body present in the chapel, the memory would not be compelled to dwell on the death of the beloved except that the inscription continually calls it back. It is the presence of the letter that refers to the absence of what it signifies. This privative power, which includes the power of inducing despair, seems to reside in the medium of presentation, the letters in stone. A further dimension of absence is added by the letters' existence consisting of empty space: unlike ink on the page, the letters here are simply articulated gaps in the stone. Thus it is that the "bitter blanks" reside *in* the marble and despair resides in the inscriptions themselves.

As artifacts of faith that induce despair, the cenotaphs in a sense represent obituaries to the Puritan tradition in America, which placed all of life within an allegory whose interpretation was supposedly already assured in advance.[19] Once the guaranty began to wear thin, however, a sense of "hollowness," always potential in things become signs, began to pervade the sensibility and numb it. That the epitaph is a fitting scene of this process that epitomizes the failure of medieval allegory in the modern world, Wordsworth gives evidence in the first of his "Essays on Epitaphs" when, praising the comforting style in inscriptions, he avers that, "if the impression and sense of death were not thus counterbalanced, such a hollowness would pervade the whole system of things, such a want of correspondence and consistency, a disproportion so astounding betwixt means and ends, that there could be no motions of the life of love."[20] This freezing of motions in the psyche describes precisely the opening tableau in the Whaleman's Chapel. In the situation Melville has constructed, the power of an allegory that no longer functions has become symbolic, speaking no message but "bitter blanks" to the mourners, and in the absence of a conscious message exerting an unconscious surrender of life from them. Memory, the cultural force that informs allegory, is now bereft of the power of life and has even become a source of petrification, as the hypnotic effect of the repeated phrase "sacred to the memory" indi-

19. Much has been written on Puritan typology and the Puritan vision of history. Among recent studies, Sacvan Bercovitch's *The Puritan Origins of the American Self* (New Haven, 1975), 35–72, presents a coherent view of this vision; while Francis Jennings' *The Invasion of America: Indians, Colonialism, and the Cant of Conquest* (Chapel Hill, N.C., 1975), demonstrates the brutal consequences of such a typology in real history. T. Walter Herbert, Jr., in *"Moby-Dick" and Calvinism: A World Dismantled* (New Brunswick, N.J., 1977), carefully and thoroughly assesses Melville's reaction to the Dutch Reformed Church of his upbringing.

20. William Wordsworth, "Essays upon Epitaphs, I," in W. J. B. Owen and Jane Worthington Smyser (eds.), *The Prose Works of William Wordsworth* (3 vols.; New York, 1974), II, 52.

cates. This phrase begins each of the cenotaphs, and its last three words are the only ones printed in the entire narrative in that "old black-letter" that is a reference point of death-obsessed Christianity.

It is perhaps a signal from the text, one of those textual self-contradictions that Philo saw as an imperative for allegory, that Ishmael claims to remember the text of the inscriptions only partially—"I do not pretend to quote"—but then spaces them out as if he were giving an accurate copy of them. The typographic reproduction of the marble tablets on the page suggests that the visible form of the words is inseparable from their linguistic content. The spacing of the letters is transferred into the book medium as if the hypnotic effect were to be transferred to the reader of these pages, recalling the hypnotic effect of the capitalized inscription over the entrance to Dante's hell—LASCIATE OGNI SPERANZA, VOI CH'ENTRATE.[21]

Indeed, the inscriptions do speak with a kind of prophetic finality about the events to come. Each tablet gives in essence a progressive revelation of the fate of the *Pequod*. The first tablet commemorates the death of a boy of eighteen, a low-ranked seaman, who was "lost overboard, / Near the Isle of Desolation, off Patagonia" (p. 39). The fate is the same as that of the sailor aloft in the chapter "The Life-Buoy," and it recalls Ishmael's own narrow escape from the same death while water-gazing aloft. "The Isle of Desolation" sums up the terrifying emptiness of the quest in which he is to take part, and the mention of Patagonia has a special irony for one who has earlier listed among his motives for the voyage "all the attending marvels of a thousand Patagonian sights and sounds" (p. 16). The phrase he reads informs him cryptically that the youthful conversion of the voyage into a primitivistic romantic quest leads ultimately to desolation and a singularly oblivious death.

The second inscription is at once more inclusive and more specific than the first, involving an entire boat's crew "who were towed out of sight by a Whale" (p. 40). Here the true agent of death is first mentioned, though the catastrophe still takes place offstage— foreshadowing the *Rachel*'s lost whale-boat, and darkly looking to-

---

21. According to John Freccero, the earliest extant manuscripts of the *Commedia* display the famous hell-gate inscription in capitals. John Freccero, seminar on the *Divine Comedy*, Yale University, 1973.

ward the disappearance of the *Pequod* in the vortex. Finally, the last inscription concerns not the body of a crew but its very head, "The late/ CAPTAIN EZEKIEL HARDY,/ Who in the bows of his boat was killed by a/ Sperm Whale." The doom of the whaling captain is now specified, identifying the type of whale and the exact manner and place of death, and providing the first foreshadowing of Ahab together with his end. Characteristically, the figural typology which the stone tablets generate is one of inexorable and violent death. These are indeed "lines which seem to gnaw upon all Faith."

The "Chapel," "Pulpit," and "Sermon" chapters (Chs. 7–9) are usually considered only as contributing to the imagery of the plot.[22] Father Mapple's sermon, in particular, is often taken to be an eloquent expression of Christian faith.[23] Taken in unison, however, these three chapters reveal the dead end of Christianity in American Calvinism. It is a multi-media show; religious works in painting, lyric, and rhetoric present themselves, each by its artistic nature suggesting a finished totality, an immutable contract of the requirements for salvation. Ishmael has already shown his disillusionment with the immutability of the established order in his Dives-Lazarus digression: "But it's too late to make any improvements now. The universe is finished; the copestone is on, and the chips were carted off a million years ago" (p. 19). Now he is to encounter this immutability like a set piece or a dream at the "extremest limit of the land," as befits his first threshold encounter.

Father Mapple's stage is bedecked with significant emblems. The pulpit itself is the first, after the cenotaphs, to meet Ishmael's eye: "Its panelled front was in the likeness of a ship's bluff bows" (p. 43). With seeming piety he comments, "What could be more full of meaning?—for the pulpit is ever this earth's foremost part; all the rest comes in its rear; the pulpit leads the world" (pp. 43–44). When Mapple steps into the pulpit and "deliberately drag[s] up the

<hr/>

22. A notable exception is Albert McLean, "Spouter Inn and Whaleman's Chapel: The Cultural Matrices of *Moby-Dick*," in Howard P. Vincent (ed.), *Melville and Hawthorne in the Berkshires: A Symposium* (Kent, Ohio, 1968), 98–108.

23. See, for example, Matthiessen's praise, *American Renaissance*, 126–27; or Howard P. Vincent, *The Trying-Out of "Moby-Dick"* (Boston, 1949), who calls the sermon "the key to Melville's deepest meaning," since it "is built on the theme most memorably stated by Dante: 'In His will is our peace'" (72).

ladder step by step, till the whole was deposited within, leaving him impregnable in his little Quebec," Ishmael muses, "there must be some sober reason for this thing; furthermore, it must symbolize something unseen." Although he speaks with no ostensible irony, it is difficult to believe that the Ishmael who only moments earlier saw into the depths of the abyss portended by the cenotaphs could readily assent to the sanctimoniousness of this staged allegory, which places the man performing it in a privileged, even inaccessible, position to the rest of mankind. Furthermore, it is difficult to square "the pulpit leads the world" with Ishmael's earlier credo that "the commonalty lead their leaders in many things," a principle he, as an outcast, is sworn to defend.

Walter Benjamin views the references to resurrection in baroque allegory as being paradoxical, maintained despite all the reasons to the contrary which have led the allegorist down the path of melancholy. What distinguishes the genuine allegory of the baroque, he maintains—genuine, that is, for the life of the mind—is that it does not affirm a "guaranteed economics of salvation."[24] Its "miracle" is always a surprise. But such an economics seems to be the message of the painting that serves as a backdrop to the pulpit, "a large painting representing a gallant ship beating against a terrible storm." In it, "high above the flying scud and dark-rolling clouds, there floated a little isle of sunlight, from which beamed forth an angel's face. . . . 'Ah, noble ship,' the angel seemed to say, 'beat on, beat on, thou noble ship, and bear a hardy helm; for lo! the sun is breaking through; the clouds are rolling off—serenest azure is at hand'" (p. 43). Here, at least, a trace of direct irony can be heard as Ishmael fabricates the pious message of the angel. Certainly this painting fails as a prediction of the *Pequod*'s voyage, unlike the ambiguous painting in the Spouter-Inn. Automatic rescue is also implied in the second and third stanzas of the hymn that precedes Mapple's sermon:

"I saw the open maw of hell,
    With endless pains and sorrows there;

24. Benjamin, *Origin of German Tragic Drama*, 216.

82

Which none but they that feel can tell—
Oh, I was plunging to despair.

"In black distress, I called my God,
When I could scarce believe him mine,
He bowed his ear to my complaints—
No more the whale did me confine."   (p. 44)[25]

The last line of the third stanza implies a vision of nature as prison that the hymn's first line reinforces—"The ribs and terrors in the whale." For Father Mapple, and for the strict New England Calvinism which he epitomizes, nature has no inherent good but has become a place of "terror" and imprisonment.[26] This "Jonah's whale," critics have rightly argued, is less approximate to Ishmael's total image of Moby Dick than is the magnificent-terrifying "Leviathan" of the Book of Job.[27] What remains to be said is that even in the Book of Jonah the image of nature is not negative. It is not God but precisely Jonah after his conversion who identifies evil with both nature and culture. Mapple's implicit metaphor in his sermon unites the converted Jonah and himself, whose task is "to preach the Truth to the face of Falsehood!" (p. 50). But Mapple has neglected—perhaps deliberately—two of the "four yarns" (i.e., four chapters) that make up his "two-stranded lesson." In the last two chapters of Jonah a fanatical self-conviction of his rightness descends on the new prophet and Jonah calls for the destruction of the sinful city of Nineveh. But the book takes a comic turn as Jonah receives his comeuppance from a bemused and slightly condescending God. The citizens heed Jonah's warning so well that God decides not to wreak destruction on them after all. Jonah is indignant:

25. David H. Battenfeld, "The Source for the Hymn in *Moby Dick*," *American Literature*, XXVII (November, 1955), 393–96, has located a hymn based on Psalm 18 in the Reformed Dutch Church as the source. Melville's changes, however, deliberately slant the hymn against a positive view of nature. Herbert, *"Moby-Dick" and Calvinism*, 111, discusses the hymn as stressing the Calvinist "progress" of the sinner.
26. See Rowland A. Sherrill's discrimination between Calvinisms in *The Prophetic Melville: Experience, Transcendence, and Tragedy* (Athens, Ga., 1979), 88–91.
27. Nathalia Wright, "*Moby Dick*: Jonah's or Job's Whale?" *American Literature*, XXXVII (May, 1965), 190–95; and Daniel Hoffman, "Moby Dick: Jonah's Whale or Job's?" *Sewanee Review*, LXIX (April–June, 1961), 205–24.

> Therefore now, O Lord, take, I beseech thee, my life from me; for it is better for me to die than to live.
>
> Then said the Lord, Doest thou well to be angry?
>
> So Jonah went out of the city, and sat on the east side of the city, and there made him a booth, and sat under it in the shadow, till he might see what would become of the city. And the Lord God prepared a gourd, and made it to come up over Jonah, that it might be a shadow over his head, to deliver him from his grief. So Jonah was exceedingly glad of the gourd. . . .
>
> And God said to Jonah, Doest thou well to be angry for the gourd? And he said, I do well to be angry, even unto death.
>
> Then said the Lord, thou hast had pity on the gourd, for the which thou hast not labored, neither madest it grow; which came up in a night, and perished in a night: And should not I spare Nineveh? (Jonah 4:3–11)

The "gourd" that God "prepares" for Jonah is a brief exemplum to teach him the goodness of creation and its fragility, for it dies the next day. By extension, God implies, cities are to be treated with the same respect. The wry tale ends before divulging whether Jonah has learned his lesson of mercy or not. Almost a parody of Jeremiah, this biblical fabliau performs a strategic opening-out of Hebrew typology to dissuade it from becoming petrified on the Jeremiad model.

This lesson was lost on the American Puritans, however. Mapple is sure of his messianic role as leader of the people, reversing the Diaspora in uniting all around him ("Father Mapple rose, and in a mild voice of unassuming authority ordered the scattered people to condense," p. 44). He is equally sure that the pre-conversion Jonah—"How plainly he's a fugitive!" (p. 46)—is, in being a fugitive, contrary to God's law. For him the very structure of the church can disclose who is good and who is bad. Ultimately he shows not a trace of uncertainty in discerning his task from God, "to preach the Truth to the face of Falsehood!" Benjamin's analysis of allegory, by contrast, emphasizes that the great advantage of the allegorical mode is its self-confessed inability to possess the Truth; its signifying technique is to represent Truth in its total act.[28] What it does *not*

28. See Bainard Cowan, "Walter Benjamin's Theory of Allegory," *New German Critique*, No. 22 (Winter, 1981), 109–22.

denominate, then, becomes its major significance. Yet to Mapple truth is merely a flag to pledge one's allegiance to. "Woe to him who would not be true, even though to be false were salvation!" (p. 50).

Mapple's twisting of the message of Jonah to its opposite in an earnest conviction of personal rightness and an intolerance of opposition suggests in its largest lineaments the attitude of Ahab. Mapple and Ahab share a hatred for profane darkness, a desire to "kill, burn, and destroy all sin," and an assumption that one can infallibly discern the ultimate import of things. Allegorical in the crude sense of substituting a value-term for a reality, theirs is ultimately a profoundly anti-allegorical attitude in rejecting the activity of interpretation as the condition whereby man lives in the world. It is a position that finally rejects all mediation—truth is not to be gained from the created world, or from the words of others, nor, finally, as with Jonah's intransigence, even from the interposing word of God.

During this hypnotic scene Ishmael has gradually dropped from view. As character he disappears after stepping into the chapel; as narrator he follows suit once Mapple begins to speak, and Mapple's words are transcribed directly, with only a few intervening stage directions. He leaves the chapel without any paraphrasing of the scene or its effect on him. As a threshold scene, in Honig's term, the episode makes the rest of the novel its explicative commentary; this text-plus-commentary structure is even more plausible if Mapple can be seen as a prelude to the spirit Ishmael will meet in Ahab. There is a further reason to the necessity of Ishmael's turning away without a word, however. In the *Inferno* words cannot save Dante from the Medusa; even Virgil, the source of Dante's language as poet, does not intervene with words but with physical action, turning Dante around and covering his eyes with his own hands. The turn to physical rather than intellectual response is here symbolic of the need for an act of absolute will to free one from the hypnosis of self, an act language cannot perform because of its origin in the desires of the self and its role in defining the self. (Dante was familiar with such an analysis of language from Augustine's *Confessions*.) Ishmael's problem at this moment, however, is not to turn away from himself, but precisely to turn away from language. The linguistic world is virtually coextensive with the Calvinistic culture that locks him in. The narrator's words of piety about the pulpit and the painting indicate his inability to revivify a tradition with its own vocabulary. On the other hand, he cannot escape a linguistic tradition by forging a new language single-handedly.

Furthermore, an appeal to other, more liberating traditions is not sufficient, though it is apparently Ishmael's natural disposition to allegorize an unacceptable text in the Philonic manner by making it square with Platonic vision. The cenotaphs induce in him a Thomas-Browne-like digression on the mysteries of mortality, on precisely the *unspeakable* nature of death. He questions "how it is that we still refuse to be comforted for those who we nevertheless maintain are dwelling in unspeakable bliss; why all the living so strive to hush all the dead; wherefore but the rumor of a knocking in a tomb will terrify a whole city. All these things are not without their meanings" (p. 41). The realm of speech seems to build comforting fictions that can only coat over the fact of death, whose mere inarticulate knocking can at one stroke sweep away the pretense of an entire linguistic community. Ishmael dispels this abyss—"But somehow I grew merry again"—by a train of reasoning from the *Phaedo*: "But what then? Methinks we have hugely mistaken this matter of Life and Death. Methinks that what they call my shadow here on earth is my true substance. Methinks that in looking at things spiritual, we are too much like oysters observing the sun through the water, and thinking that thick water the thinnest of air. Methinks my body is but the lees of my better being" (p. 41). This "merry" Platonism, however, grows quite mute when confronted by Mapple's eloquent and stony Calvinism. To escape it he must turn noiselessly to the body of Queequeg.

Queequeg alone stands outside the dumb show of the Western book, precisely because he cannot read. In the chapel he is "the only person present who seemed to notice my entrance; because he was the only one who could not read, and, therefore, was not reading those frigid inscriptions on the wall" (p. 40). To Ishmael, Queequeg represents liberation from the closed world that Western discourse has become. Not petrified by the fact of signification, the savage is immune to the "logocentrism" of looking only for the meaning signified and ignoring the means of signification. Back in the Spouter-Inn, Queequeg is able to look on the book as a material fact, somewhat comical, making it once again a potential source of metaphor as it was in the Middle Ages. In the warmth of Ishmael's friendship, he jovially performs a burlesque of the act of reading, taking up "a large book" and "counting the pages with deliberate regularity; at every fiftieth page—as I fancied—stopping a moment, looking vacantly around him, and giving utterance to a long-drawn gurgling whistle of astonishment. He would then begin again" (p. 51).

Queequeg presents less the primitivistic escape from the confining limits of cultural existence than the freedom of imagination to look on culture with a renewed eye. James Baird has pointed out that Queequeg's traits, and especially his religion, are far from typical of South Sea island religions but are obviously rather metaphorical versions of Christian and other rites.[29] Queequeg is, then, a metaphorized version of Ishmael's own culture. His native land "is not down in any map; true places never are" (p. 56). Freed from the necessity of literal interpretation, Ishmael is able to regard him as an allegory of the spirit of rejuvenation in culture. The savage is "George Washington cannibalistically developed," a rewriting of America's founding, with profound revisionary implications against nationalism and anti-naturalism necessarily carried by the *translatio* of the father of his country into a South Sea primitive.

Queequeg's companionship with Ishmael carries strong suggestions of unification of split halves of the self; critics employing archetypal analysis have expanded on the suggestions of this motif.[30] Typologically, too, the unification of the split in sacred history implied by the first sentence of the novel—"Call me Ishmael"—is given as a promise in the scene immediately following the chapel scene, when Ishmael and Queequeg smoke and worship together: "I felt a melting in me. No more my splintered heart and maddened hand were turned against the wolfish world. This soothing savage had redeemed it" (p. 53). This passage picks up two echoes from earlier moments: one is the "splintered hearts" of Ishmael and the

29. James Baird, *Ishmael* (Baltimore, 1956), 230–41.
30. *Ibid.*, 201–20.

"poor devil of a sub-sub," counterposed to the "unsplinterable glasses" of heaven. The other is Ishmael's name bearer, the son of Abraham whose "hand will be against every man, and every man's hand against him" (Gen. 16:12).

The odd thing is that the little idol Yojo whom he joins Queequeg in worshipping is not a "symbol," partaking in some greater reality. To Ishmael there is neither a presence nor anything intrinsically significant in the statue itself. Its entire worth to him consists in the occasion it precipitates for Ishmael and Queequeg to share a "pleasant, genial smoke." Queequeg's idol is not "immovable" like the stone tablets but is actually whittled at, literally being articulated by Queequeg's imagination. The central paradox of the two images and episodes becomes formulable: the tablets of inscriptions are ostensibly models for the reading process, making unavoidable an awareness of the frames within which signification functions; but the eternal immutability of the text blots out the awareness of frames and petrifies the reader. The idol traditionally declares authoritative meaning and symbolization, prohibiting free interpretation; but here it fosters a give-and-take relationship in which meaning is in process—gestures and modes of comportment, dialogue, sociable acts—in a word, the opposite of petrification.

Queequeg thus fulfills two negative figures, both speaking of a restoration of Ishmael to himself and to the people of God. In turning away from the designated carrier of the Covenant, the preacher of "the Truth to the face of Falsehood," and turning *toward* a bearer of "heathen" culture, Ishmael performs the reversal or troping characteristic of his allegory.[31] Not content to remain with Calvinism, the severe reincarnation within Christianity of the wrathful God of the Old Testament, Ishmael performs his negative act by "clearing out the seven-storied heavens," restoring the true pattern of typology

---

31. Herbert, *"Moby-Dick" and Calvinism*, 98–101, carries the defiant nature of this gesture further: to him the overtones of homosexuality in the passage are intentional floutings of Calvinist prescriptions. Melville, however, would hardly need to invoke a practice almost universally stigmatized to defy a religiosity he has already "dismantled." The roots of homosexual imagery in Melville are deep, not shallow, and relate to his understanding of the human psyche. See Edward F. Edinger, *Melville's "Moby-Dick": A Jungian Commentary* (New York, 1978), 90–91. In my line of argument it is the natural "body of man" that Ishmael discovers and, like Dante, must turn to.

—to elevate the debased people and sanctify the despised prophet—
by rejecting the cultural carrier of typology itself. Thus "whoring
after strange gods," worshipping "graven images," he begins his task
of restoring the Ark of the Covenant to its proper place.

IV

~~~

THE DREAM OF A CHART

(Moby-Dick, Chapters 24–48)

THE HYMN Bildad sings at the *Pequod's* departure marks the end of Ishmael's period of servitude to an official biblical culture:

> Sweet fields beyond the swelling flood,
>   Stand dressed in living green,
> So to the Jews old Canaan stood,
>   While Jordan rolled between.

The last line ends on a strange note of indefiniteness. Within an orthodox evocation of the Promised Land this verse seems to freeze the Jews in the midst of crossing, removing the sweet fields to a continual beyond while the Jordan that separates them forms an uncrossable between. Such is Ishmael's experience of time from this moment on. He has been delivered out of bondage both to the land and to the petrification of the word attending it, but instead of being immediately conveyed into the realm of fulfillment, he is to find himself henceforth betwixt and between, in a perilous crossing. His arrival at Canaan is indefinitely deferred.

Casting off onto the sea, Ishmael enters a marvelous indeterminacy of denomination. The biblical language of Mapple, Bildad, and Aunt Charity, mixed with its various ulterior motives, now drops away as the voyage begins. With a mixture of relief and longing he remarks, "In those for ever exiled waters, I had lost the miserable warping memories of traditions and of towns" (p. 165). The very word *exile* already leaves open the possibility of a future recovery of the biblical tradition, however transfigured, on those waters.

In the meantime, the task for the imagination can loom large: the search for a denomination and ordering that might attain a configuration of the Idea.

As old systems of reference disappear on the horizon, the temptation for the newly liberated seeker of meaning is to believe he can attain an unmediated experience of transcendence. Ishmael wants to act in the spirit of the clarion call Emerson makes in *Nature*: "Why should not we also enjoy an original relation to the universe? Why should not we have a poetry and philosophy of insight and not of tradition, and a religion by revelation to us, and not the history of theirs?" For the first time, Ishmael's field of vision is flooded by the natural world unchecked by any interpretive screen. He is overwhelmed by his first sight of the albatross as though by a revelation: "Through its inexpressible, strange eyes, methought I peeped into secrets which took hold of God. As Abraham before the angels, I bowed myself . . . I cannot tell, can only hint, the things that darted through me then" (p. 165). Alluding to the beginning of the history of revelation, Ishmael implies that his own discovery is the beginning of a wholly new epoch of revelation.

But these inexpressible secrets can induce terror as well as wonder. The rapture before the albatross is only a recollection contained in a footnote to "The Whiteness of the Whale," a chapter which in its totality may be said to be an excursus into the horror of a totally anti-revelatory order of being. The "palsied universe" of this vision reveals the impossibility of finding a text organically written on the body of nature. In and of itself nature is "a dumb blankness, full of meaning," "a colorless, all-color of atheism from which we shrink." It is both a blank page and a screen transmitting information overload to an infinite degree. Nature seems to invite writing, but on deeper inspection it mocks all articulation and peers through the page with a terrifying nothingness: its colors are "subtile deceits, not actually inherent in substances, but only laid on from without; so that all deified Nature absolutely paints like the harlot, whose allurements cover nothing but the charnel-house within" (p. 170). Seen in its nakedness, nature has no face and reflects nothing by which man can recognize his features. The seeker of meaning in nature becomes like the Narcissus figure in the first chapter, "who because he could not grasp the tormenting, mild image he saw in the fountain, plunged into it and was drowned" (p. 14). Undifferentiation spreads like a contagion, rupturing the boundaries of the self. Like an organism no longer immunologically secure, it succumbs to the outside world as to a pestilence.

Ishmael has moved toward a direct encounter with nature of the kind the Romantic symbol supposed, a unification of subject with object in one discovery of overarching harmony.[1] What he finds instead, however, is that the quest that began with a declaration of the sovereign self, establishing "an original relation to the universe," ends with the annihilation of the self. This pattern is clear and compact in "The Mast-Head," a chapter whose anti-Transcendentalist argument has long been recognized.[2] The young sailor "with the Phaedon instead of Bowditch in his head" loses himself in contemplation of the absolute. The real that would then swallow him up and destroy him, however, grants him a saving moment in which his identity "comes back in horror." It is a gratuitous moment, one should note, that might not be repeated the next time "the trance is on you." What has saved the masthead philosopher is a sudden, visceral recognition of his distance from nature and the imminent danger of that space collapsing. The abyss over which he "hovers" in this terrifying moment is ironically referred to by the narrator as "Descartian vortices." Those elegant circular paths which bodies follow in the universe, as Descartes thought, are now agents of death. The irony marks the mast-head scene as an encapsulation of Ishmael's near-seduction by abstract schematism in Chapters 24–48.

Looking for the livable middle way that will evade both the overwhelming immediacy of nature and the "miserable warping memories of traditions and of towns," Ishmael discovers in these chapters the activity of charting, a plotting of events on a spatial or space-time grid. It is a way of gaining enough distance from phenomena to escape their immediate irreducibility. By organizing them it creates a framework in which events can be made to contribute to the

1. See de Man, "Rhetoric of Temporality," 178–88, on the subject-object dichotomy in the Romantic symbol.
2. See Vincent, *Trying-Out of "Moby-Dick,"* 151–58.

working-out of an overall scheme, though that scheme ignores actual temporality and substitutes instead the abstract notion of space and time, Kant's a priori forms. The whole development of science in Kant's time, to which he responded in the first *Critique*, was to find a way of interpreting nature without dogma. The space-time paradigms of science consider an event intelligible if its "shape" in space and time fits an already known model. With this kind of knowledge the goal of a pure understanding of nature, unadulterated by intermediary texts, presents itself to the modern age.

The fascination of charting emerges full-fledged in Chapter 44, "The Chart," where Ahab is shown in his cabin raptly "marking out lines and courses on the wrinkled charts," "threading a maze of currents and eddies, with a view to the more certain accomplishment of that monomaniac thought of his soul." The scene presents an inside look at his "delirious yet still methodical scheme" and its accomplishment by coordinating space and time in a projected line of motion, a conjunction inherent in the movement of his pencil. When magnified to oceanic proportions and considered for the degree of accuracy needed to attain his purpose, Ahab's charting takes on an aura of the numerical sublime, relying on sheer incalculability to impress the ordinary mortal with his insignificance before something vast. The chapter is packed with schematic space-time terms such as *voyages, lines and courses* (twice), *threading a maze, sets of tides and currents, driftings, regular ascertained seasons . . . in particular latitudes, timeliest day to be upon this or that ground, periodicalness, migrations and migratory charts, passage, veins, ocean-line, direction, line of advance, wake, gliding along, flights, place and time himself on his way,* and, many times, *course, chart, path,* and *way.* Charting a line of motion, so difficult to do with accuracy at long distances, yet so natural and unconscious to the whale, hence requires an uncanny and obsessive consciousness from Ahab. His pursuit of Moby Dick "might seem an absurdly hopeless task" but for his possession of immense knowledge; faced with something inconceivably unreckonable, he is not lacking in intellect, will, and spirit for the endeavor.

The special terms Ishmael marks out for explanation in this chapter, *vein* and *Season-on-the-Line,* allow for a wide latitude of random motion within a certain range—a quite proper handling of

probability by modern standards. The line of migration of any single whale is straight. But, since whales swim in company, the width
as well as the direction of the group has a certain randomness and
may be "some few miles in width (more or less), as the vein is pre-
sumed to expand or contract; but [it] never exceeds the visual sweep
from the whale-ship's mastheads, when circumspectly gliding along
this magic zone" (p. 172). The Season-on-the-Line, unlike the
vein, is not a migratory line but a large area, a "place of prolonged
abode" for the sperm whale during a certain season, a "particular set
time and place . . . conjoined in the one technical phrase," where
"all possibilities would become probabilities, and, as Ahab fondly
thought, every probability the next thing to a certainty." "Fondly,"
interjects Ishmael; yet this scheme does work—a point not to be
overlooked. It is at the Season-on-the-Line that Ahab sights and
pursues Moby Dick. Moreover, he does not arrive there by instinct
or divination but because he "knows the sets of all tides and currents" and can "calculate the drifting of the sperm whale's food."
His conclusions are "reasonable surmises, almost approaching to
certainties." It is a prototype of probability theory that leads Ahab
to forecast with sufficient accuracy the chance appearance of Moby
Dick.

This ability to predict by a rational procedure fascinates the narrator, but his very fascination marks him off from Ahab's enterprise
of applied science. Ishmael's imagination always tends to ascend to
a meta-level above the action he is observing. In this chapter he is
more interested in talking about the feats of navigation than in doing navigation. Ahab, by contrast, is on the other side of the scientific imagination, doing the charting with skill but not particularly
interested in it. His quest for vengeance sharpens his acumen in
charting, making of this demanding activity a mere tool to gain his
obsessive end.

Science abstracts the event from its particularity only in order to
fold it back into an immanent framework that will make it determinable and, ideally, predeterminable. It opposes allegory in refusing to posit a disjunction between the immanent realm of events
and the transcendent realm where meaning, or "true being," exists.
A dreaming poetic eye cast on scientific thought, however, might

discover there the ground on which to construct the Romantic project of a truly new allegory for the first time since St. Paul, an allegory entirely based on the natural world.[3] Ishmael is predisposed to take this path. The spatial schematizing that distances the self from its desired objects through paradigms and charts seduces him here. His idea of control, to be sure, is not Ahab's coercive power but rather the ability to trace the paradigm within which the actions of others fit, to see their chance-seeming configurations as fixed constellations—to understand things without changing them. This desire for knowledge is his from the beginning chapter: "I think I can see a little into the springs and motives which . . . induced me to set about performing the part I did" (p. 16). This is the impulse that makes him go over his past life, finding new and "other" meanings to his experience. It is thus at the origin of his existence as a narrator and of his double existence as actor and commentator. Without the compulsion to structure and schematize, Ishmael would not be the encyclopedic allegorist that he is. In giving this impulse free reign on the waters, however, he shows he has not yet been forced to accept that other necessary dimension of allegory: the historicity of actual lived time.

Reading Ahab

Before Ishmael can apply his schematic speculations to the whale, however, he must perform a Herculean labor of the intellect to escape Ahab's pervasive influence. Though the *Pequod* allows him to approach new revelations of nature, what makes that approach possible is Ahab's will, a will diametrically at odds with nature and everywhere interposing itself between Ishmael and the whale. The chapter "Moby Dick" attests to the difficulty of going beyond Ahab's interpretation of the white whale. Ishmael describes the unifying power of Ahab's word: "My shouts had gone up with theirs . . . my

3. See Heinrich Henel, "Goethe and Science," in *Literature and Science: Proceedings of the Sixth Triennial Congress of the International Federation for Modern Languages and Literatures, 1954* (Oxford, 1955), 216–21, and Carl Grabo, *A Newton among Poets: Shelley's Use of Science in "Prometheus Unbound"* (1930; rpt., New York, 1968), for attitudes toward the sciences by the more adventurous Romantic poets. Melville contrasts with both because of his interest shown here in mathematical calculation and predictability. Goethe, everywhere limited by the aesthetics of the symbol, "rejected mathematical physics because it seemed to shatter the phenomena perceived by the senses" (Henel, 220).

oath had been welded with theirs . . . Ahab's quenchless feud seemed mine." Caught in the force field of Ahab's will, the individual almost loses all hope of forming an "original relation to the universe" or of seeing anything other than what the scheme of vengeance will allow. This force leads Ishmael to relinquish his attempt to imagine Moby Dick: "I gave myself up to the abandonment of the time and place," he admits, and all during this early stage of the voyage he "could see naught in that brute but the deadliest ill" (p. 163). His attempt to pass beyond the screen of Ahab's discourse results in the magnificent and terrifying effort of the next chapter, "The Whiteness of the Whale," which begins with that explicit purpose: "What the white whale was to Ahab, has been hinted; what, at times, he was to me, as yet remains unsaid" (p. 163). Yet it concludes with no real difference in attitude from the previous chapter: "Wonder ye then at the fiery hunt?" (p. 170). The progression of images in this chapter is not dictated by any inherent logic but by attraction and repulsion: "a colorless, all-color of atheism *from which we shrink*" (p. 159, emphasis added). Ahab asserts his presence in this chapter by these terms of force, for, though wholly absent from the images, he has gained control over what would seem most private: the unconscious imaginary order of Ishmael's thought. The terms from magnetism and electricity that repeatedly describe the captain make this point.

Stubb's nighttime encounter demonstrates this dream power. Ahab's pacing on the deck above his sleeping crew at night causes such a "reverberating crack and din" that "their dreams would have been of the crunching teeth of sharks" (p. 112). When Stubb requests the captain to stop and is intimidated by him, he reflects on those brief events as on a dream encounter and is only able to talk in mad similes: "his eyes like powder-pans! . . . his brow . . . flashed like a bleached bone" (pp. 113–14). He feels "turned inside out" afterward, and muses, "I must have been dreaming, though— How? how? how?" The "Queen Mab" chapter that follows finds Stubb recounting the actual dream he has had afterward, in which Ahab appears as a pyramid impervious to Stubb's kicks. "So confoundedly contradictory was it all," says Stubb; yet Ahab everywhere presents a monolithic power to his crew, a power that cannot be broken down and analyzed any more than it can be assailed. Nonetheless the dream symbol itself may provide the key to Ahab's decomposition, if anyone could read it: for Moby Dick is described as having a "high, pyramidical white hump" (p. 159). The image may suggest that Ahab is a double of the white whale itself and that all his power only comes from the object of his vengeance, which can by its movements dictate his every move. The white whale, as Ahab's double, decodes him, converting him from enigma to readable text.

Though Ahab is himself controlled by his own object, his power to control others is not thereby annulled but paradoxically multiplied. His quarter-deck speech to the crew seals their purpose with the aid of inverted sacramental symbolism. Turned upside down the harpoon sockets become "murderous chalices" to hold the liquor he passes among his crew. As *symbola* they annul differences by calling for an unconscious assent. The inversion of the harpoon points indicates their displacement from their cultural function, the purpose for which they were designed, and their reappropriation as imaginary objects, or images, operating in a realm where signifiers no longer exist in a conscious system of exchange but manifest the power of the other over the self, conveying the force of desire and enthrallment rather than any specific meaning. The harpoons' inversion is thus a double one: as chalices from holy to unholy, and as weapons from tool to charm.

The sailor Ishmael, who feels the strong pull of this "quenchless feud," is countered by the retrospective narrator, who can see through Ahab's maneuvers as "more or less paltry and base." He recognizes that all of Ahab's gestures of dignity or charismatic power are mere "external arts and entrenchments," and that his resorting to them differentiates his kind eternally from "God's true princes of the Empire" (p. 129). These remarks, which already suggest a more or less complete reading of Ahab's character, are made in the chapter ending in the narrator's question of how he can present Ahab—"But Ahab, my captain, still moves before me in all his grimness and shagginess." As a character Ahab still exerts his enchantment on Ishmael, and only a heroic effort can capture his nearly ineffable nature: "Oh, Ahab! what shall be grand in thee, it needs must be plucked at from the skies, and dived for in the deep, and featured in the unbodied air" (p. 130). What *shall be* grand—the task for author Ishmael thus parallels the one for sailor Ishmael: to read, and to write, Ahab. Chapter 33 chiefly succeeds in telling what Ahab is not—a "true prince"; his nature remains vague, "shaggy." The process against which his own pyramidical will militates is his decomposition into separate levels of discourse and of existence—an interpretation which would be one with an allegorization of him.

The discovery of two levels in Ahab already begins implicitly in the "Quarter-Deck" chapter that so firmly asserts his unity. Describing his very unity, however, already frames Ahab in a potentially dualistic scheme: his thought, Ishmael notes, seems to be "so completely possessing him, indeed, that it all but seemed the inward mould of every outer movement" (p. 141). This construction sets up the categories of inside and outside, thus providing the possibility of a future discernment of a discrepancy between appearance and reality in Ahab. Stubb follows suit: "'The chick that's in him pecks the shell. 'Twill soon be out.'" Both these remarks suppose a continuity between the two levels discerned: as the inner, so the outer, or first in, then out.

In the speech itself this duality continues to be paired with an assertion of continuity between levels. When Starbuck objects, "I came here to hunt whales, not my commander's vengeance," Ahab replies, "Thou requirest a little lower layer." He repeats this phrase in his great monologue:

> Hark ye yet again,—the little lower layer. All visible objects, man, are but as pasteboard masks. But in each event—in the living act, the undoubted deed—there, some unknown but still reasoning thing puts forth the mouldings of its features from behind the unreasoning mask. If man will strike, strike through the mask! How can the prisoner reach outside except by thrusting through the wall? To me, the white whale is that wall, shoved near to me. Sometimes I think there's naught beyond. (p. 144)

The metaphors of layer, mask, and wall each insist on a two-leveled model of reality. Ahab's analysis of himself discloses an ostensible motive of vengeance which is simply the outward expression and consequence of that deeper motivation, a hatred of the "inscrutable thing" that with seeming malice masks itself and presents a wall to man. The mask and the wall, however, mark discontinuities between appearance and the reality of that "unknown but still reasoning thing." To know this reality Ahab seeks to prove himself in a "living act" that will force the hidden thing to show its hand, to "put forth the mouldings of its features." The impression made on the mask of appearance is, like a stamp on wax, a negative one. Here is no symbolic unification of subject with object; here no analogical order insures the image of reality in appearance; instead a wall exists between the two, and the ultimate reality can only be known by the traces that it leaves showing where it is not.

Critics have noted that Ahab's view of the whale is an allegorical view, of the kind seen in Prudentius' *Psychomachia* where good agents war with evil agents.[4] But it cannot be said that Ahab partakes of the allegorist's mind, even though he does in a sense preserve the biblical typological view of the world by inverting it. To the Jews the epoch-making movements in their history were moments in which God intervened in secular reality to reveal Himself as other than that reality. Ahab also sees the world as significant only when an alien force intrudes to show itself; yet that force is evil. "I see in him outrageous strength, with an inscrutable malice sinewing it. That inscrutable thing is chiefly what I hate; and be the white whale agent, or be the white whale principal, I will wreak that hate upon him" (p. 144). Hatred does not lead to history, however: Ahab does not see time as patterned meaningfully by the white whale's appearance but sees its intervention in his life as a hateful originary moment. The desire to make coherent sense of one's life through retrospective interpretation is supplanted in Ahab by an obsessive, repeated return to the horrendous moment of his loss, which stands outside of time to him.

An inversion of the Jewish attitude toward God in history, Ahab's

4. Charles H. Cook, Jr., "Ahab's 'Intolerable Allegory,'" *Boston University Studies in English*, I (Spring–Summer, 1955), 45–52.

conviction is thus connected only negatively to the dim inheritance of Judaeo-Christian typology left behind on the shores of New England. He is haunted by the suspicion that there may in fact be "naught beyond." The physical world already has no significance in itself, but that lack has seemed to be in the service of some higher worth. If in fact no higher truth exists, then significance cannot return to the world but disappears entirely, making the world a pure interplay of "unreasoning" forces. This is of course the vision of the world opened up by the impact of scientific discoveries on the modern mind—Arnold's "darkling plain . . . Where ignorant armies clash by night." But it induces a deep-rooted cynicism and dishonesty in Ahab.

To judge from the way he presents himself to the crew in his quarter-deck speech, Ahab's deeper reality is undeceivingly bound up with his appearance. Further, he knows he must keep up appearances—and the principle of appearances disclosing reality—to his crew if he expects them to act confidently and obediently. Ishmael expresses this faith in a congruence between inside and outside near the end of the chapter, describing a sudden stillness that allows several ominous signs to be heard and felt at once, only to disappear just as quickly. "Ah, ye admonitions and warnings!" he exclaims, "why stay ye not when ye come? But rather are ye predictions than warnings, ye shadows! Yet not so much predictions from without, as verifications of the foregoing things within. For with little external to constrain us, the innermost necessities in our being, these still drive us on" (p. 145).

This is the retrospective narrator, commenting on the Aeschylean unity of character and fate in the completed drama. For the drama in progress, however, that unity is by no means assured, for the narrator has yet to go beyond Ahab's presentation of himself to an independent, analytic assessment of him. He has not yet shown Ahab's "innermost necessities."

He can only hope to do so by "furious tropes." Chapter 41's probing of Ahab's mind sums up, "If such a furious trope may stand, his special lunacy stormed his general sanity, and carried it, and turned all its concentred cannon upon its own mad mark" (p. 161). No explanation other than a psychomachia seems able to account for his combination of madness and sanity. Yet the narrator is still aware that "Ahab's darker, deeper part remains unhinted." Furthermore, he resorts to an elaborate two-leveled figure of the human psyche to explain his inability to expose Ahab fully:

> Winding far down from within the very heart of this spiked Hotel de Cluny where we here stand—however grand and wonderful, now quit it;—and take your way, ye nobler, sadder souls, to those vast Roman halls of Thermes; where far beneath the fantastic towers of man's upper earth, his root of grandeur, his whole awful essence sits in bearded state . . . aye, he did beget ye, ye young exiled royalties; and from your grim sire only will the old State-secret come.   (p. 161)

In this magnificent passage, reminiscent of Keats's *Hyperion*, man's conscious and everyday life is like a palimpsest written over an *Urtext*, not representing but concealing the ruined sovereign that is the original image of man.[5] Presumably Ahab has found the "old State-secret" from this deposed power within himself. The scene is allegorical not only in personifying an element in the human psyche but in referring to a past state of being which, when found, reveals one's present state to be not a plenitude but an exile. At the heart of human existence is something that Ahab has probed and that prevents Ishmael the narrator from saying explicitly what it is, because it is "vain to popularize profundities, and all truth is profound." This something, roughly phrased, consists of the realization that man in his present state not only is alienated from his original kingly image but has even forgotten this alienation. The reason for both alienation and forgetting is the too great suffering attendant on the dethronement of original man. What Ahab has come up against is the heart of what Romantic allegory realizes—that worldly existence is related only negatively to a prior,

5. Although no hard evidence exists that Melville read Keats, it is difficult to believe that his attentive study of the major and minor English Romantics, increasing steadily over the years, would leave out such a major figure. Merrell Davis points out several close parallels in *Mardi* to *Endymion*, *Lamia*, and other poems (*Melville's "Mardi,"* 75, 75n, 76, 132n, 141n). It may be that whereas Melville is compelled to mention Coleridge's prior text when writing of the unmediated experience of seeing an albatross, his obviously allegorical scene here needs no spell-breaking reference to give token of its textuality. On traces of allegory in Romantic symbolic experience, see Gayatri Spivak, "Allégorie et histoire de la poésie: Hypothèse de travail," *Poètique*, No. 8 (1971), 431–35.

more authentic experience of being. Ishmael expands this moment into an allegorical tableau in which life is characterized as a forgetting of an exile from a dethronement—a triple removal from that royal existence that would mean participation in true being.

But what this moment actually leads to in Ahab is a total break between inner motive and outer means. And the text reflects this break: Ahab is not fitted smoothly to the picture of the ancient king but is only indicated as roughly cognizant of the whole problem it denotes. "Now, in his heart," the narrative continues, "Ahab had some glimpse of this, namely: all my means are sane, my motive and my object mad." But if this is the extent of Ahab's understanding then it is poor indeed in comparison to the depths of insight which would seem to be required of one who winds his way down to the "vast Roman halls" of the psyche. The chief thing that Ahab has discerned is the discontinuity between his means and ends, because they too exist on two levels simply superimposed on one another. If his "motive and object" are to break out of the prison mentioned in his quarter-deck speech and restore himself to his throne, this end in itself is not mad but seems the natural response to a sympathetic vision of the old king. What is mad, paradoxically, is the resort to "sane" means—that is, means wholly within the control of the practical intellect—to accomplish this transcendent end. So Ahab's glimpse of himself, seen from the standpoint of the old-king-allegory, actually reverses sanity and madness.

Nonetheless, Ahab is aware of the discontinuity inherent in his project. It is a discontinuity that leads him to dissemble: "Yet without power to kill, or change, or shun the fact; he likewise knew that to mankind he did long dissemble; in some sort, did still." His attempt to mask his transcendent purpose and deny the discontinuity of his actions thus manifests that discrepancy only more surely and more dangerously.

Ishmael begins now as narrator to be aware of the gap in Ahab's character, and in Chapters 43 and 44 he presents allegorical masques of the discrepancies between the levels of his endeavor. Chapter 43 ("Hark!") makes use of the ship's two-level structure as a possible allegorical distribution. On the top level sailors are standing in a line on the deck directly above Ahab's cabin, silently passing buckets of fresh water from one of the ship's casks to another. One sailor suddenly hears a noise beneath them, coming from Ahab's cabin, that "sounds like two or three sleepers turning over" (p. 170). He is led to speculate that Ahab is hiding someone in his cabin, and thus the ostensible purpose of the chapter—suspense—is accomplished.

But the spatial, diagrammatic quality of the scene provokes a further reading. To begin with, it takes place on two levels. At the top level the chain of sailors and the exchange going on between them, always of the same buckets, suggests the circulation of an economic system and has literal ties with that system, since they are filling the ship's scuttle-butt in the interests of fulfilling their commercial mission. It is all a clear, rational, and mundane proceeding, and its continuity achieves precisely the effect Ahab looks for in his command. Below them, however, something unknown is going on, something hidden that can be discerned only vaguely but that sounds like a turning and suggests some darker purpose of Ahab's. Thus Ahab's pretense of business as usual on board a whaling ship is carried out with only momentary misgivings by the sailors; Archy, who has heard that brief hint, must drop his speculations when he is told—look to your bucket: do your job. But the murmur in that smooth-flowing circulation, even if brief, cannot be erased. It has happened, and the chapter's title reflects the moment of that break. Ahab's own darker purpose—his turning—has put forth the mouldings of its features from behind his well-constructed mask.

Chapter 44 ("The Chart") presents a further two-level look at Ahab. At the beginning of the chapter the reader is asked to follow him down to his cabin from the quarter-deck, where "that wild ratification of his purpose with his crew" took place. Once alone, he takes out "a large wrinkled roll of yellowish sea charts," evidence that Ahab's change of scene is a transfer from public to private and from oratory to writing. As an allegory of reading his language, the scene in his cabin reveals a level of thorough calculation masked by the power and spontaneity of his rhetoric. Already in the "Quarter-Deck" chapter he is portrayed as a man traced upon—"his ribbed and dented brow" marked by "the footprints of his one unsleeping, ever-pacing thought." Now, while he writes he is seen as written upon on another level, a level not inherent to himself and one of which he is unaware: "The heavy pewter lamp suspended in chains over his head, continually rocked with the motion of the ship, and for ever threw shifting gleams and shadows of lines upon his wrinkled brow, till it almost seemed that while he himself was marking out lines and courses on the wrinkled charts, some invisible pencil was also tracing lines and courses upon the deeply marked chart of his forehead" (p. 171).

In this chapter, for the first time, Ishmael takes the measure of Ahab. Previously the captain has appeared as a legend, a figure of power—and before any of these, as a difficult subject for narrating, who presents a problem for portrayal. Ahab must enter the domain of writing in order to execute his purpose. His speech could pretend the unity of his project just as it sought to effect his crew's solidarity with him, but he cannot long sustain this level. At the heart of his project are discontinuities, capable of being graphed only by the movement of his pencil. Yet as this scene implies, to write is to leave oneself open to be written on. Ahab's wordless tracing is a direct transcription of his will onto space and time, yet the very entry of his project into an explicit dimension of time reveals to Ishmael that Ahab's action has been graphed at a level beyond his own control. The shadow writing of the lamp on Ahab's forehead is a glimpse of the anagoge, a foreshadowing of Ahab's ultimate place in the temporal chart of the world.

The vision of Ahab on two levels leads at the end of this chapter to his portrayal as a double figure. He becomes increasingly allegorical as he realizes that his charting can do little to catch Moby Dick: "And have I not tallied the whale, Ahab would mutter to himself . . . tallied him, and shall he escape? His broad fins are bored, and scalloped out like a lost sheep's ear!" (p. 174). The word *tallied* suggests both the numerical enterprise of his charting and the knife wound, like a notch, he gave Moby Dick in their first encounter. Suddenly he realizes that the grid of his chart, net though it be, is not sufficiently fine to capture the whale, who will perpetually elude any systematic attempt to possess him.

And here the old biblical language enters to indicate the point at which Ahab's scientific, systematic enterprise falls short. The whale as "lost sheep" suggests Ahab as a demonic inversion of the Good

Shepherd, who in this case would find his charge only to destroy it. But despite the biblical archetype implied here Ahab cannot return the escaped beast to the fold. The whale's elusion of all preconceived systems appears inevitable to the imagination at the very point where scientific language is dropped and biblical metaphors taken up.

Ahab's muttering in this scene leads to his greater anguish at night, the torment of a man who "sleeps with clenched hands; and wakes with his own bloody nails in his palms." If the image of Christ is suggested as a play on the word "nails" here, it marks Ahab as a Romantic antitype, the would-be harrower of heaven rather than of hell, who nonetheless has his own agony in the garden. His suffering is staged within him, however, largely hidden from the conscious Ahab, revealing itself only at the threshold between sleep and waking, a continually fruitful moment for allegory in that it suggests two parallel worlds both conjoined and disjoined, able to bring out the disjunctures and doublings within the supposedly integral self. Ahab's "exhausting and intolerably vivid dreams of the night" goad him on until "a chasm seemed opening in him" and a "hell in himself yawned beneath him." When he bursts out of his stateroom into the open, Ishmael speculates that the tormented thing before him is a double (or, more accurately, one half) of Ahab, not "the scheming, unappeasedly steadfast hunter of the white whale" but "the eternal, living principle or soul in him" which "in sleep, being for the time dissociated from the characterizing mind . . . spontaneously sought escape from the scorching contiguity of the frantic thing, of which, for the time, it was no longer an integral" (p. 175).

This double Ahab is now a thoroughly conceptualized character, become so nearly an allegorical type that he can be identified, in the closing image of the chapter, with Prometheus, the *locus communus* of defiant striving. No longer an ineffable, magnetizing presence to the mind of the narrator, he has become identifiable and dissoluble into dyadic models. The fact that his decomposition can be accomplished only by an allegorical fiction, however, means that Ishmael's understanding of him cannot be the univocal possession of knowledge but only a series of dualistic schemes, in which the two components remain incommensurable with each other and ultimately inexplicable. Two chapters after "The Chart," Ahab is shown more clearly than ever in Chapter 46 to be a conniving manipulator. He considers his men "tools" that are merely "apt to get out of order" and need adjusting, and judges that "the permanent constitutional condition of the manufactured man . . . is sordidness" (p. 183). Thus he must hold up to them his promise of "cash" as a sop to their lower natures, meanwhile "observ[ing] all customary usages" of a normal whaling voyage to keep them from recalling his announced purpose and perhaps mutinying. How this debased and spiritually desolate condition squares with his terrible magnificence, Ishmael does not venture to say.

Unweaving the Mat

Ishmael's vision of the charter charted is thus able to free him from Ahab the patriarch's hypnotic power, but it cannot of itself present him with any new revelation. The product of his own abstract speculations is not itself a text but something like the writing surface on which an event can become significant once it has happened. Yet when he does experience such an event, it turns out to alter the map of his universe, and in no small particulars but in the very nature of its existence. After the intrusion of the real whale into the novice whaler's world, his space-time chart remains intact and correct in every dimension—except that it no longer exists. The whale has brought its erasing world of whiteness into the world of the mind and caused an irreversible rupture there.

Ishmael's consummate space-time chart is woven in Chapter 47, "The Mat-Maker," where, as in other nearby chapters, the illusion of timelessness prevails. As Queequeg and Ishmael busy themselves weaving a sword mat to bunt the ship's masts, the weather becomes so silent and uniform that "each silent sailor seemed resolved into his own invisible self." A strange dreaminess, "an incantation of revery," begins to reign "all over the ship and all over the sea." The repetition of consonants, particularly sibilants, and phrases places this incantatory power in the narrative as well. Removed from any landscape, with no atmospheric movements, without reference to any point of change, action begins to seem timeless. Separated from temporal context, it also becomes figurative, losing its fastness to a literally determinable surrounding. As linear time disappears, the idea of time emerges.

In Ishmael's fancy the mat is converted to "the great Loom of Time," the threads of the loom representing necessity or Fate, the shuttle with which he weaves in the cross-thread representing his free will, and the heavy blow of the wooden sword with which Queequeg drives home the interwoven ropes representing chance. "Aye, chance, free will, and necessity—no wise incompatible—all interweavingly working together." Ishmael finishes this scheme on a note of almost Oriental peace at the inexorable yet harmonious workings of time. Yet just previously he has noted that the scene into which he was entering was "so still and subdued and yet somehow preluding." And just at the point when he finishes his philosophical disquisition, a row of asterisks marks a break in the narrative, signaling the intrusion of a different kind of time:

*   *   *   *   *   *   *

> Thus we were weaving and weaving away when I started at a sound so strange, long drawn, and musically wild and unearthly, that the ball of free will dropped from my hand, and I stood gazing up at the clouds whence that voice dropped like a wing.

The irony of that row of asterisks deserves comment. Implicitly Melville has set up an analogy of the text of his novel to the weaving of the loom—an analogy as old as Homer. It would imply that the text is a uniform fabric, interweaving its elements harmoniously and continuously, fulfilling a predetermined design as it moves toward its end. Yet at the precise moment after Ishmael mentions the most disruptive element in his orderly scheme—chance, perhaps underrated if it is considered to be "restrained in its play within the right lines of necessity, and sideways in its motions modified by free will"—at the moment when he cannot help confessing that "chance by turns rules either, and has the last featuring blow at events," the fabric of the text is broken up by those asterisks.

Like divine intervention in mundane history, the chance event disrupts uniform plans of order and recenters attention on finalities.

The singing-out for the whale sounds "strange," "wild and unearthly"; it has "dropped like a wing" from the clouds. Its suddenness is
registered in terms at once enchanting and ominous: Tashtego the
lookout seems "some prophet or seer beholding the shadows of Fate,
and by those wild cries announcing their coming." At once the
metaphysical illusion of Fate as something known is broken up in
Ishmael's mind: henceforth it appears as *that which comes.*

A one-line paragraph signals the plunge into a completely different kind of time: "Instantly all was commotion." The events that
follow suggest an entirely different allegory of how the world is
woven. The whales are Necessity, the realm of nature and force; the
whaleboats are Free Will; the sudden squall that overcomes them,
leading to the whales' escape—Chance. The elements of the Loom
of Time all reappear in this drama, but the loom is permanently
invalidated because it has left out the "commotion" that is the in-
dispensable condition of experiencing reality.

What characterizes this new kind of time is urgency:

> The Sperm Whale blows as a clock ticks, with the same un-
> deviating and reliable uniformity. . . .
> "There go flukes!" was now the cry from Tashtego; and the
> whales disappeared.
> "Quick, steward!" cried Ahab. "Time! time!"
> Dough-Boy hurried below, glanced at the watch, and re-
> ported the exact minute to Ahab.   (p. 186)

The very recurrence of the isolated word *time* mocks the leisurely
accretion of threads by the Loom of Time. And Stubb's rollicking
"ambiguous jollity," as he calls his crew in an American version of
festina lente, knocks away the last vestige of dreaminess: "Easy, easy;
don't be in a hurry—don't be in a hurry. Why don't you snap your
oars, you rascals? Bite something, you dogs! So, so, so, then;—
softly, softly!" (p. 188). "But what the devil are you hurrying about?
Softly, softly, and steadily, my men. Only pull, and keep pulling;
nothing more. Crack all your backbones, and bite your knives in
two—that's all. Take it easy—why don't ye take it easy, I say, and
burst all your livers and lungs!" (p. 192).

"The First Lowering" is one of the finest narratives of action in the entire work. Traces of allegory are virtually nonexistent in the chapter until the action abates near its end, and then the allegory is of a dramatically different kind from the stratifying, analytic sort that has prevailed thus far in the voyage. Tossed out of his whale-boat, battered by a furious storm, Ishmael feels that he and his mates are burning "unconsumed" in the lightning; "immortal in these jaws of death!" (p. 194). An allegory tinged with the intimate recognition of contingency and negativity emerges out of their measures to survive:

> After many failures Starbuck contrived to ignite the lamp in the lantern; then stretching it on a waif pole, handed it to Queequeg as the standard-bearer of this forlorn hope. There, then, he sat, holding up that imbecile candle in the heart of that almighty forlornness. There, then, he sat, the sign and symbol of a man without faith, hopelessly holding up hope in the midst of despair. (pp. 194–95)

The image seems inherently allegorical, a Renaissance emblem denoting *Spes*; but Ishmael's awareness of all the "almighty forlornness" surrounding it makes of it an allegory of allegory. The "man without faith" is the allegorist contemplating death, resembling the baroque allegorists on whom Benjamin dwells.[6] Even the language here reinforces the emblem, showing a more complete comprehension of the allegorist's craft: the alliteration in "hopelessly holding up hope" underlines its antinomy-in-unity; the repetition of "There, then, he sat" doubles the image in a way that makes explicit the two-level, text-plus-commentary structure of allegory.

The squall that strands them on the ocean all night makes Ishmael realize the ever-nearness of death. Once he returns to the ship, he again undertakes a writing enterprise—but it is to make out his will. He has adopted a "free and easy sort of genial, desperado philosophy" with which to regard "this whole voyage of the Pe-

---

6. Cf. Benjamin's comment that "ultimately, the [allegorical] intention does not faithfully rest in the contemplation of bones, but faithlessly [*treulos*] leaps forward to the idea of resurrection" (*Origin of German Tragic Drama*, 233).

quod, and the great White Whale its object" (p. 196). What his realization of time and death has given him is irony, the ability to escape the seduction of timelessness in an intellectual project by seeing its worthlessness from an eternal perspective. That perspective can be brought in only by religious allusions, and they can be made to fit the situation only by means of the same jocular irony that has unseated the intellectual project in the first place. Paradoxically, this unseating is experienced as a liberation rather than a new confinement: Ishmael confides that he felt as though "a stone was rolled away from my heart" once he has written the rough draft of his will. His realization of being virtually condemned to death makes him feel as though he has been resurrected: "All the days I should now live would be as good as the days that Lazarus lived after his resurrection" (p. 197). And, in a tour de force like John Donne's "Death, thou shalt die," he declares, "I survived myself; my death and burial were locked up in my chest."

This resurrection is a return to the primacy of experience, but it is no longer the unmediated confrontation of Ego with Other that the Romantic symbol supposes. Benjamin, in tracing the development of "that untenable modern view of allegory and symbol," cites Schopenhauer's remark that the Romantic symbol could directly express the Idea, whereas allegory can only indirectly express concepts.[7] Melville demonstrates at one brilliant stroke, by making the Idea a living, breathing leviathan, the point Benjamin tirelessly argues: the Idea cannot be directly presented to the consciousness. The conceptualization inherent in allegory, however, becomes its leading epistemological advantage once one sees that the notion of "manifesting the Idea" is a delusion. For phenomena in their base state cannot participate in truth; they must first be broken up into concepts, becoming accessible to the intellect, even if that conceptual scheme is flawed.[8] In fact it must be flawed, for the final turn toward truth, as Benjamin argues, cannot be made unless one realizes that the concepts do not present real knowledge but only map

7. *Ibid.*, 161–62.
8. *Ibid.*, 33: "Phenomena do not, however, enter into the realm of ideas whole, in their crude empirical state, adulterated by appearances, but only in their basic elements, re-

out the configuration of the Idea—that they are nothing in themselves and only in their interplay do they act out a drama which can participate in truth.

The chart is thus an alternative to unmediated vision, a necessary alternative as Melville shows because the vision of absolute nature becomes an unknowable, annihilating horror, "the ungraspable phantom of life" which the Narcissan quester can find "in all rivers and oceans" (p. 14). The sublime absolute always bears the hidden face of the Gorgon.[9] Pierre's compulsion to know the truth about Isabel elicits the Gorgon allusion from him, for she opens up an undifferentiated, lawless, natural side to his thoroughly idealized father and hence to the status of his own existence. "Lo! I strike through thy helm, and will see thy face, be it Gorgon!" (*Pierre*, 66). In this line Pierre inherits the stance of Ahab the orator, who carried the Medusan quest to its ultimate end and is destroyed; the truth of his vision becomes undistinguishable from the dishonesty of his action. Ishmael presents this spiritual petrification as a series of alternative images of himself, from Narcissus to the falling masthead dreamer to the initiate at the Temple of Isis (in Chapter 76), and hence not literally as himself. His fascination with charting removes him from the immediate hypnotic power of the natural Other. However, it leaves him completely isolated, a Cartesian thinking subject, severed from even the notion of community in his thought, unable to speak, silently occupying a world which undulates between piercing rationality and lulling dream. He, too, would be lost, except that nature itself does not let him be.

Hence charting is an indispensible activity, though as an end in itself it is radical error, for it moves directly away from the experiential world. In conceptualizing the world, however—through such

---

deemed. They are divested of their false unity so that, thus divided, they might partake of the genuine unity of truth. In this their division, phenomena are subordinate to concepts, for it is the latter which effect the resolution of objects into their constituent elements."

9. On Melville's understanding of the Romantic sublime as implying annihilation, see Barbara Glenn, "Melville and the Sublime in *Moby-Dick*," *American Literature*, XLVIII (1976), 165–82. Glenn sees Melville as fully consonant with Burke, whose inquiry he read and marked. This topic deserves further attention, however, and one ought to consult Thomas Weiskel's *The Romantic Sublime: Studies in the Structure and Psychology of Transcendence* (Baltimore, 1976), to review the sublime in Melville under a fuller light.

schemes as cetology, the ship's course, the Loom of Time, and the whaling ship's chain of command—Ishmael casts the figures which, jostled out of their stately position in charts, begin to join the "dance of represented Ideas" as he enters the pell-mell world of action.[10]

10. Benjamin, *Origin of German Tragic Drama*, 29: "Truth, bodied forth in the dance of represented ideas, resists being projected, by whatever means, into the realm of knowledge."

V

~~

THE CARNIVALIZED WORLD:
DISCOVERY OF THE BODY

(*Moby-Dick*, Chapters 49–75)

The Carnival Attitude

WHEN HE RETURNS to the ship after his first whale hunt, soaked from a night in a storm-tossed whaleboat and given up for dead by his shipmates, Ishmael feels possessed by an "odd sort of wayward mood." That he is not dead is genuinely amazing to him; but that he came so close to death, and that everyone is so indifferent to the narrowness of his escape, is an equal and opposite shock. He comes to feel caught in a curious tension of internal forces:

> There are certain queer times and occasions in this strange mixed affair we call life when a man takes this whole universe for a vast practical joke, though the wit thereof he but dimly discerns, and more than suspects that the joke is at nobody's expense but his own. . . . And as for small difficulties and worryings, prospects of sudden disaster, peril of life and limb; all these, and death itself, seem to him only sly, good-natured hits, and jolly punches in the side bestowed by the unseen and unaccountable old joker. (p. 195)

This "odd sort of wayward mood . . . comes in the very midst of his earnestness, so that what just before might have seemed to him a thing most momentous, now seems but a part of the general joke." This mood he denominates a "free and easy sort of genial, desperado philosophy"; and with it he "now regarded this whole voyage of the Pequod, and the great White Whale its object" (p. 196).

The entire opening paragraph of Chapter 49, "The Hyena," betokens a radical change of attitude from the serious concerns of the foregoing chapters, with their introduction of Ahab and his obsession, the quarter-deck speech, the first presentation of the mates and harpooners, with a ringing defense of Starbuck in the name of the "great democratic God," the intimate glimpses of Ahab in "Sunset" and "The Chart," and the philosophical cast of "The Mast-Head" and "The Mat-Maker."[1] The depth of Ishmael's seriousness in those chapters is something of a problem, however. The "great democratic God" passage, for instance, is often taken as Melville's own credo, but a note of callowness does sound through this and many of the most serious passages in the early chapters.[2] It is not a case of the narrator attempting to duplicate the naïveté of the tyro sailor; the narrator himself has his own problem of inexperience in finding the imaginative and rhetorical form of the experience he has had. (Since this dynamic of the narrator is as much a fiction as the dynamic of the sailor, it is ultimately what marks off Ishmael the narrator from Melville the author, who—despite all hypotheses of "two *Moby-Dicks*" or more by reconstructing scholars—at some point must have envisioned both levels of his difficult narrative as a unity.)

What the rhetoric of those earlier chapters has been unable to do justice to is the world outside hierarchies—the oceanic world, the real object of Ishmael's narrative. Thus he must insist in Chapter 45 that Moby Dick is not a "hideous and intolerable allegory" but a real whale, about whom real legends exist, and whose cousins left their indelible marks on the *Essex*, the *Acushnet*, and many other stove ships. To be true to that segment of reality unknown to timid landsmen and somehow entrusted to him by the Fates, he must refuse the allegory that Ahab has made of the whale and that he is tempted to embrace. To counter it he must provide affidavits, bare

---

1. See Edward H. Rosenberry, *Melville and the Comic Spirit* (Cambridge, Mass., 1955), 122.

2. For the most part, this passage has been viewed as spoken with the greatest sincerity. Thus Vincent: "Melville's words are not merely the rip tide of rhetoric. They are deep belief" (*Trying-Out of "Moby-Dick,"* 105); and Henry Nash Smith: "This august dignity is the central affirmation of the novel" ("The Image of Society in *Moby-Dick*," in Tyrus Hillway [ed.], *"Moby-Dick" Centennial Essays* [Dallas, 1952], 74). Sacvan Bercovitch discusses Melville's ambivalence about the hopes of democratic society in *The American Jeremiad* (Madison, Wis., 1978), 191–94.

physical definitions ("a spouting fish with a horizontal tail," p. 119), taxonomizings, and even philological examinations of the literal whale. This literalism, furthermore, is in service of nature, which not only opposes culture but contains it and makes culture possible, and finally if gazed at long enough reveals culture to be an insubstantial affair, "a little chipping, baking, patching, and washing," in Emerson's famous *deprecatio* at the beginning of *Nature*.

But what "The Affidavit" (Chap. 45) asserts to be fully literal (again, a little too insistingly), "The Hyena" (Chap. 49) discovers to be neither wholly literal nor exactly allegorical, but rather a "general joke" in which one is inextricably involved and for which the highest mark of appreciation is laughter. According to Erich Auerbach this daring appreciation of the natural in and of itself is the hallmark of Rabelais, making him one of the great fathers of realism: "Rabelais' entire effort is directed toward . . . tempting the reader out of his customary and definite way of regarding things, by showing him phenomena in utter confusion; upon tempting him out into the great ocean of the world, in which he can swim freely, though it be at his own peril."[3] These words, though intended for another author, may serve as the indication of Ishmael's rhetorical strategy in Chapters 49 to 75.

The connection of Melville with Rabelais is not without justification, for it is Rabelais above all who revels in the physical universe as it is, who "bolts down all events, all creeds, and beliefs, and persuasions, all hard things visible and invisible, never mind how knobby" and who thus lights the way for Ishmael's imagination in perceiving the "general joke" of earthly existence. We know of course that Melville acquired a copy of the Urquhart Rabelais shortly after buying Cary's Dante in that flurry of deep reading that preceded and ran alongside *Mardi*.[4] In *Mardi* he had "grim Dante shake sides with fat Rabelais," suggesting the two great national poets as obverse sides of each other in imagination.[5] Furthermore, the form of *Mardi* seems a rough recasting of Panurge's quest-voyage

3. Erich Auerbach, *Mimesis: The Representation of Reality in Western Literature*, trans. Willard Trask (Princeton, 1953), 275–76.
4. Sealts, *Melville's Reading*, 87–88, Item 417; Davis, *Melville's "Mardi"*, 64–66.
5. Herman Melville, *Mardi, and A Voyage Thither*, ed. Harrison Hayford, Hershel Parker, and Thomas Tanselle (Evanston, Ill., 1970), 13.

in the *Quart Livre*, and this homology of pattern deepens in *Moby-Dick*, which Northrop Frye classifies along with *Gargantua and Pantagruel* as a "romance-anatomy."[6] In important ways Rabelais helped Melville attain the shape of his experience and of his fiction.

The paradox of the "genial, desperado philosophy" Ishmael now feels is this: although it reveals his life to be caught between forces that determine it and chance occurrences that will either save or destroy him, it is a liberating discovery. It frees him from the vestigial loyalties to the land-world of hierarchy and superficial piety, so that he does not have to assert a benevolent order when he needs to recognize the real malevolence that surrounds him. Again Auerbach strikes the right note in saying that the "revolutionary" thing about Rabelais is "the freedom of vision, feeling, and thought which his perpetual playing with things produces, and which invites the reader to deal directly with the world and its wealth of phenomena."[7]

Yet Auerbach's perceptive and convincing view of Rabelais is somewhat misleading because it makes Rabelais a kind of phenomenologist who simply goes "to the things themselves" and captures their essential spirit by a kind of osmosis, without any filter of tradition. The difficult work of unearthing the buried traditions that shaped the forms of play and "triumphant earthly life" in Rabelais has been accomplished by the great Russian scholar Mikhail Bakhtin. His research shows that the Rabelaisian mode of physicality and play derives from folk traditions developed over a millennium of medieval Christianity and, although suppressed by its "official culture," regarded leniently and allowed to emerge full-blown in various calendar feast days.

This "culture of folk carnival humor," as Bakhtin uncovers it, showed its signs everywhere yet has often remained invisible to modern eyes because of its fundamentally different mode of perceiving the world. In writing of the "history of laughter" Bakhtin stresses that modern intellectual culture uses laughter only negatively, to ridicule positions it disapproves of. The carnival, however, is "far distant from the negative and formal parody of modern times. Folk

6. Northrop Frye, *Anatomy of Criticism: Four Essays* (Princeton, 1957), 313.
7. Auerbach, *Mimesis*, 276.

humor denies, but it revives and renews at the same time. Bare negation is completely alien to folk culture." Thus paradoxically the carnival spirit can degrade and abuse that which is high without negating it. In carnival, truth does not express itself in one-sided postulates but is all-inclusive. Bakhtin makes this point: "As opposed to the official feast, one might say that carnival celebrated temporary liberation from the prevailing truth and from the established order; it marked the supension of all hierarchical rank, privileges, norms, and prohibitions. Carnival was the true feast of time, the feast of becoming, change, and renewal. It was hostile to all that was immortalized and completed."[8]

This hostility extended even beyond earthly institutions to the conception of God, and medieval folk festivity made fun of the central myths of Christianity just as the Greeks had their satyr dramas: "In the folklore of primitive peoples, coupled with the cults which were serious in tone and organization were other, comic cults which laughed and scoffed at the deity ('ritual laughter'); coupled with serious myths were comic and abusive ones."[9] The abuse of God is not a logical or ontological attack but a strategy of exaggeration to make the world habitable and return human nature to itself. "It is an attitude toward the world which liberates from fear, brings the world close to man and man close to his fellow man (all is drawn into the zone of liberated familiar contact), and, with its joy of change and its jolly relativity, counteracts the gloomy, one-sided official seriousness which is born of fear, is dogmatic and inimical to evolution and change, and seeks to absolutize the given conditions of the social order."[10] This "victory of laughter" "was not only a victory over mystic terror of God, but also a victory over the awe inspired by the forces of nature, and most of all over the oppression and guilt related to all that was consecrated and forbidden."[11]

The uses of this attitude on board the *Pequod* should be more than evident. The fear-inspiring forces of nature surround the ship everywhere, and Ahab's rule of magnetism and awe pervades every

8. Bakhtin, *Rabelais and His World*, 11, 10.
9. *Ibid.*, 6.
10. Mikhail Bakhtin, *Problems of Dostoevsky's Poetics*, trans. R. W. Rotsel (Ann Arbor, Mich., 1973), 133.
11. Bakhtin, *Rabelais and His World*, 90.

psychic inch wherein one might hope to find refuge from nature. Leaving the ship to hunt the whale for the first time, however, Ishmael discovers nature itself standing outside and above this oppressive hierarchy of forces, or, more accurately, including them in its own life-continuing process. Since nature itself is not exempt from death but relativizes it within a line of regeneration, disaster and death can appear to Ishmael as "jolly punches in the side" and cause for hilarity. The motif of hitting and punching captures precisely that jollity and perception of relativity that dominates the carnival, and Bakhtin documents the traditions of good-natured drubbing in medieval festivals as well as in Rabelais.[12]

The whaleboat, as temporary refuge from the ship, is the place of discovering this desperado philosophy. The flimsiness of the boat, especially when fast to a running whale by the sizzling, perilous whale-line, places everyone in it in danger of his life; yet there reign in it a curious gaiety and, as with Stubb, a notion that one is risking life and limb, breaking his back rowing while pulling headlong into the jaws of the whale, all just for fun, "for the mere joke of the thing" (p. 188). The whale-line "folds the whole boat in its complicated coils" and "silently serpentines about the oarsmen," threatening to entangle each one; yet "gayer sallies, more merry mirth, better jokes, and brighter repartees, you never heard over your mahogany, than you will hear over the half-inch white cedar of the whale-boat, when thus hung in hangman's nooses" (pp. 240–41). Any captain who attempts to maintain his dignity standing in the whaleboat on a gam finds himself knocked in the knees and the small of his back by the fore and aft steering oars and knocked off balance by the boat's pitching in the waves, and in a squall he may be forced to "seize hold of the nearest oarsman's hair, and hold on there like grim death" (p. 207).

With the realization that "all men live enveloped in whale-lines" comes a liberation from the terrors of the whale: the men in the whaleboat feel not "one whit more of terror, than though seated before your evening fire with a poker" (p. 241). Concurrent with this decontamination comes a new freedom in dealing with the im-

12. See Bakhtin on the *nopces à mitaines, ibid.*, 200–207.

age of the whale. Bakhtin describes how in the carnival "all that was terrifying becomes grotesque," and in parading the grotesque terrors of death and hell "the people play with terror and laugh at it; the awesome becomes a 'comic monster.'"[13] Up to this point, the whale has signified this metaphysical terror of death to Ishmael. The experience of the actual whale hunt teaches Ishmael a new perspective on "this business of death," whose terror he has previously been able to escape only by Platonizing the physical world and blocking it out from his ascending consciousness. Now, however, it is the physical itself that leads him to his new attitude because of its implicit gaiety, in which all the seamen participate whenever on the hunt. The whale itself becomes the "comic monster" of the folk festival: without ceasing to signify death it becomes something to be played with as well.

Chapters 65 ("The Whale as a Dish") and 67 ("Cutting In") concentrate on the body of the whale, especially connected to the carnival motif of eating. The implicit comparisons, in these chapters, of the whale's body to the human body, culminating in designating the right whale's and sperm whale's heads as Locke and Kant, provide a burlesquing of the heretofore only sublime leviathan, a comic anthropomorphizing that brings the whale down to our level. Here are the chapters that can speak of eating the whale, an act that would be gravely out of place elsewhere. The tradition of the "carnival anatomy" enters, "the enumeration of the parts of a dismembered body."[14] Ahab speaks to the sperm whale's head and enjoins it to reply. Images which make of the whale a violated and incomplete body appear here as normal and acceptable, defeating the unspeakable fear of previous chapters and free from the pathos of the later, more involved chapters.

The Whale and Allegorical Representation

A sense of play comes to dominate the image of the whale in Chapters 55 to 57, chapters free from even the unrigorous rigors of bibliotaxonomy in Chapter 32. These metamorphoses of the whale come as an explicit prologue to a later viewing of "the true form of the

13. *Ibid.*, 91.
14. Bakhtin, *Problems of Dostoevsky's Poetics*, 135.

whale . . . in his own absolute body" (p. 224). Having tossed overboard all superficial seriousness, the play of Ishmael's relativizing
desperado philosophy thus never loses sight of its role as prelude or
foreplay to the truly serious study of the whale. First the pseudo-
scientific claims of accurate drawings of the whale must be ex-
ploded. The various paintings of whales, at first on canvas and
then, as in the title of Chapter 57, "Of Whales in Paint; in Teeth;
in Wood; in Sheet-Iron; in Stone; in Mountains; in Stars," serve to
dislodge the notion of representing the whale directly (Cuvier's
drawing is "not a sperm whale, but a squash"). Not stopping there,
however, these successive images move toward the notion that the
creature can only be indicated in a self-confessed fiction. In these
playful approaches to a science of the whale, the whale becomes
something like the Platonic Idea (a "full-grown Platonian Leviathan," p. 228). What Benjamin insists on proves true again: Ideas
cannot be directly expressed but must be represented in concepts
whose form in their interplay constellates the Idea. For Benjamin
this is the task of philosophy, which is thereby awakened from its
dream of being the science of the absolute.

It is precisely this dislodging of philosophical representation from
science to art that Ishmael accomplishes in his drafts of cetology.
He ends Chapter 32 with a famous disclaimer of completion: "But I
now leave my cetological System standing thus unfinished, even as
the great Cathedral of Cologne was left, with the crane still standing upon the top of the uncompleted tower. For small erections may
be finished by their first architects; grand ones, true ones, ever leave
the copestone to posterity. God keep me from ever completing anything. This whole book is but a draught—nay, but the draught of a
draught" (pp. 127–28). The unfinished state of his science, in
other words, becomes not a simple lack indicating merely a place
where future information is to be inserted, but an artistic gesture
indicating its openness to truth. Melville's "Cetology" chapter thus
takes the form of a scientific treatise, rather than of a report or brief
which would claim to neutralize the gestural aspect of its writing.
Treatises still follow rhetorical lines of development, and they
avowedly "treat of" a subject rather than purporting to encompass
it exhaustively. The form of the treatise earns Benjamin's apprecia-

tion in the "Epistemocritical Prologue" of his *Trauerspiel* book, for it is the treatise that preserves the representational character of philosophical language and thus becomes the key to a rehabilitation of the Western philosophical tradition once the Hegelian project of absolute knowledge has failed. In Benjamin's view philosophy participates in truth insofar as it can be read as an allegory—as a drama (or, better, a masque), by the progression of its thought representing man vis-à-vis the Idea. It thus must represent the Idea by absence, for man's distance from the Idea is his governing condition.

Ishmael now sees his entire narrative work as "but the draught of a draught"—the original draught now being, presumably, the created world. If ashore he believed somewhat bitterly that "the universe is finished; the copestone is on," he now sees that creation cannot be complete, at least because it prohibits an adequate expression of itself. Thus his "draught of a draught," in the paradoxical logic of allegory, more accurately expresses the true nature of being than would a statement purporting to be complete. His incompleteness asserts his strength, the strength to be "grand" and "true," also associated with sexual potency through a hinted pun on "erections." This play on words leads us back to Rabelais and the realization that all procreative power is but an absence of satisfaction, a desire to fill a gap in being which never can be filled and thus demands endless attempts.

In Chapters 55 to 57 the quest for an adequate portrait of the whale leads to endless attempts, envisioning the whale from every imaginable perspective. The indeterminacy principle in representing the whale is as follows: "The only mode in which you can derive even a tolerable idea of his living contour, is by going a whaling yourself; but by so doing, you run no small risk of being eternally stove and sunk by him. Wherefore, it seems to me you had best not be too fastidious in your curiosity touching this Leviathan" (p. 228). To experience this reality and to attempt its representation are two incompatible activities—a fundamental truth which the modern camera can do no more than make us forget momentarily. The threshold between those activities involves a giving over of oneself, a "risk."

What has remained undetermined to this point is the place of allegory with regard to this threshold. As I have tried to show with Dante, allegory tends to depict this moment of "risk" at the threshold, the desertion of conceptual representation and the self-relinquishing turn to another power, a body not yet defined as a text. Similar moments can be found in Spenser and other allegorists, as Honig's and Quilligan's remarks on threshold dreams and texts suggest, though, it seems to me, Dante most clearly exposes this process. Nonetheless, the mode of allegorical signification remains steadfastly on the "here," earthly side of that threshold, precisely because it is the mode of writing in which the discontinuity between representation and experience of the transcendent has come to consciousness most clearly. Therefore allegory centers on an experience it cannot really present but can only represent in coded form. This paradox may help explain why allegories can become repetitious, since the very depiction of allegorical experience is its own negation; and try after try must be made to hit that experience, though each image remains equidistant from it.

As a result, allegory postulates a leap to attain that experience. This leap cannot overcome its own impossibility, because the absolute disjunction of the conceptual realm from the ideal logically precludes any crossing; hence the leap is a fictional device for an experience that cannot be formulated. The allegorist, or his protagonist, has found himself in the presence of an entity beyond naming or imagining. Dante stresses the distancing inherent in allegorical representation by making this leap a device of writing when in the *Paradiso* he states of his failure to describe the beauty of St. Peter's song, "the pen passeth on and leaves a blank" ("Però salta la penna e non lo scrivo," literally: the pen leaps and I do not write it, *Par.* XXIV, 25). Similarly, the famous threshold crossing of Julius Caesar is described in graphological terms: "What after that it [the "sacred standard" of Rome] wrought, / When from Ravenna it came forth, and leap'd/ The Rubicon, was of so bold a flight, / That tongue nor pen may follow it" (*Par.* VI, 61–64). The pure act of will can risk all and cross the threshold of true being, whereas conceptualization must remain behind. If Dante is most explicit on this point, Melville even exceeds him in graphic conciseness when in the Loom of Time episode the row of asterisks bar the conceptualizing moment from the plunge into action and risk. Such devices are signs of the arbitrariness of the sign, an indication by the writer that nothing he could put on the page would bear an inherent, mimetic connection to the experience he has had.

Ishmael in speaking of the whale confesses the inadequacy of any mimetic sign: "True, one portrait may hit the mark much nearer than another, but none can hit it with any very considerable degree of exactness." But the difference is not one of degree. All portraits remain in the realm of conceptualization, at an equally unbridgeable distance from the whale's "absolute body," and thus exactness is out of the question. Ishmael's preference, therefore, for whales "variously represented" (the running head for this chapter in the original American edition, preserved in the Hayford-Parker) in nonmimetic elements from teeth to stars, is because these do not deceive the viewer about the impossibility of accuracy but rather divulge their own status as conceptualizations.

The final example, the constellation, is the most perfect of allegorical representations of the whale because it comes closest to making evident the process of representation-by-absence that is allegory, proving that this absence is fundamental to human perception. In a constellation the lines that would define the figure of the object are absent; they are only traced by the eye from point to point. Angus Fletcher has written of the frequent reliance of allegories on stars and constellations, a double reason that Emerson explains well: "The stars awaken a certain reverence, because though always present, they are always inaccessible" (*Nature*, 9). Fletcher points out that stars have long been emblems of the Platonic ideal realm.[15] But Emerson goes on to make that characteristic naturalizing turn that enables the American writer to see the world itself as allegory: "But all natural objects make a kindred impression, when the mind is open to their influence." So Melville: "Nor when expandingly lifted by your subject, can you fail to trace out great whales in the starry heavens, and boats in pursuit of them; as when long filled with thoughts of war the Eastern nations saw armies locked in battle among the clouds" (p. 233). Here again the paradox

15. Angus Fletcher, *Allegory: The Theory of a Symbolic Mode* (Ithaca, N.Y., 1964), 95–98.

of allegory: it takes a mind that is "lifted" and "filled" with a spirit to attain an "empty" mode of perception-and-representation. "Grand ones, true ones, ever leave the copestone to posterity."

Rereading *Moby-Dick* one is repeatedly struck with brilliant passages never noticed before, as though they had been tipped into the book. Such is the kind of revelation afforded by the sentences that close the chapter on "Whales Variously Represented": "Thus at the North have I chased Leviathan round and round the Pole with the revolutions of the bright points that first defined him to me." Melville's Dantesque circumlocution for "star"—bright points— seems to capture the essence of the mode in which the Idea reveals itself in allegory. And what biographer of Ishmael has yet noticed that the constellation Cetus was what "first defined" the whale to him? That "first" has a primacy that is more than genetic. The constellated whale has been the object of transcendent desire for Ishmael all his life. It is the point that connects earth and heaven, or at least the point that would disclose to him whether there is such a connection: "Would I could mount that whale and leap the topmost skies, to see whether the fabled heavens with all their countless tents really lie encamped beyond my mortal sight!" (p. 233). The constellation is only visible in the southern hemisphere, and hence he can have seen it only on an ocean voyage. Real experience and ideal vision thus intermingle and necessitate each other in Melville's world.

So the constellated whale, the heavenly whale, is the object of Ishmael's lifelong quest-romance. But the eros that spurs him toward it does not inform him whether that quest will end in bliss or in destruction, or what form the quest ought to take, or anything about the reality of the whale and whaling. It is something of a Gnostic myth of ascent that Ishmael posits in this daring trope of climbing on the starry whale's back, again revealing his kinship with the allegorical readers of Homer. To the tyro Ishmael, who thinks "my body is but the lees of my better being"—insofar as he himself is the young, pale sailor "with the Phaedon instead of Bowditch in his head"—meaning and "true being" exist only beyond the heavens. But he is led at crucial moments to turn away from that ascent, for he realizes as the wiser, more distanced narrator that this ascent would actually be a plunge to the depths. The insight of his allegorical contemplation is that the beyond-ness of true being is not an erasable quality but its true essence: being is always beyond. But, paradoxically, he finds that only on earth and in earthly experience can he discern the traces that indicate being's beyond-ness. Thus allegory and naturalism are played off against each other until, as in his letter to Hawthorne, Melville ends with envisioning "this great allegory, the world."

The Inverted World

In one of the metamorphoses in Chapter 57, the whale appears configured in the outline of a mountain range when seen from one particular vantage point. The transformation is a purely interior one, a gestalt perceived out of an externally arbitrary collection of sense data. The constellation Cetus is essentially perceived in the same way. The free play of the whale's images is generally conceived apart from the older carnival sense of play as communal festivity and is instead a token of the mind's power to transmute any image given to it. Whatever carnival Ishmael's desperado philosophy attains must work through the interiorizing transformations the carnival attitude underwent during Romanticism.

During its time as a festival for all, the expression of the carnival attitude included the grotesque. The ideal of beauty goes hand in hand culturally with a philosophy of serenity and seriousness; the beautiful body, complete in itself, excludes new life, whereas the protrusion of new life in the body, in giving birth and in various growths bearing the folk significance of fertility, always has the marks of the grotesque. The onset of the classical attitude in seventeenth-century Europe banished grotesque forms from acceptable cultural expression. When Romantic movements overthrew the rule of the Enlightenment aesthetic, they rediscovered the grotesque; but discovered in isolation from the folk it was no longer seen within the context of carnival laughter. Bakhtin writes of this change as first appearing in Sterne and as typical of German authors from the anonymous author of the *Night Vigils of Bonaventure* to E. T. A. Hoffmann: "The Romantic genre [of the grotesque] acquired a private 'chamber' character. It became, as it were, an individual carnival,

125

marked by a vivid sense of isolation. The carnival spirit was trans-
posed into a subjective, idealistic philosophy. It ceased to be the
concrete (one might say bodily) experience of the one, inexhaustible being, as it was in the Middle Ages and Renaissance."[16]

The individual carnival in turn opens up a terrifying abyss. "The
world of Romantic grotesque is to a certain extent a terrifying
world, alien to man. All that is ordinary, commonplace, belonging
to everyday life, and recognized by all suddenly becomes meaning-
less, dubious and hostile. Our own world becomes an alien world.
Something frightening is revealed in what was habitual and secure."[17] These features describe in essence the terrors expressed in
"The Whiteness of the Whale," fully comprehended in Wolfgang
Kayser's formula: "The grotesque is the estranged world."[18] The
transformation of the grotesque into terror is also at the origin of
the conception of Ahab, the epitome of the disillusioned Romantic, a version of the German idealist turned dark and bitter. The
irrational arises to him only as a purely demonic revelation.

Even more revealing in its connection to Ahab is the transformation in meaning of the mask in Romantic grotesque. This describes
Ahab's perception when he says, "All visible objects, man, are but
as pasteboard masks. . . . *Sometimes I think there's naught beyond*"
(p. 144). The treacherous masking of the annihilative principle in
nature repeatedly presents itself as a possibility in these chapters. In
the midst of Ishmael's metamorphic mood the most destructive and
unredeemable aspects of things appear. In Chapter 51, the men
chase the spirit-spout with "a sense of peculiar dread at this flitting
apparition, as if it were treacherously beckoning us on and on, in
order that the monster might turn round upon us, and rend us at
last in the remotest and most savage seas" (p. 201). Ishmael's sense
of exile is heightened and transforms the seascape around him to
one of utter lostness. Like the spirit-spout, it leads to no end—it is
a sign like the allegorical sign, leading one continually onward from
horizon to horizon but with no content in itself and with no end in

16. Bakhtin, *Rabelais and His World*, 37.
17. *Ibid.*, 38–39.
18. Wolfgang Kayser, *The Grotesque in Art and Literature*, trans. Ulrich Weisstein
(Bloomington, Ind., 1963), 184.

view. The name of the African cape is doubled, transformed backward in time: "Cape of Good Hope, do they call ye? Rather Cape Tormentoso, as called of yore." Peeling away the name of hope to reveal an original name of torment, this recollection of an older name betokens the loss of eschatology, a loss of any continuity of history. Cut loose from the guaranties that such a continuity would offer, Ishmael is prey to the torments of an utter indeterminacy of the universe: "We found ourselves launched into this tormented sea, where guilty beings transformed into those fowls and these fish, seemed condemned to swim on everlastingly without any haven in store, or beat that black air without any horizon" (p. 201). Signs come unmoored; they signify anything whatever without any particular order, thus loosing the infinite perspectives of subjectivity.

The metamorphic visions that open Chapter 58, "Brit," lead from beauty to a bottomless ground of destruction. Covered with brit, the ocean appears as "boundless fields of ripe and golden wheat" (p. 234). Right whales feeding on the brit are like "morning mowers" in sound, but like "lifeless masses of rock" visually. The treachery of appearances confronts the landsman in "the subtleness of the sea"; "its most dreaded creatures" are "treacherously hidden beneath the loveliest tints of azure" and they themselves often have a "devilish brilliance and beauty" (p. 235). Here even beauty takes on a grotesque terror. The discontinuity of appearance and reality opens up a bottomless chasm. Behind a gleaming beauty lurks the devourer—the sea as Medusa. "The live sea swallows up ships and crews"; it is "foe to man" and "fiend to its own offspring," dominated by a "universal cannibalism" and "eternal war." By these associations it becomes clear that Ishmael is referring to the land as well, to nature in general—whose face we forever keep masked from ourselves for the sake of our sanity. "By the continual repetition of these very impressions, man has lost that sense of the full awfulness of the sea which aboriginally belongs to it."

Yet the associations of womb in "offspring" and "swallows up" indicate a subjective rather than wholly natural image. The true, inescapable enemy is within. Nature alone is not treacherous; the source of horror is the subjectivity that makes the self a victim before the imagined vision of the devouring mother. Ishmael ends the chapter by asking, "Consider them both, the sea and the land; and do you not find a strange analogy to something in yourself? . . . In the soul of man there lies one insular Tahiti, full of peace and joy, but encompassed by all the horrors of the half known life. God keep thee! Push not off from that isle, thou canst never return!" (p. 236). The irony with which this last statement is uttered becomes clear in the light of the unconscious birth imagery of the chapter. But in a sense this advice to stay inside the womb, not to "push off," is only consistent with the direction of Romantic subjectivity, which continually places the inside in primacy over the outside. The progression of this chapter follows that pattern, beginning with whales and brit and ending with "something in yourself." Ahab states the primacy of subjectivity more overtly at the end of Chapter 70: "O Nature, and O soul of man! how far beyond all utterance are your linked analogies! not the smallest atom stirs or lives in matter, but has its cunning duplicate in mind" (p. 264).

Bakhtin acknowledges that "Romanticism made its own important discovery—that of the interior subjective man with his depth, complexity, and inexhaustible resources, and that "the *interior infinite* could not have been found in the closed and finished world [of the Enlightenment], with its distinct fixed boundaries dividing all phenomena and values."[19] As Bakhtin has remarked elsewhere, "A genre lives in the present, but it always *remembers* its past, its beginnings."[20] The fully Rabelaisian carnival is thus inaccessible after new paths of interiority have been blazed. Fully unifying laughter is banished, for it would dismantle the barriers that define the self. "If a reconciliation with the world occurs, it takes place in a subjective, lyric, or even mystic sphere."[21]

Yet the world of carnival is transformed somewhat differently in Hawthorne and Melville from its transformation among European Romantics and Poe. In "The Masque of the Red Death" and "The Cask of Amontillado," the carnival trappings are preserved only to estrange both protagonist and reader, isolating the protagonist in a defenseless confrontation with death and with the destructive de-

19. Bakhtin, *Rabelais and His World*, 44.
20. Bakhtin, *Problems of Dostoevsky's Poetics*, 87.
21. Bakhtin, *Rabelais and His World*, 44.

sire of another. In Hawthorne's "My Kinsman, Major Molineux," however, the carnival retains its character as an "all-people's" celebration, tied to political life, initiation into sexuality, and uncrowning or killing the father. "The May-Pole of Merry Mount" shows the festive carnival in the very process of being "buried" by history, for reasons Hawthorne cannot see as wholly bad. Nonetheless its sudden brief appearances, as though through holes in a fabric, indicate moments of true community from which the political life of the present is unhappily distanced and which it ought to try to recapture. For Hawthorne, in other words, the old carnival becomes allegory.

With Melville it is somewhat more complicated. Ishmael experiences fully the reversals of subjectivity, but he is not caught up completely within them. One of his first examples of metamorphosis, the crippled beggar "holding a painted board before him, representing the tragic scene in which he lost his leg" (pp. 231–32), is a two-sided emblem. On the one hand, he stands implicitly as an alternative version of Ahab, one still locked into the constraints of subjectivity. He has suffered the same fate as Ahab, yet he has reacted in the opposite way—not in defiance and fury but in defeat and impotence. Standing there "with downcast eyes . . . ruefully contemplating his own amputation," he exemplifies allegorical contemplation as the melancholy contemplation of absence. His misery and humility league him with the other threshold figures, the sub-sub-librarian and the pale usher, who find no reward for their actions—for ten years he has patiently shown his painting and his stump "to an incredulous world."

On the other hand, the beggar offers hope: an opening from the subjective world into some kind of community. Poor though he may be, he has transformed the scene of his deprivation into art, and "his three whales are as good whales as were ever published in Wapping" (p. 232). This praise comes after the apocalyptic remark that "the time of his justification is now at hand"; Ishmael seems to suggest that his narrative portrait of the beggar will negate his mistreatment, just as painting has preserved his life. But while the beggar goes back to "ruefully contemplating his own amputation," Ishmael comes outside himself into at least the promise of a reuniting.

His inversions thus ultimately serve not subjectivity itself but life, death, and human society. Granted that his entry into a carnival atmosphere is accomplished internally—it is a "mood" he is drawn into, rather than an actual festival—yet its internal nature does not categorically separate it from the folk culture of laughter. For in the midst of his lonely musings he discovers the possibility of a people's carnival involving all "fellow creatures," for the first time.

The Threshold Dialogue

The pan-cultural celebration of the Middle Ages and Renaissance is not to be re-created in a time dominated by interior isolation and the Calvinist gospel of mirthless industriousness. What carnival there is aboard the *Pequod* must for the most part be created by talk. The early chapters of the voyage such as "Knights and Squires," "The Specksynder," and "The Cabin-Table" stressed the hierarchy that determines all things aboard a whaling ship. In contrast, Ishmael now discovers an equality among his shipmates when they are faced, not with Ahab and his manipulations of the imaginary whale, but with the real whale and the proximity of death. This commonality develops around forms of language stressing an equality among speakers. Ishmael's serial questioning of Queequeg, Stubb, and Flask in "The Hyena," his tale-telling with the Spanish dons in Lima, the nature of the gam and the beginning of the *Pequod*'s gams with a series of ships, and Stubb's back-and-forth skylarking with the cook and with Flask after killing a whale, all betoken the dialogue form that, according to Bakhtin, has from the earliest times of verbal art shaped the literary expression of carnival.

The dialogue form has its roots in philosophical discourse, but it was used by a number of writers besides Plato and is not necessarily bound to dialogues of Socrates nor even required to include Socrates as one of the interlocutors. The "free creative attitude" toward truth that Bakhtin cites as the dialogue's primary characteristic did not allow it to remain tied down to such apostolic duties; what it retained throughout classical antiquity was "the Socratic method of dialogically arriving at the truth, and the external form of a dialogue." The major insight of this genre is the dialogical nature of truth, the realization that "the truth is not born and does not reside

in the head of an individual person; it is born of the dialogical inter-
course *between people* in the collective search for the truth."[22]

The special setting of many of the ancient dialogues is a threshold,
especially the threshold between life and death. One can see this
form in Plato's *Apology* and *Phaedo*, especially, and in works from the
Middle Ages to the present which situate their stories in deathbeds,
graveyards, and places of danger. The course of dialogues at these
threshold moments becomes most intense and liberated because, as
Bakhtin indicates, at such a moment "there is present a tendency to
create *extraordinary* situations, which cleanse the word of all automa-
tism and objectivization and force the person involved to reveal the
deepest layers of his personality and thought."[23] In *Moby-Dick* this
kind of revelation happens, as *content*, only later, when the climactic events provoke such eloquent confessions as Ahab's great speech
in "The Symphony." As *form*, however, the dialogue appears first in
these chapters beginning with "The Hyena," and it is linked closely
to humor and the carnival spirit.

The calm composure with which both questioner and questioned
carry out their set piece after Ishmael returns from his first whale
hunt makes this scene extremely funny, and it is all the funnier because of its urgent life-and-death character:

> "Queequeg," said I, when they had dragged me, the last
> man, to the deck, and I was still shaking myself in my jacket to
> fling off the water; "Queequeg, my fine friend, does this sort of
> thing often happen?" Without much emotion, though soaked
> through just like me, he gave me to understand that such things
> did often happen.
> "Mr. Stubb," said I, turning to that worthy . . . .   (p. 196)

Here laconism and long-winded circumlocution appear together,
both of them favorite devices of the Yankee humorist and often
combined in the form of a dialogue between innocence and experience, or city versus country. Just as in jokes of this vein, the humor
here is verbal: words themselves becomes objects of humor and
hence objects of attention. In the questioner's formality—repeat-

22. Bakhtin, *Problems of Dostoevsky's Poetics*, 89–90.
23. *Ibid.*, 91.

131

ing his address to each person, and adding "my fine friend" or "that worthy"—and circumlocution, the same focus is maintained, and it is finally sealed in Flask's apt stylistic criticism of Ishmael: "Can't you twist that smaller?"

A witty focus on words shifts the emphasis in fictional representation from the persons represented to the ideas and attitudes represented. The Socratic dialogue and the Menippean satire, which ridicules intellectual rather than social conventions, are the two major forms of expression of carnival in literature. Both concern themselves with the fate of ideas in the world, most typically with degrading the monological or "one-sided" great idea down to the level of bodily reality. The typical rhetorical devices of the dialogue form to which Bakhtin points are two: syncrisis ("the juxtaposition of various points of view toward a given object") and anacrisis ("the means of eliciting and provoking the words of one's interlocutor, forcing him to express his opinion, and express it fully"). Socrates of course was the master of anacrisis. But Ishmael's threshold dialogue is a kind of reverse anacrisis: his own asking questions and receiving almost no answer, certainly no full expression of opinion, from anyone else provokes his own full expression—in five successive clauses beginning "considering"—of his predicament. Although cast in a self-satirizing vein which marks it as akin to Menippean satire and parodies the actual Socratic dialogue, this is a pivotal moment in the voyage.

The syncrisis or personification of attitudes, by contrast, is a large pattern beginning shortly after this moment and running throughout the rest of the voyage. The gams of the *Pequod* have been shown to be a structural device in the novel; they also present a progression of ideas in which each ship stands for a particular attitude, about the white whale or about life.[24] In the *Jungfrau*, the *Bouton de Rose*, and the *Samuel Enderby*, the middle three gams, the personification is especially pronounced, since each ship satirically represents a national attitude. Syncrisis becomes the dominant technique in Melville's later novel *The Confidence Man*, wherein all the

24. See James Dean Young, "The Nine Gams of the *Pequod*," *American Literature*, XXV (January, 1954), 449–63.

devices of carnival are brought in to create an ineluctable point of crisis.[25]

The gam, whose etymology connects to *game*, is a rare instance of "friendly and sociable contact" between strangers on the sea. In Chapter 53 the "godly, honest, unostentatious, hospitable, sociable, free-and-easy whaler" is contrasted to other kinds of ships which fail to make this sociable contact, and each kind of ship is satirically personified, the merchant ships, for instance, "mutually cutting each other on the high seas, like a brace of dandies in Broadway" (p. 206). The narrator's attitude does all it can to amplify the traces of symposial jolliness in these meetings, often merely by facetiousness and puns. The pirate, who thinks himself superior to the "blubber-boiler," often attains an "uncommon elevation," but only at the end of a rope; he therefore has "no proper foundation for his superior attitude" and "no solid basis to stand on." One groans; this seems like lesser rather than greater Shakespeare (Launce and Speed rather than Mercutio); yet it effectively jolts Ishmael and the reader out of a one-sided seriousness, and in juxtaposing dignified argument and the question of prestige with the ignominious death of the pirate, as well as in making a joke of death ("elevated in that odd fashion"), the joke draws on the deep roots of the carnival.

In contrast to these festive forms of upheaval, the story of the *Town-Ho* is about a serious rebellion, and its subversiveness has direct political implications. The frame of the story, however, which the narrator says he is preserving "for my humor's sake," brings in several motifs that link the story to carnival forms. The story first boards the *Pequod* during a gam with the *Town-Ho*, not by official channels—from officer to officer—but by a devious lower route. Tashtego learns the tale from one of the *Town-Ho*'s men in a secret meeting, then performs a second inversion by telling most of it in his sleep. The subversive content of the story is thus joined by a transmission that is doubly subversive (of the ship's protocol and of the waking world's priority over the dream world). Ishmael tells it in a convivial setting spiked by *chicha* and a good-natured, am-

25. James L. Babin's work in progress, "The Anatomy of Confidence," investigates the ties of *The Confidence Man* to Menippean satire.

bivalent reverence-irreverence, culminating in the mixed sacred-profane gesture of swearing on the Bible that his unholy story is true.

The note of irreverence is struck more strongly in Chapter 64, "Stubb's Supper," which moves from the grotesque horror of the shark feeding frenzy to carnival-allegorical ways of dealing with this horror. Nature in this vision of sharks is all gory maw and belly, a scandalous horror to the cultural sensibility and hence to traditional religious discourse, for it presents the pure undifferentiated at the heart of the processes of life. But to the carnival-grotesque this vision is normative, and it is only fitting that Stubb and the shark should be feasting on the same whale at the same time.

Thus likewise enlightened morality must be degraded and defeated, and spiritualist-miraculist Christianity burlesqued. Stubb orders Fleece the cook to go preach decent behavior to the maddened sharks, and as an allegorical touch, he is to carry a lantern to see—and to "enlighten"—his congregation. But soon Fleece loses heart, sizes them up, and ends: "Cussed fellow-critters! Kick up de damndest row as ever you can; fill your dam' bellies till dey bust—and den die" (p. 252). So much for enlightened Christianity. Next, the "second birth" of fundamentalist conversion becomes a joke: Fleece must be born over again, Stubb insists, because he has lived all this time and still can't cook a whale steak to Stubb's liking. Similarly Stubb makes fun of Fleece's beliefs about going to heaven, literalizing them to refer to going to the masthead. But whereas the effectiveness of moralistic enlightened religion has been disproved in this scene—for the sharks don't listen to the sermon—the motifs of rebirth and ascension are not debunked but "degraded" in Bakhtin's sense, burlesqued and carried down to the lower stratum of meaning, thereby saving these concepts from excessive spirituality and serious one-sidedness.

But the signature scene of carnival dialogue is Chapter 73, which is entirely structured by dialogues, dialectical opposites, and playful inversions. After killing a whale, Stubb and Flask stand in their boats near the massive corpse, an impressive threshold, and mix this world and the next as they discuss the oblique signs that prove Fedallah is really the devil. Religious folk motifs of tail, hooves, and serpent intertwine with nautical realities as Ahab's sinister harpooneer is imagined to coil his "'cursed tail . . . down, do ye see, in the eye of the rigging'" (p. 275). He is imagined to have struck a bargain with Ahab to surrender him Moby Dick in exchange for "'his silver watch, or his soul, or something of that sort.'" The American folk debate form par excellence is bargaining, and here it is enlisted to degrade high spiritual matters to the level of an all-reaching relativity. The debate form continues when Stubb retells the prologue to the book of Job, transposing it to the "'old flagship'" where the devil makes his demands on the "'old governor.'" All sacrosanct entities are bespattered as Stubb stretches out his yarn to include a comically and contemptibly powerless God: "Who's afraid of [the devil], except the old governor who daresn't catch him and put him in double-darbies, as he deserves, but lets him go about kidnapping people; aye, and signed a bond with him, that all the people the devil kidnapped, he'd roast for him? There's a governor!" (p. 277).

When Flask wonders where he's heard the story before, Stubb suggests not the Bible but "'Three Spaniards? Adventures of those three bloody-minded soldadoes?'" and thereby manages to get in a slap at both the Holy Trinity and the Jesuits. For all its impiety, though, this scene would make no sense if it were, as Lawrence Thompson argues, the secret place where Melville can safely discharge his hatred of God, protecting himself by an "only in fun" disclaimer. Such a univocal determination of meaning would in fact be the real target of this riotous dialogue that capsizes any serious propagator of sovereign concepts. When challenged at long last by Flask as to whether or not he really means everything he's been saying, Stubb replies, "'Mean or not mean, here we are at the ship.'" Paradoxically, to search for the meaning of meaning is to miss the whole point.

Hence the Stubb-Flask, Fedallah-Ahab, and devil-God debates must be followed by a vigorous uncrowning of philosophical controversies. When the severed heads of the sperm whale and right whale are metamorphosed into "Locke's head" and "Kant's," the real target is not so much the doctrines of association of ideas and a priori forms as it is the practice of philosophical controversy itself,

135

as narrow and quibbling as it has become in Melville's time. After the vigorous verbal workout of Stubb and Flask, these severed heads by contrast merely counterpoise each other silently; and even if they offset one another, they place the student of philosophy "in very poor plight." The conceit ends with an exhortation against scholastic philosophy: "Thus, some minds for ever keep trimming boat. Oh, ye foolish! throw all these thunderheads overboard, and then you will float light and right." The modern rationalist cast of mind, severing the head from the body, must be cast off in the Panurgian quest for the whole body, be it whole man or whole whale.

Edward Rosenberry led the way in cataloging the comic elements in *Moby-Dick*. I can only add to his thorough treatment a slight but crucial difference in point of view, where the Rabelaisian attitude serves as exemplary. The modern conviction that seriousness is unquestionably superior to laughter haunts Rosenberry's study at times, prompting him to remark, for instance, that "Stubb's laughter is a kittenish evasion of life."[26] Coming directly after he has cited Stubb's impressive refusal to be daunted in "The Candles" ("'do they only have mercy on long faces?—have they no bowels for a laugh?'") and at the moment of death ("'For all that, I would yet ring glasses with ye, would ye but hand the cup!'"), this verdict indicates a failure to recognize the worth of jollity itself. Ishmael's laughter is termed a "comic philosophy" which balances all in a wise detachedness—it is "a psychological symbol of a philosophical acceptance." To him there is thus no difference between the bodily entering into play of the "Hyena" chapter and the antiphysical recklessness of Ishmael's more inexperienced comment on the cenotaphs in the Whaleman's Chapel, when he is still land-bound: "In fact take my body who will, take it I say, it is not me."

This is the picture of Ishmael that recent criticism has tended to convey, making his "godly gamesomeness" or competent bracketing of life's abysses the premier accomplishment of his voyage.[27] The self that pretends to be able to escape any bodily woe by retreating

---

26. Rosenberry, *Melville and the Comic Spirit*, 120.
27. This is Wadlington's assertion in *The Confidence Game in American Literature*, 73–101.

into subjectivity, however, is not the Ishmael of the voyage who has discovered the esprit of the whaleboat's crew in the face of death, who "was one of that crew" and whose "oath had been welded with theirs." Even if he first experiences the unity of the *Pequod*'s crew as a negative thing, formed in fear at Ahab's bidding, he has already made the major discovery of community with Queequeg alone. Now he discovers an expansion of that "melting" he has felt earlier; and if the crew is far from the image of an ideal community, it nonetheless offers momentary flashes of that true conviviality which, after all, was only a seasonal thing even in the great age of carnival.

In the writings of Erasmus and Rabelais wisdom and foolery are not only *not* diametrically opposed but are actually made identical. As early as Montaigne, however, Bakhtin detects a slight decline from this most inclusive and scandalous of wisdoms, from which the seventeenth century is then seen as a precipitous fall. Walter Kaiser, however, would place Shakespeare and Cervantes, and to an extent Thomas More, in this tradition as well, and tie them all to a line that goes back not only to Lucian (whom Bakhtin acknowledges plentifully) but to Horace's *ridentem dicere verum*.[28] Significantly, this phrase can be read either as "to tell the truth (while) laughing" or "to tell the laughing truth"; the main line of Western literary tradition, into which Horace falls squarely, could never entirely stop seeing truth as exterior to laughter. By contrast, Rabelais does not advocate laughter as a wise corrective to harsh truths; it is not a corollary of Aristotle's "nothing to extremes." One may laugh because it is healthy to do so, but to make health the chief reason for laughing becomes as insulting as the notion that it is useful to believe in a God. Truth itself laughs. The truth is one with laughter, and it is not a sardonic laughter that derides the hopeless absurdity of existence. In the medieval festivals laughter dissolved differences and nullified the pompous hierarchies of church and feudal manor, calling forth all people to participate unafraid in the full, uncensored pageant of life. It is this all-people's laughter that Ishmael hears faintly at sea, almost three centuries after it has died out

---

28. Walter Kaiser, *Praisers of Folly: Erasmus, Rabelais, Shakespeare* (Cambridge, Mass., 1963), 103.

on land. It is the form of his escape from the "miserable warping memories of traditions and of towns," a form he searched for and failed to find while scanning the mysteries of the chart.

What Melville writes is an allegory of carnival, which does not give us the full enactment of communal festival—that would be impossible in his day—but looks toward it as a reference point, something either imagined or fleetingly achieved (as by Stubb and Flask). So Melville's use of carnival imagery, though as a nineteenth-century author he is removed from any genuine living expression of carnival in the folk, is not merely appropriated to denote subjectivity as in the other Romantics. Melville's imagination lives within this alienated world, yet his carnival-grotesque symbols and motifs emerge in mindfulness of the vanished spirit of bodily gaiety and communal life.

VI

~~~

UNVEILINGS

(*Moby-Dick*, Chapters 76–105)

THUS FAR the chapters forming the "cetological center" of *Moby-Dick* (as Howard Vincent has called it) have placed in question the possibility of knowing.[1] They have shown that one may chart the coordinates of reality, or one may attempt to know the presence of the mind to itself atop a masthead, but there is always a crucial slippage—the white whale escaping Ahab's tallies, the slipping foot of the tranced youth on the masthead. As both these moments show, this slippage is not a mere marginal element, a coefficient of friction, say, that would make the general equation come out not quite right. It is rather the escape of the very thing sought for—Ahab's whale, the youth's life. This slippage is so bound up with the attempt to know, that Ishmael finally embraces his "desperado philosophy," exulting in the chase for its own sake—and, as narrator and cetologist, exulting in the act of figuring the whale without claiming to attain a final veracity.

The voyage has deeper waters to sail, however. The nimble brilliance of the chapter "Cetology" or "Of Whales in Paint, in Teeth, &c." does not amount to the sum of *Moby-Dick*. Ishmael has not only dreamed and studied the whale; he has met it eye to eye and invaded its sanctuary. How is one to account for this intimate converse? It is impossible as long as Ishmael's discourse remains primarily conceptual, aiming to figure the whale in fixed terms or images on the page. All allegories of pilgrimage presuppose that truth

1. Vincent, *Trying-Out of "Moby-Dick,"* 119.

is not only a thing to be mapped from afar; it is centrally something to be encountered. The allegorist thus is motivated by desire, Platonic eros, to leave his writing desk and enter imaginatively into a journey toward the heart of truth. What he finds on that journey is always elusive; indeed, its elusiveness might be seen to be its final truth. Once he returns to his writing desk, at any rate, he cannot represent the experiences of the journey by using signs fundamentally different from those he uses to express cetology (or truth mapped on a page). Rather, it is the pattern of his representation that changes: the open-ended pointing of emblematic allegory, with its metamorphic images—each equally bright and equally inadequate—gives way to a mustering of signs toward the portrayal of a single experience. Though the play of conceptualizing continues throughout the book, the bulk of these passages precede, both actually and structurally, the graver, deeper, "more special leviathanic revelations" (p. 116) beginning in Chapter 76. Ishmael's cetology can thus be seen as the preliminary enlargement of a repertoire of signs, the vestibule, the prelude—in the root sense of "fore-play"— to the larger action of the voyage: unveiling the mysteries of the whale and its encounter with Ahab.

Initiation

In roughly Chapters 76–105, following the imagined jettisoning of Kant's and Locke's heads and preceding the turn to Ahab's final chase, a cluster of chapters occurs that presents the deepest insights of the book. These are the harvest fruits of Ishmael's relentless digging into the material of his whaling voyage. "Cistern and Buckets," "The Grand Armada," "The Castaway," "A Squeeze of the Hand," "The Try-Works," "The Doubloon"—each has been the subject of scores of interpretive readings; their inexhaustibility is bound up with the experience they represent and the structure with which they present it, for each is a version of approach to a mystery. All these chapters employ religious imagery to indicate this structure, and several of them, as well as other chapters in this group, suggest that the approach is analogous to the interpretation of a text.

The threshold to these chapters is the final figure of Chapter 76, a chapter in which the narrator turns abruptly away from the most openly Menippean of his facetious jousts with philosophy—the whales' heads as Locke and Kant, then as Stoic and Platonic philosophies. In "The Battering-Ram" the whale is once again a being of force and terror. The thick wall of its forehead recalls concretely the epistemological impenetrability of whiteness whose very idea terrifies Ishmael in the earlier chapter "The Whiteness of the Whale." The sperm whale's forehead is "a dead blind wall," so tough that "the severest pointed harpoon, the sharpest lance darted by the strongest human arm, impotently rebounds from it" (pp. 284–85). Because of this toughness the whale cannot be conquered by a frontal approach, and, as with later remarks that suggest the analogy of whaling to reading, the implication is that every interpretive lance darted head-on will be impotent as well. The reader cannot take the subsequent events in a normal critical way.

The ominous use of the whale's forehead implied in the chapter's title, "The Battering-Ram," is of course crucial in the last events of *Moby-Dick*. The narrator wants to prepare the reader for that event, announcing here that "I shall show you some of his more inconsiderable braining feats" (p. 285). But incredulity is not the only thing Ishmael hopes to banish in the reader's mind: one may believe in the whale's actual physical power and yet see it as though it were the void itself, the sheer destructive principle. To see only this horror limits the reader to two paths: either to shun the whale entirely and remain an ignorant landsman, or to desire to destroy it like Ahab, who in his "Quarter-Deck" speech compares man to a prisoner in the world of visible objects and the white whale to the wall that imprisons him: "To me, the white whale is that wall, shoved near to me. Sometimes I think there's naught beyond" (p. 144). Ingeniously, Ahab's metaphoric wall becomes literalized in this chapter, but in contrast to Ahab's suspicion of nothingness Ishmael emphasizes an underlying life: "Now, mark. Unerringly impelling this dead, impregnable, uninjurable wall, and this most buoyant thing within; there swims behind it all a mass of tremendous life, only to be adequately estimated as piled wood is—by the cord; and all obedient to one volition, as the smallest insect" (p. 285).

With this consideration Ishmael addresses the reader, at a turning point crucial to the entire narrative, and enjoins him to "renounce all ignorant incredulity" and to "own the whale." Here are the final three sentences of the chapter:

> For unless you own the whale, you are but a provincial and sentimentalist in Truth. But clear Truth is a thing for salamander giants only to encounter; how small the chances for the provincials then? What befel the weakling youth lifting the dread goddess's veil at Sais?

Henceforth, Ishmael indicates, he will not address his chapters to convince the uninitiated; only if the reader accepts the powers of the whale, with a leap like Kierkegaard's leap of faith, will the deeper revelations to follow allow a glimpse of that rarest essence, Truth.

The terms of this passage are highly paradoxical but contain the essential configuration of the following chapters. The claim that only "salamander giants" can encounter the Truth prompts the question of what truth is and to what extent, and in what form, man can gain access to it.

The legend of the novice at Sais, to which Ishmael alludes in the last sentence of this chapter, poses these questions in a way that determines the responses of the chapters that follow. Melville had read and marked Friedrich von Schiller's poem "Das verschleierte Bild zu Sais," evidently reading the German and Sir Edward Bulwer-Lytton's English translation simultaneously.[2] This poem most fully records the outlines of the legend: a young man, desirous of knowing the mysterious truth of Isis, is warned against impetuosity by the old sage who tends the temple. The sage quotes an inscription attributed to Isis herself:

> "Hear, and revere her hest:
> 'Till I this veil
> Lift, may no mortal-born
> Presume to raise;
> And who with guilty and unhallow'd hand

2. Sealts, *Melville's Reading*, 90–91, Items 437–39.

Too soon profanes the Holy and Forbidden—
He,' says the goddess—" "Well?"
"'SHALL SEE THE TRUTH!'"[3]

The novice, predictably unable to contain his unholy curiosity, sneaks into the temple at night and lifts the veil. Schiller does not describe what he sees, but rather its effect on him:

. . . Ever from his heart
Was fled the sweet serenity of life,
And the deep anguish dug the early grave:
"Wo—wo to him!" such were his warning words,
Answering some curious and impetuous brain:
"Wo—for her face shall charm him nevermore!
Wo—wo to him who treads through guilt to TRUTH!"

The young seeker is a prototype of Ahab, sharing with him the obsessive desire to "strike through the mask." One sees in him also the audacity of Pierre and, in all these Melvillean figures, an anti-paradigm of the reader.

In Schiller's poem the statue of Isis is veiled by a text, namely, its inscription quoted by the priest, which in turn is veiled by ambiguity. The last phrase of the inscription has to be unveiled, like the outer veil of the temple, before the statue itself can be approached. Hidden in this phrase "[He] SHALL SEE THE TRUTH" ["der *sieht* [Schiller's emphasis] die Wahrheit"]) is the corollary that the truth will blind him who desires only to see it without submitting to it unseen—in Ishmael's words, "owning" it. The novice is thus a model of the bad reader, deluded into the positivist belief that the truth is a substance—a visible thing immediately intelligible.

The figure of the weakling youth marks this threshold chapter of *Moby-Dick* with the particular stamp of a threshold image. The burden of the chapter—to implore the reader to "renounce all ignorant incredulity" about the whale and whaling—is the final step before the reader enters a new phase. At certain moments in his narrative Ishmael's eye is on his hypothetical reader. In "The Affidavit" he

3. Sir Edward Bulwer-Lytton (trans.), *The Poems and Ballads of Schiller* (New York, 1844), 178–80.

143

goes out of his way to support the events of his narrative with factual analogies and data, so that his tale will not be taken as a "hideous and intolerable allegory." By Chapter 76, however, his tone is
no longer defensive; instead he must now ascertain that the reader's
assent measures up to the chapters ahead. The lifting of the veil is
the work to be accomplished in the twenty chapters to follow—before Ahab's mania draws the narrative entirely within its wake. The
secrets to be revealed are of the very origins of nature, the hinge
points of life and death, worldly and divine. It is imperative, then,
at this point, that the reader who will follow him into this inner
sanctum grant his assent to the paradigmatic importance of this approach to the whale. Only in such a way may he "own the whale,"
and know something more of truth than the "provincials and senti-
mentalists."

Approaches to Isis

The abiding concern in the following twenty chapters is how to circumvent the disaster of Sais: to approach the truth in its full man-
ifestation, a fullness so terrifying that a direct approach would mean
annihilation. The transcendent potency of the leviathan is empha-
sized in unparalleled depth of detail. He has not a tripartite but a
"triune" tail (p. 316); he is compared favorably to Jove in the matter of a nose. The view of the sperm whale's front is sublime: "in
that full front view, you feel the Deity and the dread powers more
forcibly than in beholding any other object in living nature" (p.
292). Because of its featurelessness, man is unable to grasp it as a
face—it is "nothing but that one broad firmament of a forehead,
pleated with riddles." It is thus structured like the Temple of Jerusalem, with an outer veil to mask its real incomprehensibility—"the
whale, like all things that are mighty, wears a false brow to the common world" (p. 293). Even the spout presents a danger if it is
viewed too directly—"if the jet is fairly spouted into your eyes, it
will blind you" (p. 313).

Edwin Honig writes that the white whale "contains the purpose,
vanity, and eternal blandishments of all answers to the question of
existence. It represents, not the Deity, but the enigma which the

Deity has propounded and shaped."[4] And Marius Bewley sees Moby Dick as the embodiment of an endless dialogue: "The White Whale is Melville's profoundest intuition into the nature of creation, and it is an intuition in which God and nature are simultaneously present and commenting on each other."[5] To both critics, the whale is a kind of language in itself. Yet it is a language inaudible to human ears: the sperm whale maintains a "pyramidical silence" (p. 292). These elusive qualities are in Job's leviathan: "Will he speak soft words unto thee? . . . Behold, the hope of him is in vain: shall not one be cast down even at the sight of him? . . . Who can discover the face of his garment?" (Job 41:3, 9, 13). Ishmael extends its undiscoverability even further: "How comprehend his face, when face he has none? Thou shalt see my back parts, my tail, he seems to say, but my face shall not be seen" (p. 318). Like Job before God, Ishmael concedes a categorical defeat: "Dissect him how I may, then, I but go skin deep; I know him not, and never will."

Ishmael cannot draw out Leviathan, whether with hook or with pen. Just as his cetological attempts are "but the draught of a draught," Ishmael's rendering of the sperm whale can be only the re-presentation of a representation: "How may unlettered Ishmael hope to read the awful Chaldee of the Sperm Whale's brow? I but put that brow before you. Read it if you can" (p. 293). In such a case, he argues, the quest of literary portrayal to embody reality is vain, since it would deny its own character as representation. Further, Ishmael would reduce to a travesty the sublimely referential character of the sperm whale if he purported to present the whole of it immanently. In his brief address to the reader, then, he acknowledges that his real task is to fashion a text which leads the chain of signification outward toward the reader and presents the transcendent connections of the whale's hieroglyphics as faithfully as possible.

Once the danger of immediate approach to this sublime being has been made fully explicit, the episodes in the following chapters pre-

---

4. Honig, *Dark Conceit*, 144.
5. Marius Bewley, *The Eccentric Design: Form in the Classic American Novel* (New York, 1959), 198.

sent the models of approach to the enigma of the whale's existence. This section begins with Chapter 77, "The Baling of the Case," a delicate operation to salvage the sweet and valuable essence, spermaceti, from the dead whale's head. The cutter "has . . . to be uncommonly heedful, lest a careless, untimely stroke should invade the sanctuary and wastingly let out its invaluable contents" (p. 440). Here the whale is quite consistently an allegorical model of the text. The whalemen cutting into the whale are the interpreters, doing a careful violence to the text with their crude approximations of hermeneutic wands. The "sanctuary" of the whale's case contains a desired substance in danger of flowing away, escaping the grasp of the cutters. Their care is a minimal precaution, betokening a respect, if for nothing else than the cash value of spermaceti. Cutting-in thus constitutes a successful indirect approach to the heart of allegory. One who wishes to make an entrance into the text must violate the body, yet be "timely"; "a careful disorder is the rule." The obtaining of sperm oil is fraught with paradoxes and thus structured hermeneutically rather than purely as a scientific analysis. It requires "tact" (to use Gadamer's term).[6]

The whale, then, is a text; and, living, it is like the writing of God on Sinai or on Belshazzar's wall—terrible to see and fearful or impossible to interpret. The dead whale is another matter. Bereft of its sublime power, it still possesses its valuable substance within, spermaceti, a pure element, like wisdom in ancient allegories. No longer raw power, then, but wisdom is the content of the dead whale as text—an equation made more certain when Melville emphasizes that the end product of sperm oil is light. The approach to this valuable substance thus comes to resemble not so much worship as reading. The whalemen's cutting-in requires that they use a subtle hermeneutic, a balance of violence and care; for even the dead whale may swallow up the subject who approaches it. Reading, by implication, is still a dangerous activity. Tashtego's accident in Chapter 78, "Cistern and Buckets," graphically and comically illustrates the danger of becoming lost in a text.

6. Gadamer adopts the term from Hermann Helmholtz, explaining it as "a particular sensitivity and sensitiveness to situations, and how to behave in them, for which we cannot find any knowledge from general principles" (*Truth and Method*, 16–17).

Tashtego, "that wild Indian" (p. 288), must represent the some-what naïve reader in this allegory, because his native energy works more against him than in his favor. It is his disciplined skill and care that allow him the privilege of cutting-in. His balance of force and tenderness makes him seem like a hierophant, "highly elevated above the rest of the company" to perform his interpretive work. Indeed, "he seems some Turkish Muezzin calling the good people to prayers from the top of a tower" (p. 287). Armed more with zeal than with learning, Tashtego aligns himself with Melville's "men who dive," not the careful scholars but those who dare to grasp the sublime matter of an argument. The bucket he continually guides down into the whale's head, then puts aloft to empty, is an image of the hermeneutic circle, exegeticizing and then presenting the re-sults of exegesis to the general store of knowledge. But Melville is aware that this circle, which appears serene and secure in the the-ory of a Friedrich Schleiermacher, may be the most perilous ele-ment in interpretation.[7] Tashtego suddenly falls "head-foremost" into the whale, becoming part of the circle himself as he looks like "the twin reciprocating bucket in a veritable well." The text has absorbed him.

The precise reason for his fall is unknown; Ishmael gives three speculations, which gloss the threefold danger of interpretation. The first is practical, a lapse in attention like that of the meditative masthead sitter: Tashtego may have been "so heedless and reckless as to let go for a moment his one-handed hold." The second consid-ers the situation of the reader in positioning himself before the text, "the place where he stood . . . so treacherous and oozy." The final perspective is theological and calls to mind the fall in Eden: "the Evil One himself" may "have [had] it to fall out so" (p. 288). The reader swallowed up because of his avidity recalls the fate of the novice at Sais as well as the "earnest or enthusiastic youth" of *Pierre.* Unquestionably, a theurgic power must still lurk in the text, a power especially dangerous when the reader—lulled by the con-tinuous movement of the hermeneutic circle?—thinks the thing he

7. On the inadequacy of Schleiermacher's hermeneutics, see Gadamer, *Truth and Method,* 162–73; Cyrus Hamlin, "The Limits of Understanding: Hermeneutics and the Study of Literature," *Arion,* n.s., III (1976), 389–94.

is mining is merely a patent, lifeless source of knowledge. When Tashtego plunges, "the before lifeless head" begins "throbbing and heaving . . . as if that moment seized with some momentous idea," a movement caused by "the poor Indian unconsciously revealing by those struggles the perilous depth to which he had sunk." The reader's unconscious has been taken prisoner by a text come back to life.

Tashtego's plunge is a literalization of Melville's "deep readers" and "men who *dive*," phrases betokening his association of meaning with depth. The opposite of the naïve reader's brazen confrontation, exemplified in Pierre or the novice at Sais, this is an encounter with the deep rather than surface level of a text, and it results not in a petrification but in a liquefaction. Tashtego's fate would be "a very precious perishing," to be "smothered in the very whitest and daintiest of fragrant spermaceti, coffined, hearsed, and tombed in the secret inner chamber and sanctum sanctorum of the whale." This inner temple is then implicitly compared to "Plato's honey head," an enigmatic image that suggests not only the sweet harmony of the Platonic realm beyond the heavens but the cerebral abstractness required to think that realm.

If Chapter 78 reenacts the fatal plunge from the masthead of meditation, it ends instead with the Dantesque model of rescue by an intervening, powerful angel figure, Queequeg. "A naked figure with a boarding-sword in its hand, was for one swift moment seen hovering over the bulwarks" (p. 289). Like Dante's scornful angel, he bears a kind of wand that will allow him to open up what has been closed. Queequeg's special mark, however, is not scorn but midwifery. Dropping his sword, he reaches into the whale with his arm and draws out Tashtego. The difference is important: instead of an incorporeal angel, a "wild" (*i.e.*, non-Western) man effects a quite bodily rescue. Ishmael's pun about "the deliverance, or rather, delivery of Tashtego" knowingly unites sacred history and the biography of the individual soul (Dante's second and third levels of meaning, according to his letter to Can Grande) with biology, and the temporal structure of the natural world is now seen in Melville's epoch for the first time as intrinsically part of the process of redemption.

Chapter 78 contains in a nutshell the moments repeated metaphorically in later chapters: cutting into the whale; the unwilling slip into unmediated vision; the sublime perishing, dissolving the self by uniting with an other and being absorbed completely by it. The precipitous plunge may be a "precious" attainment of mystery, but one is not likely to return from it. The direct way of the enthusiast (the "Turkish Muezzin") is too perilous and must be replaced by a method of gradual approach. The whale hunts in these chapters provide the models that respond to this challenge. All of Ishmael's careful cataloging of the equipment and techniques of the whaleboats serves to emphasize the combination of methodicalness and mad daring involved in approaching a raging whale.

But whereas the structure of the whale hunt has been given painstakingly, its goal has not yet appeared as anything like a mystery. It is only in the first whale hunt after the Sais allusion, in Chapter 81, that the whale begins to gain the language of pathetic nature and thus to embody the divine paradox of power and suffering. The intensity of its pathos is all the more striking because it comes mixed in with Stubb's besting of the stupid "Yarman" whalemen, the "foolish virgins" of the *Jungfrau* who have lost their oil. In the midst of the fun a suddenly quite other tone appears when the mutilated whale is sighted: "It was a terrific, most pitiable, and maddening sight" (p. 298). The whale is described with the kind of repetition that has been used by poets from Virgil to Cowper to denote a pitiable erraticness and confusion: "Now to this hand, now to that, he yawed in his faltering flight, and still at every billow that he broke, he spasmodically sank in the sea, or sideways rolled towards the sky his one beating fin." The appeal to the heavens, a much used pathetic gesture, is not spared. Nor is the simile that appeals to nature, at once epic and personal: "So have I seen a bird with clipped wing, making affrighted broken circles in the air, vainly striving to escape the piratical hawks."[8] Here, out of many possible places, is where the technical information appears concerning the effect of the harpoon barbs—"it is this 'holding on,' as it is called; this hooking up by the sharp barbs of his live flesh from the back; this it is that often torments the Leviathan into soon ris-

8. Robert Zoellner has isolated the Homeric similes in this chapter. See *The Salt-Sea Mastodon: A Reading of "Moby-Dick"* (Berkeley, 1973), 176–77.

ing again to meet the sharp lance of his foes" (p. 299). More specifically, the whale has a "non-valvular structure of the blood-vessels,"
unlike other mammals, so that "when pierced even by so small a
point as a harpoon, a deadly drain is at once begun upon his whole
arterial system," and when the pressure is so immensely increased by
his sounding, "his life may be said to pour from him in incessant
streams" (p. 301). Suddenly the puny whalemen are cruel predators.

The streams of blood flowing from the whale connect it to the
divine, as another simile strongly implies: its blood flows "even as in
a drought a river will flow, whose source is in the well-springs of far-
off and undiscernible hills." The divinity tapped here is a suffering
god, and all the tropes connected with the whale bear the signature
of this combination of power and suffering. The sounding whale
suggests Samson blinded: "How vast, then, the burden of a whale,
bearing on his back a column of two hundred fathoms of ocean!"

The notion of connection to a source, as it appears in the river
simile here, is most often made to announce the Romantic symbol
and its communion with being. But at this point the contrast between the symbolic view of nature as whole and the allegorical view
of nature as wounded is at its most extreme. Melville contrasts the
two most vividly in the serenity of the sea and sky and the agony of
the whale.

> As the three boats lay there on that gently rolling sea, gazing
> down into its eternal blue noon; and as not a single groan or cry
> of any sort, nay, not so much as a ripple or a bubble came up
> from its depths; what landsman would have thought, that be-
> neath all that silence and placidity, the utmost monster of the
> seas was writhing and wrenching in agony!   (p. 300)

This sharp contrast is the basis of what Benjamin, in his analysis of
symbol and allegory, states as a contrast between two faces:

> Whereas in the symbol . . . the transfigured face of nature is
> fleetingly revealed in the light of redemption, in allegory the
> observer is confronted with the *facies hippocratica* of history as
> a petrified, primordial landscape. . . . And although such a
> thing lacks all "symbolic" freedom of expression, all classical

proportion, all humanity—nevertheless, this is the form in which man's subjection to nature is most obvious.[9]

The *facies hippocratica* is the masklike appearance of the human face in its death agony. The dying whale going into its "flurry," however, epitomizes suffering nature—or the history of nature at the mercy of humanity. Yet how different, then, from the baroque Christian view, which thinks primarily of man and *his* "subjection to nature"! Here obviously the shoe is on the other foot—or fluke. It is nature who lies in bondage to man. By reversing the agonists in the medieval death's duel, Melville again shows his mark of genius: to invert and hence negate the allegorical tradition in order to affirm its structure; to bind new matter to old form so that the resulting agony can enact the allegory for our time.

Melville's practice of reversing the direction of Christian tropes occurs in another way in this same passage, providing a more self-evident example. Here, as he has done before, Ishmael quotes the Bible against itself, mocking the notion of Leviathan as an allegory of God's power, as given in Job: "He esteemeth iron as straw; the arrow cannot make him flee; darts are counted as stubble; he laugheth at the shaking of a spear!" His comment rejects this perspective: "This the creature? this he? Oh! that unfulfillments should follow the prophets." (This last phrase, like so much of the matter with which the antithetical allegory of this "wicked book" has to do, was excised by the British publisher of *The Whale*.) "For with the strength of a thousand thighs in his tail, Leviathan had run his head under the mountains of the sea, to hide him from the Pequod's fish-spears!" (p. 300).

One misreads these sentences if one sees them as a taunt that the biblical author lied or was wrong; they show rather a dismay, and a startling recognition, that "unfulfillments" are in fact exactly what follow the prophets. In other words, it is that the great Leviathan, with all his godlike attributes, has fallen on hard times. The connection to his sacred past is not denied; the typological assertion of meaning in history is maintained; but it leads downward instead of

9. Benjamin, *Origin of German Tragic Drama*, 166.

up, not toward a culminating redemption but toward an ignominious flight, defeat, and death. The shadows cast by the whaleboats
into the depths literalize this downward foreshadowing. These
shadows, says Ishmael, "must have been long enough and broad
enough to shade half Xerxes' army." The hyperbole associates the
whalemen with the most famous terrible approaching army in history. They remind one that prefigurement is not always of a saving
shape, but may be instead the shadow of man unmaking himself,
reversing the redemption by reopening wounds in the side of creation. (Is it purely coincidental, in the light of all this, that Dante
compared his fleeting vision of the final beatitude in *Paradiso* XXXIII
to Neptune's wonder at the shadow of the Argo crossing the deep?

> One moment seems a longer lethargy,
> Than five-and-twenty ages had appear'd
> To that emprize, that first made Neptune wonder
> At Argo's shadow darkening on his flood.
> (*Par.* XXXIII, 94–96)

Here, again, if a relation between Dante and Melville pertains, it
would be one of inversion or "unfulfillment.")

The sick whale's eye-spots are finally revealed, "places where his
eyes had been," "blind bulbs"—and at this point comes the final
disclosure of absence that allows the narrator to complete the whole
circle of injustice in the business of whaling. These sightless eyes
look upon the entire dark side of the "honor and glory of whaling"
(the title, it so happens, of the next chapter).[10] Ishmael laments
that, "for all his old age, and his one arm, and his blind eyes, he
must die the death and be murdered, in order to light the gay brid-
als and other merry-makings of men, and also to illuminate the sol-
emn churches that preach unconditional inoffensiveness by all to
all" (p. 301). Like Blake's youthful harlot blighting the "marriage
hearse," the outrage of this whale's murder reaches to the farthest
corners of a hypocritical society.

---

10. Zoellner senses the chafing of these two chapters against each other; cf. his close
reading of them, *Salt-Sea Mastodon*, 170–79. Zoellner's commentary is best on the ripening
of Ishmael's awareness. I cannot agree, however, that because of the counter-turns *Moby-
Dick* makes the novel is therefore not epic; nor can I agree that the sick whale is an emblem
of suffering *humanity*.

The final unveiling in this scene occurs at the whale's death. With his Yankee curiosity, both cruel and detached, Flask lances the whale in a tumorous spot; the creature's fury is brief and soon he lies in the water, and the narrator comments that he "over and over slowly revolved like a waning world; turned up the white secrets of his belly; lay like a log, and died." Dying, he provides an emblem of the entire world as sick unto death. These are his secrets. But they are one with the structure of the whole chapter, which operates according to the religious patterns of foreshadowing and unveiling, only to end in a negativity rather than a source of power. The scene is at once a baptism and a curse, "bespattering them and their glorying crews all over with showers of gore."

An extremely curious detail of Melville's language in this chapter reinforces the overall pattern of reversal. The phrase "lay like a log" in the death scene just quoted appears *before* this scene, quite out of sense with its immediate context, several moments earlier in the chase. Flask, urging his rowers on, incites them to pull after the whale now in full flight: "What a hump—Oh, *do* pile on the beef—lays like a log! Oh! my lads, *do* spring" (p. 297). Most strange, that present tense "lays." Is this a prelusive vision Flask has of his imminent conquest? Or is it just a seeming bit of nonsense that Melville has dropped in for the retracing reader to pick up?

The whale hunt of Chapter 81 reveals that the heart of negativity in religious mystery resides in suffering nature. This negative answer cannot be sufficient in itself for the allegorical journey but inevitably leads to the question of whether there is a truth beyond the allegorical presentation of suffering. Is the contemplative image of the suffering body of the god the highest mystery to which truth can attain, or is there a center of peace and harmony beyond the spectacle of absence and loss? If such a center is not merely a chimera, is it purely unattainable to man except as he dreams it? These questions are answered, though with complex qualifications, by the next narrative episode, "The Grand Armada" (Chap. 87).

This episode begins at a perilous threshold, which, as in the *Divine Comedy*, marks the moment of departure from literalism to enter the more risky enterprise of accepting figural meanings as real. The Straits of Sunda serve as this threshold point; they "not a little correspond to the central gateway opening into some vast walled empire" of "treasures . . . guarded from the all-grasping western world" (p. 318). This exclusion of the vulgar is important; it unites *Moby-Dick* with the allegorical tradition of veiling, on which Dante and Boccaccio drew as well; and here the vulgar are identified with Western civilization in general.[11] Yet the China Sea does not become an occasion for Melville to turn to the lore of the East; as James Baird has noted, Melville uses both *oriental* and *savage* as signs meaning only: against the West.[12] And as is the case with Queequeg as "George Washington cannibalistically developed," this oriental voyage has an archetypally Western structure; it is in fact far closer to the origins of Western experience than is the contemporary West from which Ishmael flees.

At the mouth of this threshold, "a spectacle of singular magnificence" salutes the crew: "Forming a great semicircle, embracing one half of the level horizon, a continuous chain of whale-jets were up-playing and sparkling in the noon-day air" (p. 320). Picked up by a piratical party of "inhuman atheistical devils," Starbuck's crew becomes the pursued as well as the pursuers, and for a while it seems that a seductive chain of whale spouts will resolve itself into another hoax like the illusive "spirit-spout" of Chapter 51. But after the boats are lowered, the crew finds the whales leading them toward something quite different from the spirit-spout. The pursuing pirates drop away unobtrusively, and Ishmael's whaleboat is stilled by the vision of "concentric circles" it encounters—a vision whose form suggests the celestial harmony of Dante's final vision.[13]

At the center of these circles Starbuck, Queequeg, and Ishmael witness the guarded matrix of the whale's existence. The sustenance of life is carried on in a natural cycle free of decay and death. Temporality has for a moment lost all its destructiveness. Nature reveals itself in a timeless moment which in itself seems to have no dependency on death. Death lies at the extremity of experience, this revelation seems to say, but what maintains nature in existence

11. On the veil in allegory and the exclusion of the vulgar, see Michael Murrin, *The Veil of Allegory: Some Notes Toward a Theory of Allegorical Rhetoric in the English Renaissance* (Chicago, 1969), esp. Ch. I.

12. Baird, *Ishmael*, 230–41.

13. Cf. Bewley's analysis of the "Grand Armada" chapter, *Eccentric Design*, 201–205.

is love. Sexuality, birth, and nursing all find their home in a feminine world whose characteristics have been conspicuously absent on the *Pequod*.

The spectacle of files of languorous whales seems strange enough to the whalers caught up in Ahab's whale lines, but the vision at the center is even more astonishing. The usually opaque sea has become transparent in these calm waters, achieving the effect of a veil lifted to divulge "the subtlest secrets."

> But far beneath this wondrous world upon the surface, another and still stranger world met our eyes as we gazed over the side. For, suspended in those watery vaults, floated the forms of the nursing mothers of the whales, and those that by their enormous girth seemed shortly to become mothers. . . . Some of the subtlest secrets of the seas seemed divulged to us in this enchanted pond. We saw young Leviathan amours in the deep. (pp. 325–26)

For a time the whalers are drawn into this armistice of nature:

> These smaller whales . . . evinced a wondrous fearlessness and confidence, or else a still, becharmed panic which it was impossible not to marvel at. Like household dogs they came snuffling round us, right up to our gunwales, and touching them; till it almost seemed that some spell had suddenly domesticated them. Queequeg patted their foreheads; Starbuck scratched their backs with his lance; but fearful of the consequences, for the time refrained from darting it.   (p. 325)

The eternal enmity between man and nature is momentarily repealed.

The journey to the center in Chapter 87 discloses the Romantic truth that there is a center within nature where being is harmonious with itself. The equilibrium of such a world is impossibly delicate, however; since it excludes man, he destroys that harmony simply by seeing it. The whale hunts, as metaphors of the quest for truth, naturally stress the violence inherent in the desire to know. And in no chapter is it more clearly stressed that nothing other than this desire, equivalent with the nature of the human mind, is the cause of the disruption of nature's Edenic harmony. For here it is not a question of a rapacious moral attitude: the whalemen are "fearful of the consequences" of attacking any whales. But with tragic consistency the consequences of previous acts come in to disrupt their present state: a whale they had wounded earlier swims into the charmed circle, bearing the line and its anchorlike drugg as a reference mark of human violence, and involuntarily flails about, "wounding and murdering his comrades." The reenactment of the expulsion from Eden is clear: "The long calm was departing"—the static time of the central revelation is broken up by a causality as treacherous and inevitable as any in Greek tragedy, so that the tragic end of this episode lends its color to the whole. The scene must end by asserting that the fall from grace is inevitably bound up with the human and with the desire to know.

This tragic insight poses the question of whether man's very nature, tainted with an ineradicable violence as it is, categorically excludes him from all transcendence. This grave question receives a comic response, far smaller in scope but not unconnected to the "Grand Armada" events. In the gam of the *Pequod* and the *Bouton de Rose* in Chapter 91, Stubb cheats the unsuspecting French captain out of a foul-smelling whale carcass which he rightly suspects may contain ambergris, the highly valued, superfragrant substance used as the base of perfumes.

The allegorical meaning of ambergris is developed in the following chapter, which is linked to the "Rose-Bud" chapter in the manner of allegorical doubling, as commentary to text. Here Ishmael dons his mock-scholar's garb, referring to "a certain Nantucket-born Captain Coffin" and "the learned Fogo Von Slack, in his great work on smells" (pp. 342–44) as sources for his facts, but also on St. Paul and Paracelsus for expansion of his meaning:

> Now that the incorruption of this most fragrant ambergris should be found in the heart of such decay; is this nothing? Bethink thee of that saying of St. Paul in Corinthians, about corruption and incorruption; how that we are sown in dishonor, but raised in glory. And likewise call to mind that saying of Paracelsus about what it is [*i.e.*, excrement] that maketh the best musk. (p. 343)

If we are able to follow the allegory suggested here, ambergris is something like transfigured matter, redeemed through grace. The sense of "corruption" is expanded by the events in the previous chapter so that it includes not only the whale's foulness but Stubb's "unrighteous cunning" as well. If this encounter emblematizes the previous whale killings, the corruption includes both the agonies of the dying whale and the predatoriness of the crews bespattered with the whale's blood. Digging into the carcass, Stubb discovers the sublime ambergris as something discontinuous from the surroundings: "Suddenly from out the very heart of this plague, there stole a faint stream of perfume, which flowed through the tide of bad smells without being absorbed by it, as one river will flow into and then along with another, without at all blending with it for a long time" (pp. 341–42).

Here is the presence of the transcendent as envisioned by allegory. Whereas the Romantic symbol tries to see heaven and earth interblended, allegory projects them on two distinct levels. The heavenly is an invisible presence that is occasionally recognizable in its distinct otherness from its corrupt surroundings.

The ambergris episode thus comes out at the opposite end from the tragic consummation of the "Grand Armada." It looks back on both Chapter 81 and Chapter 87, culminating the *via crucis* of the persecuted whale with a scriptural rumor of resurrection. The outcome requires interpretation, however, and a concomitant leap of assent on the reader's part from text to commentary. The act of the hunt can transcend the degradation of both hunter and hunted through a process of distillation—whose exact nature, however, is still unrevealed.

After this pair of chapters the reader is left with the question of whether there can be no revelation of truth to man except indirectly, through analogy. The last three episodes, then, respond by returning to versions of unmediated vision, in order to explore its consequences. The allegorical perspective that emerges in these chapters comes only out of a series of attempts at going beyond allegory, forming a dialectical movement between mediated and unmediated vision. Unlike the humble sub-sub-librarian or the common allegorizing cleric of the Middle Ages, Ishmael must resort to allegory only after finding that the leap into being either cannot be made, results in death, or cannot be maintained long enough to be grasped in language.

The first of these leaps (Chapter 93, "The Castaway") delivers the most and destroys the most. The prime example of the consequence of direct revelation is Pip. Thrown overboard through his ineptness in the quick, unrelenting teleology of the whale hunt, "Pip was left behind in the sea, like a hurried traveler's trunk." (The simile stresses this teleological cast.) When he is recovered he has permanently lost his senses:

> The sea had jeeringly kept his finite body up, but drowned the infinite of his soul. Not drowned entirely, though. Rather carried down alive to wondrous depths, where strange shapes of the unwarped primal world glided to and fro before his passive eyes; and the miser-merman, Wisdom, revealed his hoarded heaps; and among the joyous, heartless, ever-juvenile eternities, Pip saw the multitudinous, God-omnipresent, coral insects, that out of the firmament of waters heaved the colossal orbs. He saw God's foot upon the treadle of the loom, and spoke it; and therefore his shipmates called him mad. So man's insanity is heaven's sense; and wandering from all mortal reason, man comes at last to that celestial thought, which, to reason, is absurd and frantic; and weal or woe, feels then uncompromised, indifferent as his God.   (p. 347)

In one sense this is the truly "delicious perishing" because it is the absorption of selfhood in an immense reality, not in a chimera like the spirit-spout, nor in an abyss that like the squid presents no face. Nonetheless, Pip's vision is far from a beatific vision. Rather than seeing God face to face, he sees God's foot, the place where eternity and the loom of time are connected. Left behind by man's onrushing temporality, he sees the stillness that guides it. After such comprehension, however, all the temporal instruments of man, including language, are of no use to him. He has looked into the heart of the mysteries of nature and been "converted," although the conversion is a radical discontinuity that does not permit ordered reflection or interpretation to take place.

Pip's terrible confrontation is followed by the sweet merging of
"A Squeeze of the Hand," Chapter 94. If the "Grand Armada" represents one type of beatific vision, this episode presents a beatific
nonvision; there are no concentric circles and stunning arrays of
cosmic order here, but instead an ecstatic melting into one undifferentiated whole:

> Such an abounding, affectionate, friendly, loving feeling did
> this avocation beget; that at last I was continually squeezing
> their hands, and looking up into their eyes sentimentally; as
> much as to say,—Oh! my dear fellow beings, why should we
> longer cherish any social acerbities, or know the slightest ill-
> humor or envy! Come; let us squeeze hands all round; nay, let
> us all squeeze ourselves into each other; let us squeeze ourselves
> universally into the very milk and sperm of kindness.   (pp.
> 348–49)

The healing of all animosities is an elimination of differences; but
for this reason it is a de-articulation that breaks through the structure of language and thought. It can be imagined and fleetingly experienced, but is finally "inexpressible": "I declare to you, that for
the time I lived as in a musky meadow; I forgot all about our horri-
ble oath; in that inexpressible sperm, I washed my hands and my
heart of it" (p. 348).

In fact its fleetingness soon becomes its primary characteristic.
The coda to this episode looks over all human experiences as degrees of removal from the happiness found in sperm squeezing:

> Would that I could keep squeezing that sperm for ever! For
> now, since by many prolonged, repeated experiences, I have
> perceived that in all cases man must eventually lower, or at
> least shift, his conceit of attainable felicity; not placing it any-
> where in the intellect or the fancy; but in the wife, the heart,
> the bed, the table, the saddle, the fire-side, the country; now
> that I have perceived all this, I am ready to squeeze case eter-
> nally. In thoughts of the visions of the night, I saw long rows of
> angels in paradise, each with his hands in a jar of spermaceti.
> (p. 349)

Here the retreat from the central mystery receives final emphasis, in marked contrast to the versions of approach to mystery presented thus far. The biblical phrase "in thoughts of the visions of the night" works to stress this removal, implying that intellectual reflection on, and not direct vision of, mystery is the only mode in which truth can be held in the mind. St. Augustine's comment on the nature of understanding contains these same elements, a sudden presence and a simultaneous retreat, leaving behind imprints:

> The understanding permeates the mind with a sudden flash as it were, while talk is slow and prolonged and very different from thought. While talk moves on, the thought retreats into the secret recesses. However, in a marvellous way it stamps certain impressions on the memory, and these remain for the time taken to pronounce the syllables. From these same impressions we form spoken signs which are called "language." [14]

But for Ishmael the removal does not stop at this still relatively high level of intensity. A row of asterisks intrudes in the text at the end of the passage on "long rows of angels," and it indicates an unremovable bar to the mystery. The rest of the chapter is filled with informative discourse in a list of the various substances extricable from the whale, a performance hardly as sparkling as the book-sizing taxonomy of the whale in "Cetology." It ends on a most prosaic bit of unsmiling Yankee humor: "Toes are scarce among veteran blubber-room men" (p. 350).

From this point the rest of the metaphoric episodes of mystery emphasize removal, from the advice of Chapter 96: "Look not too long in the face of the fire, O man!" (p. 354) to the much-discussed "Doubloon" chapter, to the images of the whale's skeleton as a temple in the Arsacides (Chapter 102) and in Africa (Chapter 104). The association of established religious ritual with removal from, rather than approach to, a mystery is one of the surprising revelations of these chapters taken as a whole.

Chapter 95, a quite allegorical chapter, makes this equation strongly. The whale's penis, cut off in the process of cutting in, is

---

14. St. Augustine, *The Instruction of the Uninstructed* (*De catechizandis rudibus*), in George Howie (ed. and trans.), *St. Augustine: On Education* (Chicago, 1969), 365.

stripped and its skin is used as a coat to protect the mincer, who stands near the try-pot cutting pieces of blubber into it. The skin covering the mincer makes him "invested in the full canonicals of his calling" (p. 351). He is "a candidate for an archbishoprick" (the phallic pun has been noted many times—in *our* century). And the blubber pieces he cuts are called "Bible leaves," the narrator explains, because they have to be very thin. The allegory is unmistakable, however: institutional religion lives by cutting up the dead god's body, drying out and circumcising his virile power (the coat is formed by taking the dry pelt down, "removing some three feet of it, towards the pointed extremity," and then cutting armholes), and turning the rest of his body into scripture.

With this imposing figure, the journey returns to the world of allegory described by Benjamin in the German baroque. Allegory dries and trys-out the living things of this world in order to turn them into emblems. If it empties them of all life, it fills them with significance. And this is precisely what happens, allegorically, to the whale as the pieces of his body are turned into oil to light the world. "The Whaleman, as he seeks the food of light, so he lives in light" (p. 355). The true place of the production of allegory is at the grave of the gods. But it must posit a communion with the living gods as its basis, and it asks the reader to make this unreadable leap as well.

VII

~~~

UNFULFILLMENTS AND
WHELMINGS

(*Moby-Dick*, Chapter 106–Epilogue)

THE LAST THIRTY chapters differ markedly from the culminating chapters of *Moby-Dick*'s "cetological center." Breaking with the model of initiation into unknown and unanticipated realms of being, the actions near the end of the voyage are given almost entirely to anticipation of a single thing: Ahab's confrontation with the white whale.

Ahab and Augury

Fedallah, Ahab's sinister Asiatic harpooner, pronounces to the captain that "neither hearse nor coffin can be thine," that "ere thou couldst die on this voyage, two hearses must verily be seen by thee on the sea; the first not made by mortal hands; and the visible wood of the last one must be grown in America," and that "I shall still go before thee thy pilot" (p. 410). On the last day of the chase all these prophecies are fulfilled. Fedallah, drowned the previous day, surfaces lashed to Moby Dick's back, and Ahab is led to a recognition: "'Aye, Parsee! I see thee again.—Aye, and thou goest before; and this, this then is the hearse thou didst promise'" (p. 464). As he sees the *Pequod*'s hull rammed in, he makes the last identification: "'The ship! The hearse!—the second hearse!' cried Ahab from the boat; 'its wood could only be American!'" (p. 468).

The genuine surprise of these startling identifications is challenged only by the risk Melville runs of losing credibility by introducing such theatrical effects in his climactic chapters. Yet in the antiholistic aesthetic of allegory, and especially in such a genre as the baroque allegory Benjamin delineates, the "flattening" that such stagy effects might bring about could only be advantageous. Benjamin writes that the technique of the *Trauerspiel* is "the emblematic schema from which, by means of an artifice whose effect always had to be overwhelming, that which is signified springs obviously into view."[1] Examples are the crown revealed as crown of thorns, the throne room as dungeon, the boudoir as tomb, or even a harp as an executioner's axe. The revelations of whale as hearse and of ship as hearse produce this same "overwhelming" effect in *Moby-Dick*, pulling the carpet from under the illusion of a richly textured nature with indefinitely suggestive meaning. The final events of the book do away with ambiguity and determine all meanings toward one end. They present man at odds with nature and determined by the gods but not in touch with them. This situation is reflected in the text by prophecies, auguries, haruspications, and typological *figurae*.[2]

We have not explained why Melville's imagination should draw up alongside the antiquated spirit of the *Trauerspiel*; indeed, at first blush it seems an outrageous contention, since in the nineteenth century even the Germans themselves, let alone an unmethodical American dabbler in Germanica, were ignoring this body of their literature. But in his study of the *Trauerspiel* Benjamin does far more than provide an analysis of a large body of obscure German plays; his comments strike at the heart of what is baroque; and in exposing the heart of baroque he exposes what is distinctive about Christian art. He emphatically separates *Trauerspiel* from tragedy, which remains in his view a genre with an exclusively classical outlook. His brief remarks on Shakespeare support his contention that "for *Richard III*, for *Hamlet*, as indeed for all Shakespearean 'tragedies,' the theory of the *Trauerspiel* is predestined to contain the prolegomena of interpretation."[3] Melville's deep draughts of Shakespeare have not needed further emphasis since Sedgwick's and Olson's studies in the forties, and it has often been noted that the

1. Benjamin, *Origin of German Tragic Drama*, 231.
2. On the use of figural typology in *Moby-Dick*, see the remarks of Ursula Brumm in *American Thought and Religious Typology*, trans. John Hoaglund (New Brunswick, N.J., 1970), 162–97.
3. Benjamin, *Origin of German Tragic Drama*, 228.

Shakespearean tone and allusions increase markedly in the last thirty chapters of *Moby-Dick*.[4]

But the basic thing that should lead Melville toward baroque modes of expression is the problem of the story's ending. Ishmael's quest for a final meaning, if it can be considered in such a prosaic aspect for a moment, turns into the discovery of an infinity of reference—"long rows of angels"—undelimitable but also unattainable, infinitely retreating toward the Platonic beyond. (This problem was also met squarely at the end of *Mardi*, reflected in its last sentence: "And thus, pursuers and pursued flew on, over an endless sea."[5] What limits the quest for significance cannot be anything inherent in signification, but must instead be something in the way signs appear in time.

Ahab specifically revolts against the notion of an allegorical universe and instead imagines a world with all its cards on the table, where he can confront the gods openly. Since he lives according to what he believes is a set fate, with "iron rails" carrying him to his "fixed purpose" (p. 147), he thinks he can dictate the terms of the future. The foreshadowing of events is to him not figural or prefiguring in an ambiguous and open-ended way, but univocally prophetic, recalling the augurial signs of antiquity. He defies the gods with a particularly antitypological burst of *hybris*: "Now, then, be the prophet and the fulfiller one" (p. 147) (the temporal dimension of this boast underlined by the phrase "Now, then"); and he thinks to catch the gods in a paradoxical corollary of the doctrine of predestination: "Ye cannot swerve me, else ye swerve yourselves!" In his world the rapprochement between beings, whether man and god, captain and mate, or hunter and whale, is always reducible to the sheer confrontation of wills.

Ahab seems never to doubt the continuity of history: the past exists solely to remind him of his overriding purpose projected into a definite moment in the future. An instructive passage concerning Ahab's conception of teleology is to be found in Chapter 118, "The

4. William Ellery Sedgwick, *Herman Melville: The Tragedy of Mind* (Cambridge, Mass., 1944), 82–136; Charles Olson, *Call Me Ishmael* (New York, 1947).
5. Melville, *Mardi*, 654.

Quadrant," wherein he rejects the conventional way of navigating by the stars. He addresses the quadrant:

> "But what after all canst thou do, but tell the poor, pitiful point, where thou thyself happenest to be on this wide planet, and the hand that holds thee: no! not one jot more! Thou canst not tell where one drop of water or one grain of sand will be tomorrow noon; and yet with thy impotence thou insultest the sun!" (p. 412)

Ahab attacks astral navigation with the damning charge that it can include no notion of time. Since each spot in the line of a ship's voyage is a separate point with its own coordinates, each point is absolutely disjunct from the next. (Angus Fletcher's remarks, already noted, on astronomy and astral navigation as images of allegorical wisdom and desire help draw out the implications of this scene.[6])

In contrast, the devices Ahab chooses for locating his position posit a continuity in time: "'Curse thee, thou quadrant! . . . no longer will I guide my earthly way by thee; the level ship's compass, and the level dead-reckoning, by log and by line; *these* shall conduct me, and show me my place on the sea'" (p. 412). The log and line rely completely on where the ship has been and its temporal progress through the past; the compass shows in which direction the ship is heading. It is only by conflating the knowledge from the past (as record) and the future (as direction, still potential) that Ahab will learn where he is. Tellingly, however, this method makes the *Pequod* sail off course, in Chapters 118–126, until Ahab discovers that the compass' magnetic field has been reversed by an electrical storm. In addition the line breaks, and a new one has to be made. Continuity is obviously less a truth than a noble lie, a dare by Ahab against opposing forces. Benjamin's dictum on continuity has served as the point of departure for this study: "The continuum of history is that of the oppressor."[7] The perspective of allegory reveals that the project of deriving the future directly from the

6. Fletcher, *Allegory*, 96–97.
7. Benjamin, notes to "Über den Begriff der Geschichte," 1236.

conquests of the past is what the emperor's historian always does, and it is an empty delusion. The sense of time in allegorical consciousness, by contrast, is of discontinuous moments. And against Ahab's repeated assertions of a continuous project under his direction, one detects the pressure of many signs to the contrary, signs of which Ahab is aware but which he uneasily buries. If he is drawn onward by the goal he envisions, he is driven by the tormenting suspicion of an absolute disjunction between earthly time and cosmic destiny. The "wall" mentioned in his "Quarter-Deck" speech separates this fallen world from the one beyond; however, the world beyond is not felicity but malevolence.

Ahab expresses this sense precisely as a feeling when he talks to the carpenter about his leg: "When I come to mount this leg thou makest, I shall nevertheless feel another leg in the same identical place with it; that is, carpenter, my old lost leg; the flesh and blood one, I mean. Canst thou not drive that old Adam away?" (p. 391). The phenomenon of "feeling" a missing leg is used to figure the experience of absence and incompleteness. Unexamined, in the unconscious, this desire appears to the psyche as a reverse eschatology, a nostalgia for origins and original wholeness—a "missing leg" that is one with the "old Adam." This feeling is unbearable to Ahab, and he wants it "driven away." Probing that impulse deeper, he evolves an uncanny explication: "How dost thou know that some entire, living, thinking thing may not be invisibly and uninterpenetratingly standing precisely where thou now standest, aye, and standing there in thy spite?" (p. 391). The word *uninterpenetratingly*, stressed by its mere length, emphasizes the absolute opposition to any ontology of the symbol in Ahab's world. Two beings may occupy the same body, yet even within it they remain completely distinct from each other. Furthermore, the alien presence masters the "proper" owner, the self, in its despite. The disjunction of allegory becomes a hell to Ahab, who wants to be wholly himself.

Ahab has claimed to be in more intimate communion with the "clear spirit of fire" and whatever spirits control the cosmos than to need to observe oblique hints from them. He shouts to Starbuck, "'Omen? Omen?—the dictionary! If the gods think to speak outright to man, they will honorably speak outright; not shake their

heads and give an old wives' darkling hint—'" (p. 452). Yet mean-
wh:le he is becoming increasingly aware that the gods *do* hide their
truths. He cannot, however, be converted by this awareness to a
hermeneutic respect for the world; Starbuck's more-than-respect re-
pels him, and Pip's madness, though it answers to something deep
within Ahab, must finally be rejected. So he remains in torment.
After surveying Queequeg's unreadable written body he turns away
and exclaims, "'Oh, devilish tantalizations of the gods!'" (p. 399).

Thus the language of foreshadowing and fulfillment, which he had
thought to be instruments in his own service, turns against him as he
draws nearer to the white whale. Events become more ominous in a
purely ancient sense; the doom of the *Pequod* is shadowed forth in
a number of ways large and small. The splash from the coffin of
a sailor killed by Moby Dick anoints the *Pequod*; a voice from the
ill-named *Delight* mocks the coffin-lifebuoy hanging at the *Pequod*'s stern. Prophecies are spoken, amplifying a strain that has run
through the entire narrative with Elijah, Gabriel, and others. The
Manxman hears the souls of the *Rachel*'s lost crew in the cries of
seals.

Chief of seers is the eerie figure who is such a function of Ahab's
soul that "Ahab seemed an independent lord; the Parsee but his
slave," or rather "both seemed yoked together, and an unseen ty-
rant driving them" (p. 439). Fedallah's other name—"the Parsee,"
by which he comes to be called exclusively as the novel advances—
indicates the Zoroastrian sect, with its belief in a world equally balanced between good and evil forces; but, if one takes into consideration Melville's capacity for wordplay, it is not too outlandish to
note that *Parsee* is homophonic with the English-American pro-
nunciation of *Parcae* current in his day—the Greek divinities of
fate.[8] Fedallah is the only finally antirealistic character in *Moby-
Dick*; one has to presume that he is in special contact with the Fates
because he knows when Ahab's life thread is to be cut. He seems an
emissary sent not to divert the captain from his catastrophic course
but rather to inform him of it in a way that will not help him avoid
it. The witches' prophecies in *Macbeth*, the Delphic oracle, and Roman augury all share in common the closed universe of fate within

8. See Noah Webster, *A Dictionary of the English Language* (Springfield, Mass., 1852).

which Fedallah lives, and into which Ahab enters more irrevocably each time he chooses to steer his way toward the white whale. Prophecy in such a universe is oblique and deliberately misguiding, in order that doom may be foreshadowed but not foreknown until its prevention is impossible.

The omen of the hawk and Ahab's hat presents a clear rehearsal of a Roman haruspication scene. Significantly recalling Rome's origins, Ishmael muses:

> An eagle flew thrice around Tarquin's head, removing his cap to replace it, and thereupon Tanaquil, his wife, declared that Tarquin would be king of Rome. But only by the replacing of the cap was that omen accounted good. Ahab's hat was never restored; the wild hawk flew on and on with it; far in advance of the prow: and at last disappeared; while from the point of that disappearance, a minute black spot was dimly discerned, falling from that vast height into the sea. (pp. 440–41)

The bird dramatizes the totally external working of fate and the open undermining of Ahab's claims of autonomy during his last days. Itself a semi-divine creature, it swoops down from above to touch the earthly figure at only one point, for only one instant—then flies off into the heights again, carrying the emblem that by long-established synecdoche designates a man's office and function. At the farthest possible remove still visible from the ship, the bird announces Ahab's doom in a figure "dimly discerned" and not heeded by Ahab, a figure at once synecdochic and metaphoric of Ahab falling from the hands of the gods.

Ahab himself becomes more aware of an external control as he approaches his end. When he asks, "Is Ahab, Ahab? Is it I, God, or who, that lifts this arm?" (p. 445), he is at a turning point at which he begins to realize the impossibility of achieving a totally integrated, totally dominant self. Earlier he has said, as one who makes good his own boasts, "Ahab must have the doubloon!" (p. 439). But when the white whale is at last sighted, he declares something slightly different: "—no, the doubloon is mine, Fate reserved the doubloon for me" (p. 446).

Chapter 132, "The Symphony," culminates all of Ahab's late realizations in one grand excursus. The conversation between Starbuck and Ahab is in part a disguised debate between models of human desire—whether it is of "natural" or of "other" origin. Ahab first is enchanted by Starbuck: "'Close! stand close to me, Starbuck; let me look into a human eye; it is better than to gaze into sea or sky; better than to gaze upon God. By the green land; by the bright hearth-stone! this is the magic glass, man; I see my wife and my child in thine eye'" (p. 444). This "magic glass" almost induces him to set sail for home, ending what he now recognizes as forty years' exile. Starbuck caps his appeal with a poignant image: "'See, see! the boy's face from the window! the boy's hand on the hill!'"

But Ahab does not reach out to grasp that hand. The dynamics of this scene strangely parody the movement of the threshold scene of allegory, wherein one must turn away from a petrifying text to embrace a living body. At the moment Starbuck makes his climactic plea, "Ahab's glance was averted"; he turns from the warm world of hearth and progeny to face that faceless monolith that drives him on: "'What is it, what nameless, inscrutable, *unearthly* thing is it; what cozening, hidden lord and master, and cruel, remorseless emperor commands me; that against all natural lovings and longings, I so keep pushing . . . recklessly making me ready to do what in *my own, proper, natural heart,* I durst not so much as dare?'" (pp. 444–45, emphasis added). He turns to face this Gorgon head on; but it is Starbuck who shows the effects of petrification: "blanched to a corpse's hue with despair, the mate had stolen away" (p. 445). And one other figure seems petrified, also providing an arresting contrast to Starbuck's "human eye"—"two reflected, fixed eyes in the water there. Fedallah was motionlessly leaning over the same rail." Fedallah is called the "shadow" to Ahab's "substance"; he is a double who, like the allegorical doubling in text and commentary, partially explicates his original. Still, Ahab does not escape a kind of petrification in the moment he averts his glance from Starbuck: "like a blighted fruit tree he shook, and cast his last, cindered apple to the soil" (p. 444). He is the barren fig tree cursed in the gospels.

But the fulfillment of the Parsee's enigmatic oracles signals the carriers of his death to him in a way he could not have known beforehand. A whale as hearse or a sailing ship as hearse is a metaphor that fits the definition of *katachresis*, since (in Doctor Johnson's memorable phrase) they "yoke together by violence" two meanings so disparate that they could not have been associated before their actual occurrence. The radical newness of allegory thus ensures that Ahab will not foresee the pattern until the final moment. This newness is distinctly allegorical because the integrity of things in their self-intended meanings, Aristotle's "final cause," is violated in order to enlist them in a plot which cuts across natural history. The canceling of natural intentionality in objects thus ensures that their new intentionality will be pure, their new function related solely to the end of the allegory.

The Romantic Morality Play

If Ahab's world is to himself a Plutarchan *bios*, with Nietzschean overtones, it is a morality play to Ishmael, though it is one without clear labels and assurances. Without describing anything that might not naturally take place, he enlists the sea's inhabitants in a theological drama. When Moby Dick first reveals himself as "the grand god" (p. 448), the seabirds throng about him like the heavenly host.

> "The birds!—the birds!" cried Tashtego.
> In long Indian file, as when herons take wing, the white birds were now all flying towards Ahab's boat; and when within a few yards began fluttering over the water there, wheeling round and round, with joyous, expectant cries. Their vision was keener than man's; Ahab could perceive no sign in the sea. (p. 448)

The "long rows of angels," only envisioned in Chapter 94, are now incarnate on the first day that Moby Dick appears. On the third day, however, the devils rise up from below, in a supernatural symmetry with the angels:

> "The sharks! the sharks!" cried a voice from the low cabin-window . . .
> . . . scarce had he pushed from the ship, when numbers of sharks, seemingly rising from out the dark waters beneath the

hull, maliciously snapped at the blades of the oars, every time they dipped in the water; and in this way accompanied the boat with their bites. (p. 463)

Moreover, they gather around only Ahab's boat: "—however it was, they seemed to follow that one boat without molesting the others." Ishmael somehow manages to manufacture some possible rational explanations for this phenomenon. Above all, he seems to insist, these strange events *are* "phenomena": they unquestionably happened, and any explanation comes after the fact and tentatively. "It is a thing not uncommonly happening to the whale-boats in those swarming seas."

Though the tale of Ahab's demise may resemble Marlowe's *Faustus* in many respects and be delivered in Shakespearean language, it is crucial that no outright allusions to any dramatic works be made in these last chapters. Any quality of the stage that this last act bears must be seen to be entirely its own and not imposed, hideously and intolerably, by a moralizing author. The sense of actuality in the scene exemplifies the Romantic discovery of allegory in nature itself. The carnivalizing chapters have already done the work of cutting away all conventional ties of signifier to signified. The "most doleful and most mocking funeral" of the whale's carcass in Chapter 69 shows a complete *mundus inversus* with birds and sharks each seen as versions of each other: "The sea-vultures all in pious mourning, the air-sharks all punctiliously in black or speckled" (p. 262). All the more impressive, then, that they now wear the robes of angels and devils and the robes seem to fit. Nature's order is glimpsed only in fleeting moments, but when seen it is aligned perfectly for that moment with the old, dust-worn, "black-letter" visions of heaven and hell. The realms to which this allegory points are in the here and now; yet, characteristically for the allegory of our age, even when brought down from the skies this realm is no less in stature than before—and it is equally unattainable.

In the last chapters the contrast in human terms to Ahab's glorious impiety is not an overtrumping pious glory but an unobtrusive and unimportant humility such as is embodied in the ship's carpenter. Just as in baroque allegory, the religious world has become

"mundane" in the sense of trite and stale; but whereas its still hon-
orary position in letters made poets like Donne and Crashaw reach
for the outlandish to catch the element of surprise in the miraculous, Melville finds a truth in the very lowliness and stupidity of
the religious presence. In the company of geniuses, old articles of
faith no longer claim any regard. The carpenter is unable to comprehend Ahab's flights of Promethean daring and wonders openly,
"Now, what's he speaking about, and who's he speaking to, I should
like to know?" (p. 390). And when the captain spins out his mech-
anistic fantasy of a "complete man, after a desirable pattern"—fifty
feet tall, "no heart at all," and so on—and, wanting a skylight for
the head, muses, "I must have a lantern," the carpenter simply
hands him one (p. 391).

Counterposed, in other words, to Ahab's titanic world is the
humble world of the downtrodden and persistent. They are a scattered people—the blacksmith is another of them—and Ishmael
wastes no sentimentality on them but lets them stand exposed in all
their dullness. The carpenter's slow-wittedness is nonetheless what
makes him comic and links him to the sources of Christian comedy
in the medieval morality play. (The whole exchange between Ahab
and the carpenter is given in dramatic format, employed here for
the first time since Chapter 40.) The carpenter's profession is a patent emblem of Jesus' *humilitas*, but its very obviousness renders it
unable to offer any challenge to Ahab's imagination. "Carpenter?"
he says, "why that's—but no" (p. 391). Every religious emblem or
doctrine is reduced in stature and resides only in what is not regal,
noble, or imaginative. It remains as almost nothing but a verbal tic:

> "Faith, sir, I've—"
> "Faith? What's that?"
> "Why, faith, sir, it's only a sort of exclamation-like—that's
> all, sir." (p. 432)

Ahab's grim joking and the carpenter's playing straight man provide no genuine turn into comedy but only an interlude like the
gravedigger's scene in *Hamlet*, which Ahab himself specifically recalls: "The grave-digger in the play sings, spade in hand. Dost thou
never?" (p. 432). The carpenter cannot even begin to fence with

Ahab's wit, but the stage directions in Chapter 108 leave him the closing soliloquy. As he sets to work on Ahab's new leg, he imagines the resurrection as an inglorious and even routine affair. "Let's finish it," he says of the leg, "before the resurrection fellow comes a-calling with his horn for all legs, true or false, as brewery-men go round collecting old beer barrels, to fill 'em up again" (p. 392).

In Chapter 127, however, it is Ahab's turn for the soliloquy, and he is more deeply attracted by the notion of resurrection. In the coffin made into a lifebuoy he sees "the very dreaded symbol of grim death, by a mere hap, made the expressive sign of the help and hope of most endangered life" (p. 433). He then asks, "Does it go further? Can it be that in some spiritual sense the coffin is, after all, but an immortality-preserver! I'll think of that. But no." Again the quick rejection, "But no," as in Chapter 108; but this time it is not a dismissal of something trivial; it is an act of will, and of despair. "So far gone am I in the dark side of earth, that its other side, the theoretic bright one, seems but uncertain twilight to me." This "uncertain twilight" is the region where religious allegory remains in our day. Ahab's denial paradoxically reveals that his moral vision is not beyond good and evil, that he does not anticipate Nietzsche in considering the resurrection merely a delusion born of fear, but he sees it rather as requiring too great a turn off course from the "dark side of earth" where he is. Besides, the resurrection remains "theoretic," an unproven postulate.

Remnants

In the end, *Moby-Dick* circles back to its opening problem, the problem of what community an exile may join. Chapter 128, "The Pequod Meets the Rachel," looks gravely at the problem of tradition—whether it is possible for one generation to hand down its authority and its identity to the next in an unbroken line. The *Rachel* is a ship with a mission, and its intense but pathetic Captain Gardiner is no less driven than Ahab, though in the opposite direction. His young son has disappeared, towed out of sight with a whaleboat's crew that had got fast to Moby Dick. The reason for the boy's presence on the boat is a testimony to the father's desire: "A little lad, but twelve years old, whose father with the earnest but unmisgiving hardihood of a Nantucketer's paternal love, had thus early sought to initiate him in the perils and wonders of a vocation almost immemorially the destiny of all his race" (p. 435).

If Captain Gardiner's name means anything, it does so because he would like to think himself able to reap what he has sown, to ensure the full harvest of days in his own progeny. This desire runs poignantly throughout the last chapters of *Moby-Dick*, often represented in the figure of a boy, as when Ahab and Starbuck recall their sons left behind. Starbuck's exhortation to Ahab ends with the vision of "the boy's face from the window! the boy's hand on the hill!" (p. 444), and this image reappears in his despairing commands on the day of his death: "'—Mast-head there! See ye my boy's hand on the hill?'" (and commenting on himself he adds, "'—Crazed'") (p. 463). The hand represents movingly the all-too-human hope of handing down one's life to the sons, of living on in the flesh and blood of one's own making.

Like the handclasp, the metaphor of harvest expresses the hope of a continuity in family and culture. But the harvest the captains so earnestly hope for is only achieved in an ironic simile: the *Rachel*'s "masts and yards were thickly clustered with men, as three tall cherry trees, when the boys are cherrying among the boughs" (p. 436). Behind this hopeful image, however, stands the grim reality that it is the loss of the boy that has crowded all the men onto the masts and transformed the ship into an orchard. The implication is that life is not the mortal gardener's to harvest. In the matter of this trope it is rather Pip who has already stated the evident truth: "'God goes 'mong the worlds blackberrying'" (p. 363).

Ishmael identifies Captain Gardiner's ship as "Rachel weeping for her children, because they were not" (p. 436). The passage he recalls in Jeremiah speaks of a voice "heard in Ramah, lamentation, and bitter weeping," and continues, "Rachel weeping for her children refused to be comforted for her children, because they were not" (Jer. 31:15). The general concern of this section in Jeremiah, however, is the gathering together of the remnant of scattered Israel—"I will turn their mourning into joy" (31:13); "and their soul shall be as a watered garden; and they shall not sorrow any more at all" (31:12). In its context here, however, the garden has become purely an image of hopes not to be realized.

The passage in Jeremiah refers to a legend in the time of exile according to which Rachel's voice was heard weeping near the traditional locale of her tomb. She was considered the ancestress of the nation of Israel, and her tears thus stand not for a private or familial grief but for the uprooting of an entire people. The verse in Jeremiah is quoted by Matthew after he gives the account of the massacre of the innocents under Herod: "Then was fulfilled that which was spoken by Jeremy the prophet" (Matt. 2:17). While narrating an incident just before the encounter with the *Rachel*, Ishmael refers to the massacre of the innocents: "the watch—then headed by Flask—was startled by a cry so plaintively wild and unearthly—like half-articulated wailings of the ghosts of all Herod's murdered Innocents" (p. 428). Though the Manxman later identifies these cries as those of the *Rachel*'s drowned crewmen, Ishmael discerns that they are in fact the wails of "some young seals that had lost their dams, or some dams that had lost their cubs" (p. 429).

The motifs leading out from the biblical Rachel thus embrace both man and nature in suffering. The insistence in Matthew that the murder of the innocents was the fulfillment of the figure of Rachel weeping reminds one again that the fulfillment of sacred history can often be negative, for no guaranty of a positive progress through history exists. The wails are taken as one more omen about the doom of the *Pequod*.

The general inefficacy of religious practice to stall the *Pequod*'s fate is evident in the broken rite which the *Delight*'s captain performs on his dead crewman:

> Then turning to his crew—"Are ye ready there? place the plank then on the rail, and lift the body; so, then—Oh! God" —advancing towards the hammock with uplifted hands—"may the resurrection and the life—"
>
> "Brace forward! Up helm!" cried Ahab like lightning to his men.   (pp. 441–42)

The continuity that religious ritual hopes to effect between the here and the beyond is not allowed to develop. Ahab's will intrudes to break up the sentence that would promise a transition into the next life.

The promise of a smooth passage, in the final analysis, is something that religion cannot fulfill. In his final moment Starbuck asks, "'Is this the end of all my bursting prayers? all my lifelong fidelities?'" (p. 467). And in fact it is. The dream of a foreseeable rescue, a salvation according to plan, is burst. The god that reveals himself at the end is terrible: "Retribution, swift vengeance, eternal malice [are] in his whole aspect" (p. 468) as Moby Dick rams the *Pequod*, the "god-bullied hull" in Ahab's phrase. Even the concentric circles that figured an anagogic peace in the whales' bower now compose a vortex dooming all hands and present nature's final form as universal destruction.

But an invisible, unmanifested god prevails in the last page, a page that makes several gestures to present itself as though it were outside the text: it is printed entirely in italics, is titled "Epilogue," and begins, "The drama's done. Why then here does any one step forth?" (p. 470). And of course it was omitted entirely in the English edition, in a kind of ultimate ambiguity that may never be resolved. But even Melville's contemporary reviewers pointed out that a first-person account could not logically end with the death of all hands. More, however, is involved in the ending than mere survival. The "invisible police officer of the Fates" mentioned in the first chapter apparently once again has jurisdiction, for the sharks seem to have "padlocks on their mouths" and the seabirds "sheathed beaks." This seems a god who operates only in the margins of the text, just where the readable actions of human purpose stop. And he seems to operate only by chance—"It so chanced," Ishmael begins his explanation of how he survived. But as he has asserted in his model of the loom of time, "chance by turns rules either [*i.e.*, fate and free will], and has the last featuring blow at events" (p. 185).

The notion of a saving remnant implies an outline of history that is not a straight, magnificent unfolding—the line figured in the straight wake of the *Pequod*—but is instead a series of last-minute rescues, or, more centrally, a gathering up of survivors after a series of plunges into destruction. In the narrative it is the "devious-cruising Rachel" that traces this more erratic line, giving the visual equivalent to the biblical Rachel's unforeseen legacy of unfulfillment and displacement.

In the allegory of interpretation that Ishmael makes of every episode in *Moby-Dick*, the "retracing search" of the *Rachel* also suggests a rereading of the text. And it may provide an answer to what motivates allegorical interpretation. The *Rachel* reverses its course, going over waters it has traversed before, but now it is in search of something it has lost. The son represents the captain's own continuity with the future generation, and as such he represents the idea of continuity with *all* generations. If the father cannot pass on his calling to his son, then the very notion of tradition as a continuity is broken. Deluded as this desire for continuity may be, it is what causes the *Rachel* to reverse its course, without which reversal Ishmael would have drowned, exhausted, at sea. The motive for rereading a text, then, in this allegory of interpretation, may be said to be mistaken; but it is a felicitous mistake.

The *Rachel* is motivated by a desire for origins, for in representing the link of generations the son represents as well the link with the original ancestor. The alternative is the "orphan's" existence of Ishmael. The desire for origins may be equated with what we have called allegorical desire. Allegories could never get under way if from the beginning the allegorist were totally conscious that the gap in being is unbridgeable; he is spurred on by a hope of crossing that gap. In fact it is the sense of loss—what Thomas McFarland has called the "meontic mode" of Romantic writing, a pervasive sense of nonbeing—that finally determines the movement of allegories toward an origin in which they hope they might be saved.[9] Interpretation is born of this desire, for it comes only in a "retracing search" through the text of experience. One may say that interpretation occurs in the hope of finding a continuity of meaning with the origin of meaning in one's experience. Yet what one per-

9. Thomas McFarland, "The Place Beyond the Heavens: True Being, Transcendence, and the Symbolic Indication of Wholeness," *Boundary 2*, VII (Winter, 1979), 283–319. Joel Fineman links allegory with the desire for origins in "The Structure of Allegorical Desire," unpublished paper given at the English Institute, 1979.

sistently finds upon rereading—that is, if one's eyes are open—is
the unexpected, the radically unconnected element. Ishmael is
such a fragment; he is literally "unreadable" in the script of history
projected by the *Rachel.* The "miracle," then—what is truly unexpected and unaccountable—is that Ishmael is taken on board. He
becomes part of a text he has radically altered by his mere existence; the text is saved by the realization that it cannot be a pre-
scription, a script, for history.

What the *Rachel* does, then, only typifies what the reading of allegory, in the cultural context, has always done: to reread the past
out of a desire to save the future. Ishmael's rescue thus to an extent
performs the conservative function that allegorizing has done since
the Stoics. Yet it is just as surely a break with that conservative tradition as well; it is the sign that something radically discontinuous
has been taken into the heart of the text. Ishmael's rescue is the
kind of "conservative revolutionary" gesture that Benjamin's writing expresses.[10] It is the way, as we are just coming to realize, that
we all have to read the past now.

How far this realization is carried out is of course what *Moby-Dick*
does not venture to say. The triumph of Ishmael would be the widespread recognition that community is genuinely constructed not
out of fathers and sons but out of exiles and orphans, not on the
land, in Nantucket or New Bedford, but only on exiled waters. Yet
this understanding has great difficulty fitting itself to the fathers'
structure of power without negating itself. Ishmael does not become
a captain; instead he becomes a fabulator, and his empire is not
maritime but discursive. His is a city that like the proto-allegorist
Plato's will exist only in discourse.

Critics who claim that Ishmael's rescue is not real—that it cannot represent "salvation," or even "survival," or even that it does
not happen—are probably led to such conclusions by detecting the
disjunctions in the rhetoric and structure of *Moby-Dick.*[11] At that

10. Cf. Irving Wohlfarth on Benjamin's image of interpretation as "saving destruction"
rather than Derridean deconstruction: "Walter Benjamin's Image of Interpretation," *New
German Critique*, No. 17 (Spring, 1979), 70–98.
11. This is Paul Brodtkorb's conclusion in *Ishmael's White World: A Phenomenological
Reading of "Moby-Dick"* (New Haven, 1965). See also Howard C. Horsford, "The Design of
the Argument in *Moby-Dick,*" *Modern Fiction Studies*, VIII (1962), 233–51; James Guetti,

point, however, they fail to base their own critical judgments on the double, "unreadable" stance that allegorical commentary demands; instead they suppose that the only alternative to an unequivocal affirmation must be total negation. From that perspective *Moby-Dick* can only appear as nihilism. But it appears so only to the critic who has seen the new ground that Melville breaks but has refused to enter that land. Put another way, these critics have begun to see the insurmountable difficulties in creating an empire governed by the virtues Ishmael imagines during his voyage. But it is they, not Melville, who have supposed that Ishmael was to be an imperialist of the imagination. The failure they see is the failure of the Romantic project of universal historical progress through the synthesis of opposites in the imagination. This is a project, however, which many of the Romantics themselves, from Rousseau onward, had already seen through.

Ishmael not only survives in the end. What he has gained may be seen by contrasting the first chapters with the last ones—and not only the character Ishmael, but the narrator as well, has gained. The isolato of the first chapter, scorning the "crowds of water-gazers" and more willing, out of an almost surly instinct of self-preservation, to trust himself to the imperiousness of "some old hunks of a sea-captain" rather than continue to be a face in the crowd—disaffected, alienated, cynically witty—has changed, by the end, not only into one who can see the greatness in a captain he condemns but into one who can join the community of the bereft which the *Rachel* represents. The few glimpses of Ishmael after the *Pequod*'s voyage reveal one devoted to the temporary construction of communities in discourse and drink: the coterie of Peruvian dons who listen to the *Town-Ho*'s story; the "fine gam" he has with the crew of the *Samuel Enderby*, "long, very long after old Ahab touched her planks with his ivory heel" (p. 370). His phrasing (the

The Limits of Metaphor: A Study of Melville, Conrad, and Faulkner (Ithaca, N.Y., 1967); and Dryden, *Melville's Thematics of Form*. All these studies refute, justly enough, the notion of an ending harmonious with the project of the voyage, but to varying degrees all mistakenly equate the failure of Ishmael's epistemological quest with a failure to survive. The problem may be traced back to Charles Feidelson's seminal study, *Symbolism and American Literature* (Chicago, 1953), which, in opening new paths to the study of signification and imagination in *Moby-Dick*, began a reduction of Ishmael to the personified "voyaging imagination."

repetition in "long, very long," the reference to Ahab as "old," and
the image of the ivory heel on the ship's floor) expresses the won-
dering, ruminative, almost fond mood of his recollections. At least
in his remembering Ahab has become somewhat mellow, and Ishmael has managed to incorporate Ahab's tragic course into his own
understanding of the meaning of the *Pequod*'s fate. There would be
no opportunity for such recollection, however, without "the noble,
solid, Saxon hospitality of that ship [the *Samuel Enderby*]," about
which Ishmael adds, "May my parson forget me, and the devil remember me, if I ever lose sight of it."

What Ishmael has learned is that community exists most permanently in remembrance. It has no charter for establishment on
earth and can only be re-created by those who recall it and reclaim
it out of the past, seeing those saving moments in the past as models
and as promises. Hence Ishmael tells stories, giving witness to
things that he swears—both to the Spanish dons and to us his readers—are true.

As Dante's pilgrim returns to earth to write his poem, Ishmael
returns to the land to bear witness to the whale and truth. In both
poems the only evidence of that return is the work itself that tells of
the journey and mission. For both protagonists two determining
events have happened. Thematically, they have been given a mission, and both know that their earthly lives continue only to fulfill
that mission. Ishmael's earlier playful reference to Lazarus now rings
fully true: "All the days I should now live would be as good as the
days that Lazarus lived after his resurrection; a supplementary clean
gain of so many months or weeks as the case might be" (p. 197).
Consequently, both poets' omission of any detail about life after
their voyages, except what pertains immediately to their job of
writing or telling, demonstrates an awareness of what their narratives are for—not "my life story," autobiography, but testimony to
an unexpected reality in which they participated, a grander, truer
reality that had both a beginning and an end in their temporal experiences—and that their lives as survivors are justified only in
their product, the text. The other event is that structurally both
protagonists have merged with the narrators of their stories. Their

existence is now fully "achieved," and, being completed, it is fully engaged in the production of their narratives. History is composed of fragments, but in the allegory of history nothing remains that is not finally gathered into the weaving of the text.

BIBLIOGRAPHY

Abrams, M. H. *Natural Supernaturalism: Tradition and Revolution in Romantic Literature*. New York: Norton, 1971.

Auerbach, Erich. *Mimesis: The Representation of Reality in Western Literature*, trans. Willard Trask. Princeton: Princeton University Press, 1953.

Augustine, St. *The Instruction of the Uninstructed (De catechizandis rudibus)*. *St. Augustine: On Education*, ed. and trans. George Howie. Chicago: Regnery, 1969, pp. 365–69.

Baird, James. *Ishmael*. Baltimore: Johns Hopkins Press, 1956.

Bakhtin, Mikhail. *Problems of Dostoevsky's Poetics*, trans. R. W. Rotsel. Ann Arbor, Mich.: Ardis, 1973.

———. *Rabelais and His World*, trans. Hélène Iswolsky. Cambridge, Mass.: M.I.T. Press, 1968.

Bateson, Gregory, *et al.* "Toward a Theory of Schizophrenia." *Behavioral Science*, I, 4 (1956), 251–64.

Battenfeld, David H. "The Source for the Hymn in *Moby Dick*." *American Literature*, XXVII (November, 1955), 393–96.

Baudelaire, Charles. *Les Fleurs du mal. Oeuvres complètes*, ed. Claude Pichois. Bibliothèque de la Pléiade. Paris: Gallimard, 1975. Vol. I, pp. 3–145.

Benjamin, Walter. *Charles Baudelaire: A Lyric Poet in the Era of High Capitalism*, trans. Harry Zohn. London: New Left Books, 1973.

———. Notes to "Über den Begriff der Geschichte." *Gesammelte Schriften*, ed. Rolf Tiedemann and Hermann Schweppenhäuser. Vol. I. Frankfurt/Main: Suhrkamp, 1972.

———. *The Origin of German Tragic Drama*, trans. John Osborne. London: NLB, 1977.

————. "Theses on the Philosophy of History." *Illuminations*, trans. Harry Zohn. New York: Harcourt, Brace, Jovanovich, 1968.

————. "Zentralpark." *Gesammelte Schriften*, ed. Rolf Tiedemann and Hermann Schweppenhäuser. Vol. I. Frankfurt/Main: Suhrkamp, 1972.

Bercovitch, Sacvan. *The American Jeremiad*. Madison, Wis.: University of Wisconsin Press, 1978.

————. *The Puritan Origins of the American Self*. New Haven: Yale University Press, 1975.

Bewley, Marius. *The Eccentric Design: Form in the Classic American Novel*. New York: Columbia University Press, 1959.

Blake, William. *The Letters of William Blake*, ed. Geoffrey Keynes. Cambridge, Mass.: Harvard University Press, 1968.

————. *The Poetry and Prose of William Blake*, ed. David Erdman. Rev. ed. Garden City, N.Y.: Doubleday, 1970.

————. *The Writings of William Blake*, ed. Geoffrey Keynes. 3 vols. London: Nonesuch, 1925.

Bloom, Harold. *The Visionary Company: A Reading of English Romantic Poetry*. Rev. ed. Ithaca, N.Y.: Cornell University Press, 1971.

Brodtkorb, Paul. *Ishmael's White World: A Phenomenological Reading of "Moby-Dick."* New Haven: Yale University Press, 1965.

Brooks, Peter. "Romantic Antipastoral and Urban Allegories." *Yale Review*, LXIV (Autumn, 1974), 11–26.

Brumm, Ursula. *American Thought and Religious Typology*, trans. John Hoaglund. New Brunswick, N.J.: Rutgers University Press, 1970.

Coleridge, Samuel Taylor. *Confessions of an Inquiring Spirit*, ed. H. StJ. Hart. Stanford: Stanford University Press, 1957.

————. *The Statesman's Manual*. In *Lay Sermons*, ed. R. J. White. Princeton, Princeton University Press, 1972. Vol. VI of *Collected Works*, ed. Kathleen Coburn.

Cook, Charles H., Jr. "Ahab's 'Intolerable Allegory.'" *Boston University Studies in English*, I (Spring–Summer, 1955), 45–52.

Cowan, Bainard. "Walter Benjamin's Theory of Allegory." *New German Critique*, No. 22 (Winter, 1981), 109–22.

Dante Alighieri. *The Divine Comedy*, ed. and trans. Charles S. Singleton. 6 vols. Princeton: Princeton University Press, 1970–75.

————. *The Vision: or, Hell, Purgatory, and Paradise of Dante Alighieri*, trans. Henry Francis Cary. New York: Appleton, 1845.

Davis, Merrell R. *Melville's "Mardi": A Chartless Voyage*. New Haven: Yale University Press, 1952.

De Man, Paul. *Allegories of Reading: Figural Language in Rousseau, Nietzsche, Rilke, and Proust.* New Haven: Yale University Press, 1979.

————. "The Rhetoric of Temporality." *Interpretation: Theory and Practice,* ed. Charles S. Singleton. Baltimore: Johns Hopkins University Press, 1969.

Dieckmann, Liselotte. *Hieroglyphics: The History of a Literary Symbol.* St. Louis, Mo.: Washington University Press, 1970.

Dillingham, William B. "The Narrator of *Moby-Dick,*" *English Studies,* XLIX (February, 1968), 20–29.

Dryden, Edgar A. *Melville's Thematics of Form: The Great Art of Telling the Truth.* Baltimore: Johns Hopkins University Press, 1968.

Edinger, Edward F. *Melville's "Moby-Dick": A Jungian Commentary.* New York: New Directions, 1978.

Eldridge, Herbert G. "Careful Disorder: The Structure of *Moby-Dick.*" *American Literature,* XXXIX (May, 1967), 45–62.

Emerson, Ralph Waldo. "Compensation." *Essays, First Series,* ed. Alfred R. Ferguson and Jean Ferguson. Cambridge, Mass.: Harvard University Press, 1979. Vol. II of *Collected Works,* ed. A. R. Ferguson.

————. *Journals and Miscellaneous Notebooks,* ed. William H. Gilman *et al.* Vol. V. Cambridge, Mass.: Harvard University Press, 1965.

————. *Nature.* In *Nature, Addresses, and Lectures,* ed. Robert E. Spiller and Alfred R. Ferguson. Cambridge, Mass.: Cambridge University Press, 1971. Vol. I of *Collected Works,* ed. A. R. Ferguson.

Fanger, Donald. *Dostoevsky and Romantic Realism: A Study of Dostoevsky in Relation to Balzac, Dickens, and Gogol.* Chicago: University of Chicago Press, 1965.

Fineman, Joel. "The Structure of Allegorical Desire." Unpublished paper given at the English Institute, 1979.

Fletcher, Angus. *Allegory: The Theory of a Symbolic Mode.* Ithaca, N.Y.: Cornell University Press, 1964.

Freccero, John. "Medusa: The Letter and the Spirit." *Yearbook of Italian Studies: 1972,* ed. Dante della Terza. Florence: Casalini, 1974.

Frei, Hans W. *The Eclipse of Biblical Narrative: A Study in Eighteenth and Nineteenth Century Hermeneutics.* New Haven: Yale University Press, 1974.

Friedman, Maurice. *Problematic Rebel: Melville, Dostoievsky, Kafka, Camus.* Chicago: University of Chicago Press, 1970.

Frye, Northrop. *Anatomy of Criticism: Four Essays.* Princeton: Princeton University Press, 1957.

————. *Fearful Symmetry: A Study of William Blake.* Princeton: Princeton University Press, 1947.

Gadamer, Hans-Georg. *Truth and Method*, trans. Garrett Barden and John Cumming. New York: Seabury, 1976.

Garrison, Daniel H. "Melville's Doubloon and the Shield of Achilles." *Nineteenth-Century Fiction*, XXVI (September, 1971), 171–84.

Gasché, Rodolphe. "The Scene of Writing: A Deferred Outset." *Glyph*, I (1977), 150–71.

Glenn, Barbara. "Melville and the Sublime in *Moby-Dick.*" *American Literature*, XLVIII (May, 1976), 165–82.

Golemba, Henry L. "The Shape of *Moby-Dick.*" *Studies in the Novel*, V (Summer, 1973), 197–210.

Goodenough, Erwin R. *By Light, Light: The Mystic Gospel of Hellenistic Judaism.* New Haven: Yale University Press, 1935.

Grabo, Carl. *A Newton among Poets: Shelley's Use of Science in "Prometheus Unbound."* Originally published 1930. New York: Cooper Square, 1968.

Guetti, James. *The Limits of Metaphor: A Study of Melville, Conrad, and Faulkner.* Ithaca, N.Y.: Cornell University Press, 1967.

Habermas, Jürgen. *Toward a Rational Society: Student Protest, Science, and Politics*, trans. Jeremy J. Shapiro. Boston: Beacon, 1970.

Hamann, Johann Georg. "Aesthetica in nuce." *Sämtliche Werke*, ed. Josef Nadler. Vol. II. Vienna: Herder, 1950.

————. "Über die Auslegung der heiligen Schrift." *Sämtliche Werke*, ed. Josef Nadler. Vol. I. Vienna: Herder, 1949.

Hamlin, Cyrus. "The Limits of Understanding: Hermeneutics and the Study of Literature." *Arion*, n.s., III, 4 (1976), 389–94.

Hatch, Edwin. *The Influence of Greek Ideas on Christianity.* Originally published 1888. New York: Harper & Row, 1957.

Hayford, Harrison. "'Loomings': Yarns and Figures in the Fabric." *Artful Thunder: Versions of the Romantic Tradition in American Literature, in Honor of Howard P. Vincent*, ed. Robert J. DeMott and Sanford E. Marovitz. Kent, Ohio: Kent State University Press, 1975.

Henel, Heinrich. "Goethe and Science." *Literature and Science: Proceedings of the Sixth Triennial Congress of the International Federation for Modern Languages and Literatures, 1954.* Oxford: Basil Blackwell, 1955.

Herbert, T. Walter, Jr. *"Moby-Dick" and Calvinism: A World Dismantled.* New Brunswick, N.J.: Rutgers University Press, 1977.

Hoffman, Daniel. "Moby Dick: Jonah's Whale or Job's?" *Sewanee Review*, LXIX (April–June, 1961), 205–24.

Honig, Edwin. *Dark Conceit: The Making of Allegory*. Evanston, Ill.: Northwestern University Press, 1959.

Horsford, Howard C. "The Design of the Argument in *Moby-Dick*." *Modern Fiction Studies*, VIII (Autumn, 1962), 233–51.

Humboldt, Wilhelm von. *Humanist Without Portfolio: An Anthology of the Writings of Wilhelm von Humboldt*, ed. Marianne Cowan. Detroit, Mich.: Wayne State University Press, 1963.

Irwin, John T. *American Hieroglyphics: The Symbol of the Egyptian Hieroglyphics in the American Renaissance*. New Haven: Yale University Press, 1980.

———. "The Symbol of the Hieroglyphics in the American Renaissance." *American Quarterly*, XXVI (May, 1974), 103–26.

Jaeger, Werner. *Early Christianity and Greek Paideia*. Cambridge, Mass.: Harvard University Press, 1961.

Jennings, Francis. *The Invasion of America: Indians, Colonialism, and the Cant of Conquest*. Chapel Hill, N.C.: University of North Carolina Press, 1975.

Kaiser, Walter. *Praisers of Folly: Erasmus, Rabelais, Shakespeare*. Cambridge, Mass.: Harvard University Press, 1963.

Kayser, Wolfgang. *The Grotesque in Art and Literature*, trans. Ulrich Weisstein. Bloomington, Ind.: Indiana University Press, 1963.

———. *Die Vortragsreise: Studien zur Literatur*. Bern: Francke, 1958.

Kierkegaard, Søren. *Kierkegaard's Attack upon "Christendom," 1854–1855*, trans. Walter Lowrie. 2nd ed. Princeton: Princeton University Press, 1968.

Kuhn, Thomas S. *The Structure of Scientific Revolutions*. Chicago: University of Chicago Press, 1962.

Lewis, C. S. *The Allegory of Love: A Study in Medieval Tradition*. London: Oxford University Press, 1936.

Löwith, Karl. *From Hegel to Nietzsche: The Revolution in Nineteenth-Century Thought*, trans. David E. Green. New York: Holt, Rinehart, & Winston, 1964.

Marrou, Henri-Irénée. *A History of Education in Antiquity*, trans. George Lamb. 2 vols. New York: Sheed & Ward, 1956.

Mathews, J. Chesley. "Melville's Reading of Dante." *Furman Studies*, n.s., VI (Fall, 1958), 1–8.

Matthiessen, F. O. *American Renaissance: Art and Expression in the Age of Emerson and Whitman*. New York: Oxford University Press, 1941.

Mazzeo, Joseph A. *Varieties of Interpretation*. Notre Dame, Ind.: University of Notre Dame Press, 1978.

Mazzotta, Giuseppe. *Dante, Poet of the Desert: History and Allegory in the "Divine Comedy."* Princeton: Princeton University Press, 1979.

McCarthy, Paul. "Elements of Anatomy in Melville's Fiction." *Studies in the Novel*, VI (Spring, 1974), 38–61.

McFarland, Thomas. "The Place Beyond the Heavens: True Being, Transcendence, and the Symbolic Indication of Wholeness." *Boundary 2*, VII (Winter, 1979), 283–317.

McLean, Albert. "Spouter Inn and Whaleman's Chapel: The Cultural Matrices of *Moby-Dick*." *Melville and Hawthorne in the Berkshires: A Symposium*, ed. Howard P. Vincent. Kent, Ohio: Kent State University Press, 1968.

Melville, Herman. *The Letters of Herman Melville*, ed. Merrell R. Davis and William H. Gilman. New Haven: Yale University Press, 1960.

———. *Mardi, and A Voyage Thither*, ed. Harrison Hayford, Hershel Parker, and Thomas Tanselle. Evanston, Ill.: Northwestern University Press, 1970.

———. *Moby-Dick*, ed. Harrison Hayford and Hershel Parker. New York: Norton, 1967.

———. *Pierre, or The Ambiguities*, ed. Harrison Hayford, Hershel Parker, and Thomas Tanselle. Evanston, Ill.: Northwestern University Press, 1971.

Meyer, Hermann. *The Poetics of Quotation in the European Novel*, trans. Theodore and Yetta Ziolkowski. Princeton: Princeton University Press, 1968.

Murrin, Michael. *The Veil of Allegory: Some Notes Toward a Theory of Allegorical Rhetoric in the English Renaissance.* Chicago: University of Chicago Press, 1969.

Nelson, Raymond J. "The Art of Herman Melville: The Author of *Pierre*." *Yale Review*, LIX (Winter, 1970), 197–214.

Novalis [Friedrich von Hardenberg]. *Die Lehrlinge zu Sais.* In *Novalis Schriften*, ed. Paul Kluckhohn and Richard Samuel. Vol. I. Stuttgart: Kohlhammer, 1960.

Olson, Charles. *Call Me Ishmael.* New York: Reynall & Hitchcock, 1947.

Parker, Hershel. "Melville." *American Literary Scholarship: An Annual, 1975*, ed. James Woodress. Durham, N.C.: Duke University Press, 1977.

Pavese, Cesare. *American Literature: Essays and Opinions*, trans. Edwin Fussell. Berkeley: University of California Press, 1970.

Philo Judaeus. *Philo*, trans. F. H. Colson and G. H. Whitaker. Loeb Classical Library edition. 10 vols. New York and Cambridge, Mass.: Putnam and Harvard University Press, 1929–62.

Plato. *The Republic*, trans. Allan Bloom. New York: Basic Books, 1968.

Quilligan, Maureen. *The Language of Allegory: Defining the Genre*. Ithaca, N.Y.: Cornell University Press, 1979.

Rabinbach, Anson. "Critique and Commentary/Alchemy and Chemistry: Some Remarks on Walter Benjamin and This Issue." *New German Critique*, No. 17 (Spring, 1979), 3–14.

Rose, Edward J. "Los, Pilgrim of Eternity." *Blake's Sublime Allegory: Essays on "The Four Zoas," "Milton," "Jerusalem,"* ed. Stuart Curran and Joseph Anthony Wittreich. Madison, Wis.: University of Wisconsin Press, 1973.

Rosenberry, Edward H. *Melville and the Comic Spirit*. Cambridge, Mass.: Harvard University Press, 1955.

Sandmel, Samuel. *Philo of Alexandria: An Introduction*. New York: Oxford University Press, 1979.

Scheick, William J. *The Slender Human Word: Emerson's Artistry in Prose*. Knoxville, Tenn.: University of Tennessee Press, 1978.

Schiller, Johann Christoph Friedrich von. *The Poems and Ballads of Schiller*, trans. Sir Edward Bulwer-Lytton. New York: Harper and Bros., 1844.

Schlegel, Friedrich. *Dialogue on Poetry and Literary Aphorisms*, ed. Ernst Behler and Roman Struc. University Park, Pa.: Pennsylvania State University Press, 1968.

———. "Gespräch über die Poesie." *Kritische Friedrich-Schlegel-Ausgabe*, ed. Ernst Behler. Vol. II. Munich: Schöningh, 1967.

———. "Ideen." *Kritische Friedrich-Schlegel-Ausgabe*, ed. Ernst Behler, Vol. II. Munich: Schöningh, 1967.

Schless, Howard. "*Moby-Dick* and Dante: A Critique and Time Scheme." *Bulletin of the New York Public Library*, LXV (May, 1961), 289–312.

Sealts, Merton M., Jr. *Melville's Reading: A Check-List of Books Owned and Borrowed*. Madison, Wis.: University of Wisconsin Press, 1966.

Sedgwick, William Ellery. *Herman Melville: The Tragedy of Mind*. Cambridge, Mass.: Harvard University Press, 1944.

Seelye, John. *Melville: The Ironic Diagram*. Evanston, Ill.: Northwestern University Press, 1969.

Shaffer, Elinor S. *"Kubla Kahn" and "The Fall of Jerusalem": The Mythological School in Biblical Criticism and Secular Literature, 1770–1880*. Cambridge: Cambridge University Press, 1975.

Sherrill, Rowland A. *The Prophetic Melville: Experience, Transcendence, and*

Tragedy. Athens, Ga.: University of Georgia Press, 1979.

Smith, Henry Nash. "The Image of Society in *Moby-Dick*." *"Moby-Dick" Centennial Essays*, ed. Tyrus Hillway. Dallas: Southern Methodist University Press, 1952.

Smith, Ronald Gregor. *J. G. Hamann, 1730–1788: A Study in Christian Existence*. New York: Harper & Row, 1960.

Sowers, Sidney G. *The Hermeneutics of Philo and Hebrews*. Richmond, Va.: John Knox Press, 1965.

Spivak, Gayatri. "Allégorie et histoire de la poésie: Hypothèse de travail." *Poétique*, No. 8 (1971), 431–35.

———. "Thoughts on the Principle of Allegory," *Genre*, V (December, 1972), 327–52.

Stanzel, Franz. *Narrative Situations in the Novel*, trans. James P. Pusack. Bloomington, Ind.: Indiana University Press, 1971.

Thompson, Lawrance. *Melville's Quarrel with God*. Princeton: Princeton University Press, 1952.

Vincent, Howard P. *The Trying-Out of "Moby-Dick."* Boston: Houghton-Mifflin, 1949.

Wadlington, Warwick. *The Confidence Game in American Literature*. Princeton: Princeton University Press, 1975.

Webster, Noah. *A Dictionary of the English Language*. Springfield, Mass.: Merriam, 1852.

Weiskel, Thomas. *The Romantic Sublime: Studies in the Structure and Psychology of Transcendence*. Baltimore: Johns Hopkins University Press, 1976.

Willey, Basil. *Nineteenth Century Studies: Coleridge to Matthew Arnold*. New York: Columbia University Press, 1949.

Williamson, Ronald. *Philo and the Epistle to the Hebrews*. Arbeiten zur Literatur und Geschichte des hellenistischen Judentums, Vol. IV. Leiden: Brill, 1970.

Wohlfarth, Irving. "On the Messianic Structure of Walter Benjamin's Last Reflections." *Glyph*, III (1978), 148–212.

———. "Walter Benjamin's Image of Interpretation." *New German Critique*, No. 17 (Spring, 1979), 70–98.

Wordsworth, William. "Essays on Epitaphs, I." *The Prose Works of William Wordsworth*, ed. W. J. B. Owen and Jane Worthington Smyser. 3 vols. New York: Oxford University Press, 1974.

Wright, Nathalia. "Moby-Dick: Jonah's or Job's Whale?" *American Literature*, XXXVII (May, 1965), 190–95.

Young, James Dean. "The Nine Gams of the *Pequod*." *American Literature*, XXV (January, 1954), 449–63.
Zoellner, Robert. *The Salt-Sea Mastodon: A Reading of "Moby-Dick."* Berkeley: University of California Press, 1973.

INDEX